With his insightful analysis of the Funeral Oration of St. Vincent de Paul, Rev. Udovic, in three introductory chapters, lays the groundwork for the reading of the actual Oration, placing it in the context of the history of Church and State in the seventeenth century. He shows also how Maupas du Tour carefully crafted his panegyric to avoid the censure of church authorities in his depiction of Vincent de Paul and his works, while, at the same time, artfully giving the Crown, Mazarin, and the nobles a place of honor in the text. Copious illustrations of significant persons and places give life to the book. A must for any serious study of Vincentian historiography.

—Marie Poole, D.C.
Historian and Author; Editor of *Vincent de Paul: Correspondence, Conferences, Documents*

Everyone with an interest in Vincent de Paul will welcome this English translation of Maupas du Tour's funeral oration. Since it is in some way the first biography of Vincent de Paul, it must be consulted for details about his life. This translation, with important introductory materials, will become the standard text. It is sprinkled with citations from its subject, even single sentences that are practically unknown to scholars that can now be added to the canon of Vincentian materials. Maupas du Tour's text, of course, reflects his own perspectives and method of presentation, which can seem laborious and overblown. Nonetheless, it reveals to modern readers a world that, like certain citations from the saint, is likewise unknown.

—John E. Rybolt, C.M.
Historian and Author; Editor of *The Vincentians: A General History of the Congregation of the Mission*

This small volume makes a substantial contribution to the literature about Vincent de Paul, particularly in the way it advances the project of delineating Vincent's person from the wider myth about him. Rev. Udovic provides the first annotated English translation of the "Oraison Funèbre" and, as valuable as the sermon itself, three introductory chapters which situate it. He examines the life and career of Maupas du Tour, and gives an extensive analysis of his address detailing the important role it played in shaping subsequent portrayals of Vincent, notably Abelley's biography. Rev. Udovic's presentation is thorough and the translation smoothly readable. His book is a valuable and original addition to the historiography of Vincent de Paul.

—Thomas F. McKenna, C.M.
Provincial Director of the Daughters of Charity
Province of St. Louise

HENRI
DE MAUPAS
DU TOUR

✝

The Funeral Oration
for Vincent de Paul

23 November 1660

HENRI
DE MAUPAS
DU TOUR

†

The Funeral Oration for Vincent de Paul

23 November 1660

Introduction, Translation, and Annotation

BY

EDWARD R. UDOVIC, C.M.

Edited by Nathaniel Michaud

Cover illustration Courtesy Vincentian Studies Collection, Special Collections and Archives,

DePaul University, Chicago, Illinois

DePaul University Vincentian Studies Institute

Chicago, Illinois

Henri de Maupas du Tour (1606-1680).
Engraving by Michel Lasne. Dated 1645. Courtesy © Fitzwilliam Museum, Cambridge, United Kingdom

TABLE OF CONTENTS

LIST OF ILLUSTRATIONS

PREFACE

More than twenty years ago I first came across a copy of the published text (1661) of Henri de Maupas du Tour's *Oraison Funèbre* for Vincent de Paul. I immediately recognized its importance as the first public presentation of Monsieur Vincent's life and works after his death. As I read the manuscript, and did some preliminary research, I became just as interested in the panegyrist and author Bishop Henri de Maupas du Tour, and the genre of the *oraison funèbre*. In addition, the lengthy and fulsome dedication of the published work to Cardinal Mazarin was intriguing, as were the other textual references which opened windows into Vincent's seventeenth-century French world and his place in it. I was convinced of the importance of undertaking the first English translation of the *oraison funèbre*, fully annotating the text and suggesting its contextualization in Vincentian historiography.

At the time I had just finished the comprehensive exams for my doctorate and had some breathing space until my dissertation topic was approved. I finished an English translation of Jacques-Bénigne Bossuet's sermon *On the Eminent Dignity of the Poor in the Church*[1] and produced a rough translation of the *oraison funèbre*, and then began work on the annotation. Since this was the pre-internet era, work on the notes was painfully slow and I despaired of ever being able to interpret or even find some of the more obscure textual references.

As often happens in research; life, work, and other projects intervened. I turned my attention to my doctoral dissertation. Over the years I would periodically rework the translation, continue research on Henri de Maupas du Tour, and add to the notes. During this period I regularly taught a course at DePaul University entitled "The Life and Times of Vincent de Paul." In preparing for this class I continually strived to separate the Vincent of "myth" from the Vincent of "history," and to understand Vincent the "person" as distinct from Vincent the "saint." Much of this research ended up in the 2010 documentary film *Vincent de Paul: Charity's Saint*,[2] for which I served as executive producer and principal writer.

With the completion of the documentary a gap appeared in my research agenda and I decided to come back to this project. The translation was relatively easy to finish. In this era of Google searches, the massive digitization of primary texts, and the availability of e-books and e-journals, the barriers and difficulties to an extensive annotation of this text largely melted away in a few simple clicks.

I am very indebted to my able research assistant Edward Young for his expert eye and good judgment in checking notes, tracking down obscure patristic quotes (especially from the Greek Fathers), and suggesting additional notes. Any errors of course remain my own. Finally, my thanks to Nathaniel Michaud for his steady hand in editing a complex manuscript.

The translated and annotated text is preceded by three introductory chapters. In the first I outline the life and career of Henri de Maupas du Tour, to explain how he came to be chosen to deliver Monsieur Vincent's *oraison funèbre*. In the second chapter I review and analyze the content of the funeral oration and its distinctive contribution to Vincentian historiography. In the final chapter I summarize the course of the canonization cause of Vincent de Paul, for which the *oraison* served as the starting gun.

I am grateful to the Vincentian Studies Institute of the United States for its patience in waiting many years for the delivery of this oft-promised manuscript.

---

[1] Jacques-Bénigne Bossuet, "On the Eminent Dignity of the Poor in the Church," Trans. and Annotated by Edward R. Udovic, C.M., *Vincentian Heritage* 13:1 (1992): 37-58.

[2] See: **https://mission.depaul.edu/AboutUs/documentary/Pages/default.aspx** (accessed 4 February 2014).

Chapter 1

THE PANEGYRIST

In the early hours of 27 September 1660, after a long period of failing health, Vincent de Paul died at the age of seventy-nine at the priory of Saint-Lazare just outside Paris.[1] After being prepared by the lay brothers, his body remained in the room where he died. His fellow missionaries kept vigil and recited the Office of the Dead for the repose of his soul. As word spread throughout the city, people from all ranks of society filed past his bed to pay their last respects. Later that day, after the customary autopsy,[2] the body was placed in a double coffin of wood and lead and brought to the mother-house chapel.[3]

On the morning of 28 September the chapel of Saint-Lazare on the rue Saint-Denis was filled beyond capacity by a crowd that included the papal nuncio,[4] six bishops, many other ecclesiastical dignitaries, members of the nobility,[5] as well as Ladies of Charity, Daughters of Charity, Vincent's own missionaries, "along with

The death of Vincent de Paul. Late nineteenth-century French holy card.
Courtesy Vincentian Studies Collection, Special Collections and Archives,
DePaul University, Chicago, Illinois

the common people, who were there in a large crowd."[6] Following the requiem mass, the coffin was sealed and placed in a stone vault in the choir of the church.[7]

As was customary, the funeral was followed at a later date by a public memorial service at which an *oraison funèbre* was preached. The choice of both the preacher and the site of the discourse were always an indication of the deceased person's status. In addition, these *oraisons funèbres* were typically published later for wider distribution.[8]

Vincent de Paul's memorial service was held on 23 November 1660 and was arranged under the sponsorship of the Tuesday Conference of Ecclesiastics in Paris. This group, founded by Vincent in 1633, included many of the most influential prelates of the kingdom.[9] Although several Parisian pastors offered their churches, the choice fell upon Saint-Germain-l'Auxerrois in the heart of Paris across from the Louvre Palace.

Given Monsieur Vincent's fame, and his many years of service to the Church and Crown, it was appropriate that a royal parish church was chosen. The choice of the preacher was just as fitting: Henri Cauchon de Maupas du Tour the bishop of Le Puy.[10] Vincent de Paul's eighteenth-century biographer Pierre Collet, C.M., commented on the choice of Maupas du Tour:

> One could not conceive of a better choice. This prelate possessed considerable talents which were put to good use by the French Church in the canonization of François de Sales. He had an affection, esteem, and singular veneration for Vincent de Paul. His audience was composed of a great number of Prelates, Ecclesiastics, Religious, and an incredible crowd of people. The admired orator spoke with a zeal, piety, and feeling which edified those who heard him. His discourse lasted for more than two hours and despite this length there was much more he could have said; so much so that he avowed that he could have spoken for an entire Lenten season.[11]

MAUPAS DU TOUR'S BACKGROUND

Henri de Maupas du Tour was born in 1606 at Cosson near Reims. The bishop's mother had been Anne de Gondi, whose father was a cousin of Vincent's great patron, Philippe-Emmanuel de Gondi, Duc de Retz, Comte de Joigny, Baron de Montmirail, and Général des Galères de France.[12] In 1613, Vincent de Paul became the chaplain to the Gondi family and tutor to their three young sons. The family was frequently in residence at their estate at Montmirail in Brie.[13] No doubt Vincent would have had the opportunity here, or elsewhere, to make the acquaintance of the young Maupas du Tour who lived relatively nearby on his family's estate at Cosson.[14]

Maupas du Tour's grandfather, Charles Cauchon, baron du Tour en Champagne, served Henry of Navarre before his accession to the French throne.[15] His father, Charles Cauchon de Maupas (1566-1629), had supported Henry in his struggle to obtain the French throne. Rewarded for his bravery and services-at-arms, especially at the siege of Amiens in 1598,[16] he served as a councilor-of-state[17] and three times served as the ambassador to the court of James I of England. In 1606, Henry IV served as the godfather to Maupas' infant son, Henri, who was named in the king's honor.[18] After the king's assassination in 1610, Maupas became disillusioned with the regency of Marie de Medici[19] and served the Duc de Lorraine as *chef du Conseil de Lorraine*.[20] He later retired to his country estates where he pursued his seigneurial[21] and literary interests until his death in 1629.[22] Thus, on both his father's and his mother's sides, Maupas du Tour was well-connected to the highest levels of the French nobility and to the Crown.[23]

MAUPAS DU TOUR'S ECCLESIASTICAL CAREER

As was typical in French noble families of the time who had more than one son, Henri was destined from childhood for an ecclesiastical career.[24] In 1616, at the age of ten, Louis XIII appointed Maupas as the commendatory abbot of

right Marie de Medici (1573-1642).
Vincentian Studies Institute Collected Illustrations

left Louis XIII (1601-1643).
Courtesy Vincentian Studies Collection, Special Collections and Archives, DePaul University, Chicago, Illinois

Saint-Denis at Reims. [25] The young cleric studied at the Jesuit college in Reims,[26] and then at the University of Pont-à-Mousson in Lorraine.[27] He received his bachelor's degree in philosophy in 1622, his licentiate in theology a year later,[28] and his doctorate in 1635.[29] Ordained to the priesthood in 1629, he was almost immediately named the vicar-general of the archdiocese of Reims at the death of Archbishop Guillaume de Gifford. This appointment began his predictable rise through the hierarchy.[30]

Coming from a *dévot*[31] family committed to the Tridentine reform of the French Church, Maupas du Tour took his responsibilities towards the abbey of Saint-Denis seriously. When he came of age, he took an active interest in the institution's spiritual as well as its temporal affairs. In 1636, he supported its reform according to the principles that had been introduced by Cardinal de la Rochefoucauld among the Canons Regular of Sainte-Geneviève at their abbey in Paris.[32]

In 1634, Maupas received an appointment as *première aumônier* to the Queen, Anne of Austria.[33] That same year, Louis XIII nominated him to be the coadjutor to the archbishop of Reims, Henri II de Lorraine-Guise. This nomination was withdrawn because of the opposition of Charles de Lorraine Duc de Guise, who wished to keep this powerful position within his family. Maupas du Tour remained in Paris serving at the court. His biographer, Abbé Chaumiel, commented, "While at court, M. l'abbé de Maupas edified everyone

Vincent de Paul. Founder of the Congregation of the Mission (1625) dedicated to the evangelization of the poor people of the countryside. Eighteenth-century engraving; The official Seal of Saint-Lazare.
Courtesy Vincentian Studies Collection, Special Collections and Archives, DePaul University, Chicago, Illinois

by his modesty, and priestly virtues. After having fulfilled his public duties as *première aumônier* he spent his spare time in the exercises of piety and the study of the ecclesiastical sciences."[34]

MAUPAS DU TOUR AND VINCENT DE PAUL

While in Paris, Maupas du Tour often crossed paths with his cousins' former tutor and chaplain, Vincent de Paul. In April 1625, Monsieur Vincent founded the Congregation of the Mission with the financial support of Philippe-Emmanuel de Gondi and his wife Marguerite de Silly. Headquartered in Paris, and established as a group of itinerant missionaries who would evangelize the abandoned rural poor, the Congregation expanded its mission, in light of the need for good priests, to include ordination retreats, spiritual conferences, seminaries, and continuing education opportunities for ecclesiastics that came to be known as the "Tuesday Conferences."[35]

Vincent de Paul clearly influenced Maupas du Tour's priestly and episcopal ministry, imbuing him in particular with a lively concern for ministry to the poor. After the bishop's death his panegyrist would comment, "There is nothing more edifying in the life of the prelate whom we mourn than the paternal care he took to personally instruct the poor in the hospitals and the inhabitants of the mountains. He paid no regard to the lowliness of their birth, or of their education.

Anne of Austria (1601-1666).
Courtesy Vincentian Studies Collection, Special Collections and Archives, DePaul University, Chicago, Illinois

He respected the image of the Creator wherever he found it... the poor were his friends and were the recipients of a good part of the income from his benefices."[36]

Along with Vincent de Paul, Maupas du Tour also was a member of the influential Company of the Blessed Sacrament.[37] Founded in 1627 by Henri de Lévis, duke de Ventador, this group of *dévots* was composed of elite laymen and secular priests. Their aim was to bring about a thorough religious renewal in France by leading lives of holiness expressed in good works, the improvement of public morals, and a devotion to the Blessed Sacrament.[38] The secrecy surrounding the group, its aims, and its activities, raised the suspicions of Cardinal Mazarin and eventually led to its suppression.[39]

MAUPAS DU TOUR: BISHOP OF LE PUY

On 30 August 1641, Louis XIII named Maupas du Tour to be the bishop of Le Puy.[40] The Crown submitted the nomination to the Holy See for canonical investiture.[41] After almost a year with no sign of the required bulls being forthcoming from Rome, Vincent de Paul instructed the superior of the Congregation's house in Rome, Bernard Codoing, to do all he could to expedite

This page, opposite page Views of the church of St. Paul-St. Louis, Paris. *Courtesy Vincentian Studies Collection, Special Collections and Archives, DePaul University, Chicago, Illinois*

ÉGLISE DE ST PAUL-ST LOUIS À PARIS.

the sending of the needed documents. Vincent's letter of 20 June 1642 reads, "The Abbé de Saint-Denis, the Queen's chaplain, who belongs to our assembly at Saint-Lazare, one of the most capable and virtuous priests in this kingdom, was appointed to the bishopric of Le Puy in Auvergne seven or eight months ago. I entreat you, Monsieur, to do what you can to hasten the sending of his Bulls."[42] By the end of 1642 the bulls had still not arrived and Anne of Austria wrote again to Rome urging action.[43]

In January 1643 the papal documents finally arrived. On the feast of Francis of Assisi, 4 October 1643, Henri de Maupas du Tour was ordained a bishop in the Jesuit church of St. Paul-St. Louis on the rue Saint-Antoine in Paris. On the night before his ordination he wrote to his sister Marie, a Benedictine nun in Reims:

> My hand trembles and my heart pounds when I reflect upon this high dignity which the angels revere and which makes the strongest shoulders droop. This livery that I wear and that delights the eyes of my household startles my poor heart. This heavenly color reproaches me for the attachments which have so long bound me to creatures; and

this red which teaches me that I must be ready to give my blood for God and the service of souls upbraids me for not having suffered anything for God's cause.[44]

Finally, on 27 January 1644 the new bishop entered his diocese and took canonical possession of his cathedral of Notre Dame du Puy.[45] Although Maupas du Tour retained his position as *premiér aumônier* to Anne of Austria after his elevation to the episcopacy, he threw himself into the governance and reform of his diocese according to the Tridentine model of episcopal leadership.[46]

During the episcopacy of his predecessor, Just de Serres,[47] the diocese had experienced the ministry of the famous Jesuit evangelist, Jean-François Regis.[48] Regis had "inaugurated a program of social work and Christ-like mercy which had done much to alleviate their (the poor's) misery. Primitive equivalents of today's soup kitchens and houses of hospitality had been set up."[49] The several years of his service in the diocese created a charitable legacy upon which the new bishop built. According to the bishop's biographer Canon Blois:

> He was scarcely installed when he began to travel through his diocese like a true missionary, preaching for whole weeks in the most abandoned parishes, catechizing the children, and remaining long hours in the confessional. The little schools of the village or hamlet, where pious young women gathered the children during the winter months to teach them their letters or to instruct them in Christian doctrine, were the object of his special solicitude.[50]

This special solicitude for the instruction of children would lead Maupas, together with the Jesuit Jean-Pierre Médaille, to found the Sisters of Saint Joseph of Le Puy.[51]

In the course of his missionary activities in the region, Médaille had encountered a number of pious women serving the poor, the orphaned, and prisoners. These women told him of their desire to dedicate their lives to "*les œuvres de miséricorde tant spirituelles que corporelles*,"[52] but they were frustrated by the financial, social, and educational requirements of a traditional vocation to the cloister.[53]

Médaille conceived an idea which he referred to as his "*petite dessein*," quietly gathering together a group of these women to explore a new more public and less restrictive type of vocation for women in the Church.[54] The exact date when Médaille revealed his plans to Maupas du Tour is not known, though a possible date would be 1648 when the bishop invited him to deliver the Lenten sermons in the cathedral.[55] In any event, Maupas du Tour would work closely with Médaille to found the new congregation and obtain royal approval.[56] The congregation grew quickly with thirty-one foundations in France by 1680.[57]

As a member of the Tuesday Conferences of Saint-Lazare, and as a disciple of Vincent de Paul, the new bishop entered his diocese determined to improve the quality of his clergy. A diocesan synod convoked by Maupas du Tour established a conference for ecclesiastics modeled on that of Saint-Lazare.[58] The bishop next turned to the establishment of a diocesan seminary.

Jean-Jacques Olier[59] (the commendatory abbot of the Canons-Regular at Pebrac in Velay) had a special connection with the diocese. In 1642 he founded a seminary at the parish of Saint-Sulpice in Paris where he was pastor.[60] Maupas du Tour had known Olier as a fellow member of the conference at Saint-Lazare, and had been in Paris at the time of the foundation of the seminary of Saint-Sulpice. The bishop now appealed to Olier for personnel to staff his new seminary. Olier agreed, and in 1653 the seminary began operation.[61]

FRANÇOIS DE SALES AND JEANNE-FRANÇOISE FRÉMIOT DE CHANTAL

Maupas du Tour was also profoundly influenced, as Vincent de Paul had been, by François de Sales and Jeanne-Françoise Frémiot de Chantal.[62] After the death of Jeanne de Chantal at the Visitation monastery in Moulins, France, on 13

Jean-Jacques Olier, S.S. (1608-1657).
Public Domain

December 1641, Maupas du Tour delivered the funeral oration at her memorial service held in Paris early in the new year. He also began work on a biography. The work, published in 1644 and dedicated to Anne of Austria, was an immediate success, quickly going through five editions and appearing in Italian, Spanish, and German translations.[63] The bishop's admiration and devotion for these two luminous figures extended to the order of the Visitation of Holy Mary they had founded.

Maupas du Tour's complete personal devotion to François de Sales and his canonization cause was sealed when having fallen seriously ill he received the last sacraments only to make an unexpected recovery. He attributed his healing to the intercession of the "Blessed Bishop of Geneva."[64] He was also present at Annecy for the first opening of the bishop's tomb in 1656 when the bishop's galero (which had been hung directly over the tomb) was reported to have swayed to and fro as if buffeted by a strong wind. All those present had immediately declared the phenomenon to be miraculous. Maupas du Tour interrogated the sister-sacristan and even climbed up a ladder to examine the hat. His own conclusion was that the incident was inexplicable.[65]

Chapel of the First Visitation Monastery of Paris. Constructed 1632-1634. Francois Mansart, architect. Early nineteenth-century French engraving. *Courtesy Vincentian Studies Collection, Special Collections and Archives, DePaul University, Chicago, Illinois*

In 1657 he published a biography of De Sales entitled, *La vie du vénérable serviteur de Dieu, François de Sales, évêque de Genève, fondateur des religieuses de la Visitation Sainte-Marie*, which he dedicated to Pope Alexander VII. However, Maupas du Tour allowed his great devotion to François de Sales and an eagerness for his canonization to overwhelm the careful neutrality required by the regulations of the canonization process. The bishop's biography was denounced to Roman authorities for violating these regulations.[66] The delation to Rome centered on his use of the term "blessed" to refer to François more than four hundred times in the course of the biography, as well as the use of the term "saint" at least twenty four times. The book's frontispiece engraving also pictured the bishop with what appeared to be a halo.[67]

Maupas du Tour thusly placed himself in danger not only of losing his position as a promoter of the canonization but also of delaying the canonization itself. In the midst of this difficult situation Vincent de Paul came to the bishop's assistance.[68] In a letter of 12 October 1657 to Edme Jolly, the superior of the congregation's Roman house, Vincent instructed Jolly to see if he could secretly arrange a compromise that would save both Maupas du Tour's reputation and the progress of the de Sales cause.[69] Maupas did continue his role in the canonization cause, which was only somewhat delayed by the controversy over his biography.[70]

In 1662 Maupas du Tour and Charles Bourlon, the bishop of Soissons, were delegated by Louis XIV and the Assembly of the Clergy of France to travel to Rome to urge the canonization of François de Sales. In early 1665 he was dispatched again by the king to press the cause.[71] He was present in Rome as the representative of Louis XIV[72] and took part in the canonization at Saint Peter's Basilica on 19 April 1665.[73] He wrote the next day to the king, "This great ceremony took place yesterday with an extraordinary solemnity. The arms of your Majesty were displayed most prominently in the church of Saint Peter. The glory of this happy outcome is in part the result of the care and piety of Your Majesty."[74]

MAUPAS DU TOUR EMBROILED IN POLITICAL POWER STRUGGLES

Maupas' ecclesiastical reforms, not unexpectedly, met with opposition from a variety of vested interests. Yet, in the end, his greatest struggles would not be in the area of the religious affairs of his diocese, but in the temporal affairs and politics of the province of Velay. In addition to his ecclesiastical responsibilities, the bishop of Le Puy was also a temporal lord of the province in accord with his title as the Count of Velay. It was in defending the prerogatives of his joint temporal-ecclesial position that Maupas would become embroiled in, and eventually lose, a high-stakes power struggle.

The bishop's most powerful political opponent was Louis-Armand de Polignac (1606-1692), the head of an old noble family of the Velay.[75] Louis XIV had named the Prince de Polignac as Governor of Velay, and he used the powers of this position to challenge the temporal authority of Maupas du Tour as Comte du Velay. The dispute between the two became so strident that at one point Polignac blockaded the city, and supporters of the two disputants fought in the streets of Le Puy.

The only way for this dispute to be settled was by royal authority. At this time, although the young Louis XIV had reached the age of his majority, the real power behind the throne was Cardinal Mazarin who served as the king's first minister.[76] Maupas du Tour, supported by his fellow French bishops, appealed to Mazarin for the defense and recognition of the temporal rights of his see. Polignac, for his part, relied on his favor with Cardinal Mazarin and appeals to royal authority. In June 1656, the cardinal relayed the order of the king, which called on the bishop and the prince to reconcile their past differences and live in peace.[77] This was advice neither side accepted and the fighting and constant appeals to Paris continued.[78]

When Maupas du Tour published his funeral oration for Vincent de Paul early in 1661 he extravagantly dedicated the work to Cardinal Mazarin, who also had been praised by the bishop in the *oraison funèbre*. The prelate's political

Cardinal Mazarin (1602-1661). Engraving, dated 1659, by Robert Nanteuil.
Vincentian Studies Institute Collected Illustrations

difficulties, and his hope for support from Mazarin, clearly colored the the tone and content of his funeral oration.

In the end, Maupas du Tour miscalculated the strength of his position. On 9 March 1661 Cardinal Mazarin died. On 1 July 1661 the king transferred Maupas du Tour from the diocese of Le Puy to the diocese of Évreux.[79] The bishop's acquiescence to his defeat helped to keep him from falling out of royal favor, as did his successful diplomatic efforts in support of the canonization of François de Sales.

BISHOP OF ÉVREUX

Once in Évreux, Maupas du Tour threw himself into his episcopal duties, pastoral visitations, and care for the poor, with the same reforming zeal he had shown at Le Puy. In his new see he collaborated with Jean Eudes[80] in the foundation of a diocesan seminary in 1667.[81] He even attempted to have the future saint named as his coadjutor.[82] He also established conferences of ecclesiastics in his diocese, as well as publishing a monumental edition of the diocesan synodal statutes.[83]

His collaborator in this work was the grand-vicar of the diocese, the celebrated Henri-Marie Boudon who had a reputation as "*un mystique de grande race et un saint.*"[84] Together they not only worked for the reform of the diocese, but also to oppose the growing influence of the Jansenists in Normandy.[85] In 1666, Boudon found himself accused of a grave moral offense by his Jansenist enemies. He refused to respond to the charges. Maupas du Tour, who came to believe the charges, refused to defend him. Eight years later the bishop discovered that the accusations had indeed been false. He tried everything in his power to restore Boudon's honor.[86]

Maupas du Tour's reforming zeal as a bishop and pastor of souls was nourished by a spirituality that was as impressive in its breadth, as it was in its depth. A prayerful priest and zealous bishop, deeply immersed in Scripture, the Fathers of the Church, and the Tridentine reforms, he came into contact with some of the most luminous names in the history of French Catholicism: François de Sales, Jeanne-Françoise de Chantal, Vincent de Paul, Jean-Jacques Olier, and Jean Eudes among others. He took from each of them something which sustained and guided his life and ministry as a priest and most of all as a bishop.

Age and growing infirmities did little to slow him down. In December 1677 he wrote, in now trembling hand, to his nephew, "God sends each of us a cross and we must ask him for the patience to carry it for the sake of his love and his glory."[87] At the end of 1679 the carriage in which he was riding overturned, badly bruising him and breaking one of his arms. Early in the new year he submitted his resignation to the king.

On 20 April 1680, Louis XIV accepted Maupas du Tour's resignation and named a successor, Louis-Joseph Adhémar de Monteil de Grignan. While waiting for the papal confirmation of his successor Maupas du Tour continued on, to the best of his abilities, with his duties. On 8 August 1680, while on the way to a parish visitation his carriage went out of control and crashed. The aged bishop was thrown from the coach and suffered a fractured skull and several wounds. Taken back to his palace in a coma, the next night he regained consciousness long enough to receive the last rites. At noon on 12 August 1680, Henri de Maupas du Tour died from his injuries.[88]

The bishop's panegyrist[89] would comment:

> As we remember that terrible accident of two months ago, that cruel moment which proved to be the last for a life that was so precious to us as evidenced by the tears in our eyes, the sighs coming from our mouths, and the pain in our hearts. We have lost our illustrious and honored Lord and prelate Henri de Maupas du Tour, Bishop of Évreux. The poor have lost their friend, the defenseless their protector ...the clergy its star, and all of the diocese their father.[90]

A later biographer would also comment:

> M. de Maupas was known in his century as an extraordinary man as much for his virtues as for his accomplishments.... He was universally remembered for his eminent piety, his apostolic zeal, his true erudition, and the charitable institutions he established.... Today we can say that M. de Maupas was a holy bishop, and he did tremendous good during the years of his episcopacy whether at Puy or at Évreux.[91]

---

[1] For more on the controversy surrounding Vincent de Paul's year of birth and age at death, see Maupas du Tour, *Funeral Oration for Vincent de Paul*, **p.153**, n. 215, *infra*. Hereafter: du Tour, *Funeral Oration*.

[2] During the autopsy Vincent's heart was set aside. The Duchesse d'Aiguillon commissioned a silver reliquary to hold the organ. This reliquary is presently preserved in the treasury of the cathedral in Lyon, France. Vincent's heart is now preserved in a nineteenth-century reliquary and displayed in the chapel of the mother house of the Daughters of Charity in Paris. Vincent's remains are housed in a famous silver reliquary and venerated at the chapel of the mother house of the Lazarists in Paris. See also Alphonse Sachet, *Le cœur de Saint Vincent de Paul à Lyon* (Lyon: G. Patissier, 1929).

[3] See Document 57, "Journal Of The Last Days Of Saint Vincent," 4 June 1660, in *Vincent de Paul: Correspondence, Conferences, Documents*, ed. and trans. by Jacqueline Kilar, D.C., Marie Poole, D.C., et al, 1-14 (New York: New City Press, 1985-2014), 13a:208. Hereafter cited as *CCD*.

[4] Celio Piccolomini served as nuncio to France from 1656-1662.

[5] Including most notably Armand de Bourbon, the Prince de Conti, and Marie-Madeline de Vignerot, the Duchesse d'Aiguillon. See Pierre Coste, C.M., *The Life & Works of St. Vincent de Paul*, 3 vols. (New York: New City Press, 1987), 3:399. Hereafter cited as Coste, *Life*. See also Louis Abelly, *Life of the*

Venerable Servant of God: Vincent de Paul, trans. by William Quinn, F.S.C., and ed. by John E. Rybolt, C.M., 3 vols. (New York: New City Press, 1987), 1:113-118 and 3:262. Hereafter cited as *Abelly*. Unless otherwise noted, all citations to *Abelly* will be taken from this English translation of the 1891 Pémartin French edition.

[6] Document 57a, "Obituary Of Saint Vincent And Accounts Of His Memorial Services In The *Gazette de France*," *CCD*, 13a:209.

[7] The inscription on the tombstone read: *Hic jacet venerabilis vir Vincentius a Paulo, presbyter, fundator seu institutor et primus superior generalis Congregationis Missionis nec non Puellarum Charitatis. Obiit die vigesima septima septembris, anno millesimo sexcentesimo sexagesimo, ætatis vero suæ octogesimo quinto.* Coste, *Life*, 3:399. See also *Abelly*, 1:262.

[8] The *oraison funèbre* form has roots in antiquity. It became popular in France during the seventeenth century, reaching its height in the *oraisons* of Jacques-Bénigne Bossuet. These *oraisons* offered the preacher an opportunity not just to publicly mourn the passing of notable figures, but also to reflect on the life of those being eulogized from the perspectives of the moral, religious, and/or political lessons to be gleaned from their lives. See, for example, Jacques-Bénigne Bossuet, *Oraisons Funèbres de Bossuet* (Paris: Librairie de Firmin Didot Frères, 1847).

[9] For more information on the Tuesday Conferences see *Abelly*, 1:144-147; and Coste, *Life*, 2:118-149. See also Alison Forrestal, "Venues for Clerical Formation in Catholic Reformation Paris: Vincent de Paul and the Tuesday Conferences and Company," *Procedings of the Western Society for French History* 38 (2010): 44-60. Hereafter cited as Forrestal, *Venues*.

[10] The *Gazette de France* reported:

> On (November) 23, at Saint-Germain l'Auxerrois Church, a solemn memorial service was held for Father Vincent de Paul, Superior General of the Priests of the Mission. The Bishop of Le Puy preached the eulogy with the zeal and piety worthy of the occasion, omitting no trait necessary to fill out the picture he was painting to describe the great, heroic virtues of that holy man.
>
> This received the applause of the whole congregation, especially the large number of priests and religious who were there to honor the memory of the person to whom they felt obliged for the reform of the entire ecclesiastical Order, to which he devoted himself with all the success one could desire.

Document 57a, *CCD*, 13a:209.

[11] Pierre Collet, C.M., *La Vie de St. Vincent de Paul: Instituteur de la Congrégation de la Mission et des Filles de la Charité*, 2 vols. (Nancy: A. Lescure, imprimeur ordinaire du Roy, 1748), 2:181-182. Hereafter cited as Collet, *La Vie*. Another member of the Tuesday Conferences present for the service was Jacques-Bénigne Bossuet, who was on the verge of beginning his long and famous episcopal career. Bossuet had this to say about the service:

> Ce service funèbre fut magnifique; l'oraison funèbre de Monseigneur l'évêque du Puy, que nous entendimes dura deux heures, et la connaissance particulière que Monseigneur l'évêque du Puy avait du serviteur de Dieu, jointé aux autres illustres qualities de ce prélat, lui attirérent ce jour-là une attention extraordinaire de son auditoire, fort nombreux et célèbre. Il y eut là beaucoup de larmes répandues, particulièrement au sujet de l'humilité profonde et de l'incomparable charité envers les pauvres qu'il découvrit en la personne du vénérable serviteur de Dieu.

Jacques-Bénigne Bossuet, *Témoignage sur la vie et les vertus éminentes de Monsieur Vincent de Paul (1702)*, Armand Gasté, ed. (Paris: Alphonse Picard, 1892), 9-10. Hereafter *Bossuet*.

[12] For a genealogy of the House of Gondi see Jean de Corbinelli, *Histoire genealogique de la maison de Gondi*, 2 vols. (Paris: Jean-Baptiste Coignard, 1705), 1:ccxxxi, ccxliii, cclxi; 2:1, 12, 37, 50. Anne de Gondi, mother of Henri de Maupas du Tour, was related to Philippe-Emmanuel de Gondi as a second cousin once removed. Philippe-Emmanuel and Anne de Gondi's father, Jérôme

de Gondi, baron de Codun (c. 1550-1604), were second cousins. See **http://gw3.geneanet. org/pierfit?lang=en&m=NG&n=de+Gondi&t=N** (accessed 29 May 2012).

For a brief description of the office of *Général des Galères* see Jean-Marie Thiébaud, *Dictionnaire de l'Ancien Régime du Royaume de France* (Besançon: CÊTRE, 2009), 136. Hereafter cited as Thiébaud, *Dictionnaire*.

[13] See Marguerite Robert Mathieu, *Monsieur Vincent chez les de Gondy: les missionnaires et les Filles de la Charité à Montmirail* (Paris: Brodard-Taupin, 1966).

[14] Abbé Chaumiel, *Vie de Mgr. Henri de Maupas, évêque de Puy et Fondateur de la Congrégation des Dames Religieuses de Saint-Joseph* (St. Flour: Chez l'auteur, au convent de Saint-Joseph, 1837), 22. Hereafter *Chaumiel*.

[15] For a contemporary biographical sketch of Charles Cauchon, baron du Tour en Champagne et Maupas, see G. Baussonnet, *Reste des Vers de la Composition de feu tres-genereux Seigneur, Messire Charles de Maupas, Chevalier, Baron du Tour: Seigneur dudit Maupas, du Cosson, Montaneux, & Sainct Imoges: Conseiller du Roy en ses Conseils d'Estat and Privé, Plus un Elogue pour le mesme Seigneur* (Reims: Chez François Bernard, 1638). Hereafter *Baussonnet*.

[16] *Chaumiel*, 13.

[17] For a brief description of the office of councilor-of-state (French: *Conseil d'en-Haut* or *Conseil d'État*) see Anne Conchon, Bruno Maes, et al., *Dictionnaire de l'Ancien Régime* (Paris: A. Colin, 2004), 75. Hereafter cited as Conchon, *Dictionnaire*.

[18] Marie Chalendard, *La Promotion de la Femme à l'Apostolat, 1540-1650* (Paris: Éditions Alsatia, 1950), 174. Hereafter *Chalendard*.

[19] *Chaumiel*, 14.

[20] *Chalendard*, 177.

[21] For more information on seigneurial duties and responsibilities see Conchon, *Dictionnaire*, 266-267.

[22] For examples of Charles de Maupas du Tour's poetry see *Baussonnet*, 7-23.

[23] For more information concerning Maupas du Tour's family background and biography see *Chaumiel*, 11-16. Also see *Baussonnet*, 27-46.

[24] Born 15 November 1606, Henri was the second son of Charles Cauchon, seigneur de Maupas (1566-1629), and Anne de Gondi who were married in 1600. His older brother was Jean-Baptiste Cauchon de Maupas, baron du Tour. See **http://gw3.geneanet. org/pierfit?lang=en;p=henry;n=cauchon+de+maupas+du+tour** (accessed 29 March 2012).

[25] *Recueil de pieces concernant Henri de Maupas du Tour, Abbé de Saint-Denis de Reims, évêque du Puy et d'Évreux*, Bibliothèque Nationale de France 20636.1. Hereafter BN FR. Note: reference to individual documents or collections of documents in the Bibliothèque Nationale de France will be made citing the call number of that document or set of documents in the library. In cases where a book or journal in these archives is referenced, the title of that book or journal will be used rather than its call number. Note also: Maupas du Tour succeeded his paternal uncle Claude de Maupas as commendatory abbot of Saint-Denis at Reims. See *Baussonnet*, 40. For a more detailed history of this practice, see J. Gilchrist, "Commendation," in *New Catholic Encyclopedia, Second Edition*, 17 vols. (New York: McGraw-Hill, 1967-1996), 4:9. Hereafter *NCE 2nd*.

[26] Founded in 1606.

[27] Founded in 1572.

[28] BN FR 20636.2, 20636.3.

[29] *Chalendard*, 178.

[30] *Chaumiel*, 18.

[31] For more information on the *dévots* see Conchon, *Dictionnaire*, 98.

[32] For a biographical sketch of François de la Rochefoucauld see Letter 146, "To Alain De Solminihac," Paris, 23 August 1633, *CCD*, 1:209, n. 10. For details on the reform activities of Cardinal de la Rochefoucauld, see Joseph Bergin, *Cardinal de La Rochefoucauld: Leadership and Reform in the French*

Church (New Haven: Yale University Press, 1987), 170-172. Hereafter cited as Bergin, *Rochefoucauld*.

[33] For more information on the staffing of a French queen's household, and the role of *première aumônier* during this period, see Caroline zum Kolk, "The Household of the Queen of France in the Sixteenth Century," *The Court Historian* 14:1 (June 2009): 3-22.

[34] *Chaumiel*, 21-22.

[35] For more information on the foundation and works of the Congregation of the Mission see du Tour, *Funeral Oration*, footnotes 46 and 48 (Parish Missions); 62 and 122 (work with Galley Slaves); 49 and 55 (Tuesday Conferences); 47 (relief to war-torn areas of France); 50 (establishment of Tridentine-style seminaries); 51 (Ordination Exercises); 63 and 64 (General Hospitals and contemporary health-care issues); 52 (Spiritual Retreats for Ecclesiastics); 65 (Confraternities of Charity); 68, 72 and 73 (Foreign Missions); and 90 (aid to refugees fleeing religious persecution), *infra*.

[36] BN FR LN [27] 13814.20, Monsieur de St.-Michel, *Oraison funèbre prononcée dans l'eglise paroissiale de St. Nicolas d'Evreux, aux service solennel fait par Messieurs les Ecclesiastiques de la conference d'Évreux, le 8 Oct, 1680, pour Msgr. L'Illustrissime, & Reverendissime évêque d'Évreux, Henry de Maupas du Tour* (À Rouen, chez la veuve de Louis du Mensil, 1681). Hereafter cited as St.-Michel, *Oraison*.

     For more information concerning the *bénéfice ecclèsiastique* see Conchon, *Dictionnaire*, 34. See also Thiébaud, *Dictionnaire*, 36.

[37] For a detailed history of the Company of the Blessed Sacrament, see Alain Tallon, *La Compagnie du Saint-Sacrement, 1629-1667: spritualité et société* (Paris: Cerf, 1990).

[38] An account of the Company's motivation and action in the seventeenth century to ban Moliere's play, "Tartuffe," can be found in Sheryl Kroen's *Politics and Theater: The Crisis of Legitimacy in Restoration France, 1815-1830* (Berkeley: University of California Press, 2000).

[39] For more details see Coste, *Life*, 3:271-285. For the classic (though dated) study of the Company see Raoul Allier, *La compagnie du Très Saint-Sacrement de l'autel: La "cabale des dévots" 1627-1666* (Paris: A. Colin, 1902).

[40] Secret Vatican Archives, *Acta Camerararii Sacri Colegi S.R.E. Cardinalum*, "Henricus (de Cauchon) de Maupas du Tour, Aniciensis (Le Puy en Velay)," AC 18f. 159. *Processus Episcoporum Sacræ Congreg. Consistoralis*, P. Con. 42ff. 72, 82-83. See also **http://www.catholic-hierarchy.org/bishop/bcauc.html** (accessed 15 March 2012).

[41] In line with the terms of the Concordat of Bologna (1516), the French Crown had the right of nomination to all high ecclesiastical offices in France. The Holy See alone, however, had the right to bestow ecclesiastical jurisdiction on the nominees which allowed them to exercise their office. See Joseph Bergin, *The Making of the French Episcopate, 1589-1661* (New Haven: Yale University Press, 1996). Hereafter cited as Bergin, *Episcopate*. See also C. Berthelot du Chesnay and J. M. Grès-Gayer, "Gallicanism," *NCE 2nd*, 6:75.

[42] Letter 594, "To Bernard Codoing, Superior, In Rome," Saint-Lazare, 20 June 1642, *CCD*, 2:296. See also Letter 609, "To Bernard Codoing, Superior, In Rome," Paris, 19 August 1642, *Ibid.*, 2:319.

[43] BN FR 20636.28, *Copie d'un lettre de la Reine-Mère escrite au Pape en fauver de M. Évêque du Puy, 31 December 1642*. In this letter she noted that Maupas du Tour "should be recognized for the continual services that he gives to the Church of God to the great satisfaction of everyone at this Court."

[44] BN FR 20636.30. See also Dolorita M. Dougherty, C.S.J., Helen A. Hurley, C.S.J., Emily Joseph Daly, C.S.J., St. Claire Coyne, C.S.J., *et al.*, *Sisters of St. Joseph of Carondelet* (St. Louis: B. Herder Book Co., 1966), 9. Hereafter *Sisters*.

[45] For more background on the diocese of Le Puy in this era, see *Chalendard*, 162-174.

[46] See Paul Broutin, *La Réforme Pastorale en France au XVIIe siècle: recherché sur la tradition pastorale après le concile de Trente*, 2 vols. (Tournai, Belgium: Desclée & Co., 1956), 1:26, which states:

I. Les artisans de la réforme pastorale.

Au premier chef, ce sont les évêques réformateurs. De leur grand nombre nous n'avons retenu qu'une vingtaine, d'une personnalité suffisamment marquante, pas toujours les plus saints, ni les plus célèbres, mais ceux dont l'action pastorale et l'œuvre réformatrice sont signficatives de l'esprit tridentin. Ils ne sont pas les seuls.

Si nous écrivions une histoire de l'épiscopat français aux XVIIe siècle, il faudrait encore évoquer le souvenir de... H. de Maupas... au Puy....

[47] Just de Serres, O.S.B., was appointed as coadjutor in 1616. He succeeded to the see in 1621, and served until his death in 1641.

[48] Jean-François Regis, S.J. (1597-1640). By coincidence he was canonized in 1737 at the same ceremony as Vincent de Paul. See *Superna Hierusalem*, in "Circular of Mr. Couty," *Circulars of the Superiors-General and the Superioresses to the Daughters of Charity: and notices upon the deceased Sisters of the Community* (Emmitsburg, Md.: St. Joseph's, 1870), 41. Hereafter, *Superna Hierusalem*.

[49] *Sisters*, 10. For additional details of his work see *Chalendard*, 170-174.

[50] *Return to the Fountainhead*, Tercentenary Addresses published by the Sisters of St. Joseph of Carondelet (St. Louis, Missouri, 1952), 59.

[51] Jean-Pierre Médaille, S.J., was born on 6 October 1610 in Carcassone, France. Ordained in 1637, his first assignment was at the college at Aurillac. In 1641, he was assigned to give missions in the diocese of Saint-Flour, and in 1643 was named minister of the college at Saint-Flour. He died in 1669 at Billom. See *Sisters*, 11-14.

[52] *Chalendard*, 184.

[53] Chalendard concludes:

Reportons-nous aux origines: est-ce le cheminement des faits qui a permis l'épanouissement normal de la fondation de Monseigneur de Maupas et du Père Médaille: plus d'étonnement, plus de résistance de la part de l'opinion.

Est-ce l'expérience acquise en la question, par l'Évêque du Puy, dans le commerce de deux Fondateurs: saint François de Sales et saint Vincent de Paul?

Est-ce la collaboration du Jésuite cofondateur, member d'un Ordre moderne à la vitalité et au dynamisme communicatifs?

C'est probablement l'action combinée de ces trois facteurs qui a ... rendu les Filles de Saint-Joseph bénéficiaires de la Promotion de la Femme à l'apostolat.

Ibid., 198.

[54] *Sisters*, 16.

[55] *Ibid.*, 21-22.

[56] *Chaumiel*, 41-45. See also *Chalendard*, 182-192.

[57] *Chalendard*, 190.

[58] See Marguerite Vacher, *Nuns Without Cloister: Sisters of St. Joseph in the Seventeenth and Eighteenth Centuries*, Patricia Byrne et al., trans. (Lanham, Md.: University Press of America, 2010), 56. Hereafter cited as *Vacher*.

[59] For a biographical sketch of Jean-Jacques Olier, see Letter 146, *CCD*, 1:208-209, n. 8. See also the draft unpublished English translation, "Notebooks of Brother Louis Robineau: Notes concerning the actions and words of the late Monsieur Vincent de Paul our Most Honored Father and Founder," John E. Rybolt, C.M., trans., originally published as Louis Robineau, *André Dodin, C.M., présente Louis Robineau. Monsieur Vincent: Raconté par son secrétaire; Remarques sur les actes et paroles de feu Monsieur Vincent de Paul, notre Trés Honoré Père et Fondateur* (Paris: O.E.I.L., 1991), 94. Hereafter the English translation is cited as *Robineau*. Citations to manuscript texts in the draft English translation maintain the same numbering as in the Dodin edition.

[60] *Vacher*, 166-170.

[61] M. Antoine Jacotin, *Inventaire-Sommaire des Archives Départementales: Haute-Loire, Archives Ecclesiastique - Série G: Clergé Seculier, antérieur à 1790.* L [43] 12, f. 178, 233, 238.

[62] See André Dodin, C.M., *François de Sales, Vincent de Paul: les deux amis* (Paris: O.E.I.L., 1984). Hereafter Dodin, *François de Sales*. For more on François de Sales and Jeanne-Françoise Frémiot de Chantal, see du Tour, *Funeral Oration*, p. 159, n. 275, and n. 280, respectively, *infra*.

[63] Henri de Maupas du Tour, *La vie de la vénérable mère leanne Françoise Frémiot: fondatrice, première mère & réligieuse de l'Ordre de la Visitation de Saincte-Marie* (Paris: Simeon Piget, 1647). Hereafter cited as du Tour, *Vie de Frémiot*.

[64] Ernestine Lecouturier, *Françoise-Madeleine de Chaugy et la Tradition Salesienne au XVIIᵉ siècle*, 2 vols. (Paris: Bloud et Gay, 1933), 1:132. Hereafter cited as *Lecouturier*.

[65] *Ibid.*, 1:229.

[66] *Ibid.*, 1:235.

[67] Marie-Patricia Burns, V.S.M., *Françoise-Madeleine de Chaugy, dans l'ombre et la lumière de la canonisation de François de Sales* (Annecy: Académie Salésienne, 2002), 85. Hereafter cited as *Canonisation*.

[68] Early in the canonization process (17 April 1628), Vincent de Paul gave lengthy sworn testimony as to his personal knowledge of the sanctity of François de Sales. See Document 29, "Deposition At The Process Of Beatification Of Francis de Sales," [17 April 1628], *CCD*, 13a:80-96. In 1641, Vincent de Paul added the account of a mystical vision that he had at the time of death of Jeanne-Françoise de Chantal. See also Document 34, "Vision Of The Three Globes," [1641], *Ibid.*, 13a:137-139.

[69] Letter 2411, "To Edme Jolly, Superior, In Rome," Paris, 12 October 1657, *Ibid.*, 6:541-543.

[70] See *Canonisation*, 89. See also *Chaumiel*, 73-74.

[71] See *Chaumiel*, 89-91.

[72] See *Canonisation*, 187.

[73] See *Chaumiel*, 91-93.

[74] Quoted in *Canonisation*, 190.

[75] For more information on Maupas du Tour's struggles in Le Puy, see BN FR L[30] 228 BIS: Ch. Rocher, "Un Évêque et un Conspirateur en Velay," in *Annuaire de la Haute-Loire* (Le Puy: M.D. Marcessou, ed., 1877). See also BN FR L[27]N 11387.235: Anonymous, *Vie de M. De Lantages: Prêtre de Saint-Sulpice, Premier Supérieur du séminaire de Notre Dame du Puy* (Paris: Adrien le Clere, 1830).

[76] Maupas du Tour's standing at court had not been helped when, in June 1649 at the beginning of the Fronde, he gave the opening address at the Estates General of Languedoc. His remarks were taken out of context and immediately reported to the queen and Cardinal Mazarin as a challenge to their authority. Although Maupas du Tour went to great pains to deny this implication, the damage to his reputation at court was real. See BN FR L[30]c 228 BIS: Paul le Blanc, *Annuaire de la Haute-Loire* (Le Puy: Marchessou Fils Ed, 1879), 12-17. See also J.A.M. Arnaud, *Histoire du Velay, jusqu'à la fin du regne de Louis XV*, 2 vols. (Le Puy: J.B. La Combe, 1816), 2:180-185. Hereafter cited as Arnaud, *Histoire*. For a brief description of the Fronde, see Conchon, *Dictionnaire*, 134-135.

[77] BN FR 20637.111.

[78] Arnaud, *Histoire*, 185-189.

[79] *Chalendard*, 193. Interestingly, Le Puy was smaller than Évreux and farther from Paris, and Le Puy offered greater revenues. See Bergin, *Episcopate*, 118. So, in financial terms, Évreux was certainly a less desirable diocese for any bishop, and somewhat of a demotion for Maupas du Tour.

[80] John Eudes was born 14 November 1601. Ordained 20 December 1625 as a member of the Congregation of the Oratory of Jesus in France, he gained a reputation for his work with victims of

the plague. He left the Oratorians and founded the Congregation of Jesus and Mary (Eudists), as well as the Sisters of Our Lady of Charity of the Refuge. Like Vincent de Paul, he was active in the establishment of seminaries according to the Tridentine model and he opposed Jansenism. He died on 19 August 1680, and was canonized 31 May 1925.

[81] See, for example, Antoine Montigny, S.J., *Vie du Père Jean Eudes, missionaire apostolique, instituteur de la Congrégation de Jésus et Marie et de l'Ordre de Notre-Dame de Charité* (Paris: Adrien Le Clere, 1827), 355-363. Hereafter cited as Montigny, *Vie du Père*. See also Pierre Hérambourg, *Le Révérend Jean Eudes apôtre des SS. Cœurs de Jésus et de Marie,...ses vertus* (Paris: P. Lethielleux, 1869).

[82] Montigny, *Vie du Père*, 382-383.

[83] Chanoine Bonnenfant, *Histoire Générale du diocèse d'Évreux*, 2 vols. (Paris: Auguste Picard, 1933), 1:174-175.

[84] Albert Bois, *Les sœurs de Saint-Joseph:Les Filles du petit dessein: de 1648 à 1949* (Lyon: Ed. du Sud-Est, 1950), 27. Hereafter *Bois*.

[85] For a thorough explanation of Jansenism, its history and teachings, see J. Carreyre, "Jansénisme," *Dictionnaire de Théologie Catholique*, A. Vacant, et al., eds., 15 vols. (Paris: Letouzey et Ané, 1903-50), 8:318-529. Hereafter cited as *DThCatholique*.

[86] Pierre Collet, C.M., *La vie de M. Henri-Marie Boudon, grand archidiacre d'Évreux*, 2 vols. (Paris: Jean-Thomas Herissant, 1753), 2:192-197.

[87] Quoted in *Bois*, 29.

[88] See *Chaumiel*, 98.

[89] Maupas du Tour's panegyric was delivered by Monsieur de Saint-Michel, a priest from the seminary of Évreux. See St.-Michel, *Oraison*.

[90] *Ibid.*, 13814.5.

[91] *Chaumiel*, 7-8.

Chapter 2

THE ULTIMATE GOAL:
VINCENT DE PAUL'S CANONIZATION

"He is canonized."[1] With these triumphant words, Jean Couty, the seventh Superior General of the Congregation of the Mission and the Company of the Daughters of Charity[2] announced what "all the true children of our holy Founder have always and ardently desired:"[3] the canonization of Vincent de Paul. The elaborate, hours-long ceremony, led by Clement XII took place on 16 June 1737, the Feast of the Most Holy Trinity, at the Basilica of Saint John Lateran in Rome.[4] An impressive octave of ceremonies celebrating the canonization also took place in Paris, notably at the new saint's reliquary-shrine at the maison-mère of the Lazarists on the rue Saint-Denis.[5] Vincent de Paul had been dead for almost seventy-seven years.

Official portrait of Jean Couty, C.M.
Vincentian Studies Institute Collected Illustrations

The "vivid and lifelike"[6] portrait of Monsieur Vincent presented to such great effect "and without any exaggeration"[7] by Henri de Maupas du Tour in his *oraison funèbre* was filled out and completed at great length and with great skill by Louis Abelly[8] in his 1664 biography.[9] Both panegyrist and biographer were selected carefully. Each brought impeccable credentials and the necessary skills to their important tasks.[10] Published as quickly as possible after Vincent de Paul's death, these works took advantage of heightened public attention and presented a seamless narrative designed to support the weight of an eventual canonization cause.[11] In fact Maupas du Tour's *oraison funèbre*, as the first published account of Vincent's life and virtues, should be recognized for what it was: the unofficial opening of Vincent's cause.[12]

In the last decades of his long public life, Vincent de Paul achieved a national prominence for his role in the successful Tridentine reformation of the Catholic Church in France.[13] This long-delayed, and desperately-needed reformation was an essential part of the Bourbon monarchy's long term goal, beginning with Henry IV, of building a strong kingdom under an absolutist king. A strong kingdom needed to be supported by a reformed Gallican Church which was proud of its unique traditions, doctrinally orthodox, loyal to the papacy, but under the firm control of the Crown.[14]

Louis XIV (1638-1715). Portrait by Hyacinthe Rigaud.
Public Domain

At the dawn of the seventeenth century, after decades of bitter religious warfare intertwined with an equally bitter war of succession, there were high odds to be overcome for the success of both the Church's reformation and this Bourbon state-building. Yet by the late 1650's and early 1660's, as the young Louis XIV emerged from the shadows of the regency of his mother Anne of Austria (aided by Cardinal Mazarin), these odds had largely been beaten,[15] albeit at a high cost.[16] The supremely self-confident and brilliant France of the Sun King, "Ludovico Magno,"[17] was very different from the kingdom that had stumbled so haltingly and painfully into the new century. By mid-century the Gallican Church had also emerged with its own self-confidence and brilliance restored.[18] It can be argued that Vincent de Paul became the symbol of the glory of French religious achievement, and its impact not only on France, but also on the Universal Church[19] which found in him the last of the great reformers of the Counter Reformation.[20]

VINCENT DE PAUL'S HUMILITY: RESISTING A CULT OF PERSONALITY

During his many years on the public stage of Altar and Throne, Vincent de Paul steadfastly resisted anything smacking of even the slightest personal

Blessed Vincent de Paul. French engraving c. 1729.
Vincentian Studies Collection, Special Collections and Archives,
DePaul University, Chicago, Illinois

recognition, or the marks of public deference and special privileges naturally accorded to, and generally expected by, leaders in a hierarchical society and church.[21] Indeed, he had a visceral reaction to receiving any praise, as Maupas du Tour notes, "in fact, anyone who said anything favorable about him cruelly tortured his humble soul. *'Qui me laudat, me flagellat.'*"[22] Instead, the genuinely humble Monsieur Vincent always tried to focus attention away from his person to the mission of ecclesial reform (especially of the priesthood), evangelization of the countryside, and charity toward the most abandoned of the poor that motivated all of his efforts and all of the groups he founded.[23]

Always minimizing or even completely discounting his own role, Vincent instead publicly gave credit for all his successes to God and the guidance of Divine Providence,[24] and then to the efforts of generous supporters and faithful collaborators.[25] He claimed that any accomplishments had taken place in spite of his ever-present faults, failings, and sinfulness.[26] He also took responsibility for any failure, once noting: "But what else can come from a miserable sinner except failures and faults in every matter?"[27] Vincent's favorite adjective to describe himself was "wretched."[28]

Loath to talk about himself in any positive or revealing way, Vincent's humility naturally piqued the very interest and personal attention he wanted so much to avoid. This interest was also heightened by his reputation for holiness accorded by public opinion despite his repeated disclaimers. Thus, given his reputation and the success of his multiple activities, his words and actions were

Antoine Portail, C.M. (1590-1660).
Vincentian Studies Institute Collected Illustrations

largely matters of public record, of current memory, and ultimately beyond his control.[29]

However, it must also be remembered that Vincent de Paul (1581-1660) lived much longer than the average life-span of a man of his time.[30] This meant that the details of the first half of his life (generally speaking the period prior to 1617, and especially prior to 1610), before he came to Paris, remained unknown and inaccessible.

Vincent occasionally revealed small details of his early life, sometimes said in passing to illustrate some contemporary issue or question, or if he could use the revelation to illustrate the guidance of Divine Providence, or to demonstrate his own personal unworthiness.[31] Interestingly, he chose to minimalize the level of his educational accomplishments in service of his sense of humility.[32] Some missing details undoubtedly could have been filled in by a handful of his oldest and closest collaborators like Antoine Portail,[33] Louise de Marillac,[34] and Philippe-Emmanuel de Gondi.[35] However, even these longtime friends had no direct knowledge of Vincent's life before he arrived in Paris in late 1609 or early 1610.[36]

Among those who would have been most desirous to know the full life-story of Monsieur Vincent were his followers, especially the members of the Congregation of the Mission and the Company of the Daughters of Charity.[37] For these men and women the biography of Monsieur Vincent took on a personal significance as the inspiration of their own vocational choices.[38] There is evidence that this devotion and curiosity led, even during Vincent's lifetime, to the construction by his followers of a biographical narrative — an activity they kept hidden to avoid their founder's inevitable dismay, embarrassment, and disapproval.[39]

THE EXAMPLE OF VINCENT'S "TUNISIAN CAPTIVITY"

Early in 1645, the unrelenting pace and volume of his correspondence finally led Vincent de Paul to begin relying on the services of a secretary. The man Vincent chose was a trusted and talented lay-brother[40] of the Congregation of the Mission named Bertrand Ducournau.[41] As historian Stafford Poole, C.M., has pointed out: "To his boundless personal devotion to Saint Vincent, Brother Bertrand joined a zeal for preserving everything that the Saint wrote and said." In the following year a second equally-devoted and talented secretary was added, Brother Louis Robineau.[42]

In addition to his roles as Vincent de Paul's correspondence secretary and personal assistant, Ducournau also concerned himself with documenting all aspects of Monsieur Vincent's activities.[43] It was at his urging, for example, that in 1657 the members of the Congregation of the Mission finally began to surreptitiously record the spiritual conferences given to the community by its aging founder.[44]

Sometime in the first half of 1658, only two years before his death, Vincent de Paul received a letter from the Canon Jean de Saint-Martin, an old friend in his home region of Dax in Gascony in the southwest of France.[45] The letter upset him greatly. The Canon de Saint-Martin[46] had written with the news that his nephew had recently made the discovery, among the family papers, of two letters written (in 1607 and 1608 respectively) by Vincent to his first patron in Dax, Monsieur de Comet.[47] He enclosed copies of these letters believing that his friend would enjoy seeing them again after so many years. He was wrong.

In these missives, long-lost and long-forgotten, the young Vincent had told Monsieur de Comet in great detail of an incredible two year saga (1605-1607). It began with his capture at sea by the dreaded Barbary pirates,[48] then being sold into slavery at Tunis, his subsequent life as a slave under several successive masters, a miraculous escape in a "skiff" across the Mediterranean Sea back to France (accompanied by his last master, a renegade Christian), and finally his travels to Avignon and Rome.[49]

Vincent de Paul immediately burned the letters and wrote to his old friend asking for the originals. Unbeknownst to Vincent, his secretary under the direction of the Congregation's senior leadership (Antoine Portail, Jean Dehorgny,[50] and René Alméras[51]) wrote immediately to the Canon and asked him not to honor Vincent's request, but rather to send the originals directly to him. The Canon complied.[52]

Official portrait of René Alméras, C.M.
Vincentian Studies Institute Collected Illustrations

As late as May 1660, only months before his death, Vincent was still writing asking to be sent the originals of the letters. "I implore you by all the graces God has been pleased to grant you, to do me the favor of sending me that wretched letter which mentions Turkey — I mean the one that M. d'Agès found among his father's papers. I beg you again, by the bowels of Jesus Christ Our Lord, to do me this favor I ask of you as soon as possible."[53]

In August 1658, Brother Ducournau wrote to the Canon de Saint-Martin thanking him for sending the original letters. His letter is worth quoting at length:

M. Portail, M. Dehorgny, and M. Alméras, with whom you are acquainted, have asked me to write to you, until the time they can do so themselves, to thank you most humbly for the letters you sent them. Nothing in this world could be more precious to them than those letters because *their contents will one day add luster to the holy life of the person who wrote them* [emphasis added].

Certainly, none of us ever knew that he had been in Barbary... I assure you, however, that I admire still more his constraint in never breathing a word of all these things to anyone in the Company, although he has had hundreds of occasions to do so when speaking of the assistance to the captives that he undertook twelve to fifteen years ago.[54]

He told us quite often that he was the son of a plowman, that he herded his father's swine, and other humiliating details, but he kept silence about anything that could bring him honor, such as having been a slave, so he would not have to tell the good ensuing from it....

So, the captivity of this charitable man gained for him the knowledge of alchemy, but he made better use of it than those who try to change the nature of metals; for he has converted evil into good, the sinner into a just man, slavery into freedom, hell into paradise through the many works undertaken by his Company and by the ingenuity of which a zealous man is capable. He has discovered the philosopher's stone because his charity, inflamed by a divine fire, has changed everything into pure gold....[55]

Monsieur in sending us those letters you have revealed to us a hidden treasure, and you will greatly console those priests if you can send them any others, even though they contain nothing extraordinary... They would very much like to know.... when he came to Paris and why, in what year and where he became a priest. In addition, Monsieur, if you know other details about his youth, we will be most grateful if you inform us of them. He never talks to us about himself except to humble himself, and never to reveal the graces God has given him nor those granted to others through him.

Had those two letters fallen into his hands no one would ever have seen them, so those priests have judged it advisable to hold on to them without mentioning them to him. And so that he will have no idea that we have them, they have even destroyed your letter, thinking that you will not be offended by that... If he should ask you again for them, you could write him that you sent them to him and are very chagrined that he did not receive them. We ourselves are really sorry to deprive him of the consolation he would have in reading his past history, and, in his old age, to see himself as a young man, but we had either to make that decision or lose the original letters — which would have been far worse....[56]

Irrespective of the ongoing debate about the historicity of Vincent's so-called "Tunisian captivity"[57] this incident reveals that given Vincent de Paul's own almost complete silence about his past, his followers and admirers had no choice but to reconstruct it as best they could without his knowledge, cooperation, explanation, or correction.[58]

Engraved depiction of Vincent as a slave in North Africa.
Nineteenth-century French print.
Courtesy Vincentian Studies Collection, Special Collections and Archives,
DePaul University, Chicago, Illinois

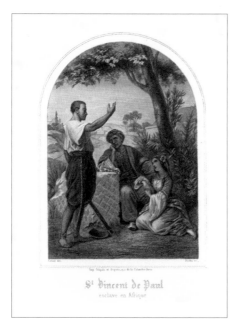

THE PRESUMPTION OF SANCTITY: "THE EMINENT VINCENT DE PAUL WHO I ESTEEM AS A SAINT AND WHOM YOU HAVE SO OFTEN ADMIRED..."[59]

The conviction shared by Maupas du Tour, Abelly, their audiences, as well as Vincent's numerous followers, was that the recently-deceased Vincent de Paul had lived a long life that demonstrated heroic levels of personal virtue, especially humility. This personal virtue was what had enabled him, with God's grace, to accomplish the prodigious feats of Church reform, evangelization and charity to the glory of God, and the glory of France.[60] They reached an inevitable conclusion with respect to Vincent's sanctity:[61] "This is the miraculous genius of the great Vincent de Paul whose grace, fidelity, and courage today is the object of our wonder, and who for countless centuries to come will receive the admiration of God's Church."[62] This conclusion, after all, was based on what they had heard with their own ears, and seen with their own eyes.[63] As Maupas du Tour notes, "We could say of him, even though his modesty would never have allowed it, that all the flowers growing in all the most beautiful gardens have neither the variety, nor the beauty, of his virtues that were displayed for everyone to see."[64] Now that Vincent was dead, the time had come to tell this story of sanctity publicly and without restraint.

In telling Vincent's story, Maupas du Tour knew he had to walk a fine rhetorical line. He could suggest that public praise of Vincent's heroic virtue and his life's work were reasonable and merited; however, he could not suggest that this public opinion (no matter how wide-spread) constituted proof of a sanctity which the Church alone could judge infallibly through its rigorous canonization process with its certification of numerous miracles.[65] In fact, one of the early stages of the canonization process required the judgment *de non cultu* that there had been no such premature claim.[66]

Maupas du Tour, therefore, planned both the content and tone of his *oraison funèbre* very carefully. His choice of a thematic scriptural quotation was designed to establish the religious premise he was proposing for understanding the true significance of the late Vincent de Paul: "*...cuius laus est in evangelio per omnes ecclesias.*" (...[the brother] who is praised in all the churches for his preaching of the gospel.)[67] Having revealed his scriptural theme, Maupas du Tour prefaced his remarks about the deceased with a rhetorical riff on the philosophical and theological bases upon which one could discern the difference between true praise (never sought after but truly deserved because of virtue, and offered with no selfish motivation) and other so-called "praise" (often debased and commonly offered for mercenary and unworthy human motives). According to Maupas du Tour, the praise to be offered to Vincent de Paul in the *oraison* was "praise that is due to the story of his rare virtues, since it can be said of his very holy life and his very happy death that they were designed by grace, and crowned by the gospel."[68]

In the first section of the *oraison funèbre* Maupas du Tour describes the commonly-held opinion of Vincent de Paul as having been "a person of eminent virtue"[69] (indeed an "inexhaustible fountain of virtues"[70]). He was "the instrument chosen by the greatest designs of Divine Providence (chosen by the 'hand of God'[71]) to be involved in all the most important activities that have given glory to God, been advantageous to our faith, and brought honor to the state. Nevertheless, even though this great man deserved many glorious rewards for his actions ("displayed for everyone to see"[72]) he kept his merits completely hidden from view under the veil of his humility."[73] According to Maupas du Tour, "both heaven and public opinion"[74] (including the court and Crown) recognized Monsieur Vincent as having been an "admirable," "literal," "rare," and "perfect example" of Christian humility.[75]

In Maupas du Tour's view, evidence of Vincent's "profound humility [included the] perfect scorn this great man had for himself during his entire life,"[76] and the fact that he even went so far as to "welcome scorn,"[77] "having a fervent desire to be treated only as an object of the greatest contempt."[78] The ultimate proof, however, was to be found in the fact that although "he was entirely radiant and his face shone with light like another Moses. Yet, he was the only one who could not see, or appreciate the beauty of his own eminent virtues,"[79] as he "glorified his lowliness, and... made himself poor in order to enrich the poor."[80]

Vincent the Evangelizer. Early nineteenth-century Italian holy card.
Courtesy Vincentian Studies Collection, Special Collections and Archives, DePaul University, Chicago, Illinois

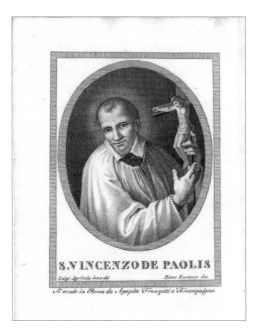

S. VINCENZO DE PAOLIS

According to the bishop, this example of the "miraculous genius"[81] of Monsieur Vincent's humility was something which "was difficult... to understand."[82] Yet, this initial incomprehension was itself evidence of the luminosity of Vincent's virtue, it could not be understood from the perspective of "merely human considerations."[83] Thus, Maupas du Tour proceeded to explain, "the constancy of his (Vincent's) humility"[84] is the only way that it could be explained; from the perspective of faith. Vincent de Paul's fervent desire to be dismissed as a person "of no real importance,"[85] was the necessary result of his desire above all else to seek only the glory of doing God's will in his life.[86] Maupas du Tour notes:

> In effect, Messieurs, wasn't it necessary that a soul so dedicated to self-abandonment, and which throughout every moment of life had sought nothing other than the glory of God, would have had to descend far into the deepest abyss to establish the source of its humility? And, Messieurs, what is the ultimate abyss at the bottom of the earth? It is hell, that sad, eternal dwelling place for God's enemies... Messieurs, I dare to say that this great man, revealed what he honestly thought about himself when he said he was worse than the devil... This was astonishing to witness, Messieurs, because through his incredible humility he was able to compartmentalize his heart. On the one hand he could feel the fires of hell. Simultaneously, however, because of the ardor of his zealous charity he could also feel those very different flames which resemble the innocent flames of the Seraphim that burn in Heaven.[87]

Vincent knew "that human beings are always prone to seek that which is... the most advantageous to their own interests, even above the interests of God's glory."[88] This sinful tendency "was a terrible danger"[89] to be avoided at all costs because the "illusions"[90] it created "threatened the entire ruin"[91] of all that one tried to accomplish in God's name and in fulfillment of his will.

Vincent de Paul's personal humility and meekness provided him with a "perfect temperament,"[92] a self-emptying stance that led him "to strip himself of his human spirit"[93] and gave him a remarkable amount of confidence,[94] freedom, and strength to depend on Jesus Christ alone, "and the inspirations provided by God's spirit."[95] According to Maupas du Tour:

> I know it is easy to be astonished by the success of all the activities he undertook in ways that were so totally contrary to the means which ordinarily would have been suggested by mere human prudence. This great success came about because.... God for his part, draws near to those who search for him and he fills them with the light of his wisdom. He then brings about favorable conclusions to even the most difficult

affairs having but the gloomiest prospects of success, which would ordinarily make even the most prudent spirits grow faint[96]

"THE ENTIRE WORLD WAS WARMED BY THE HOLY ZEAL OF HIS CHARITY"[97]

In the second half of his *oraison funèbre* Maupas du Tour undertook a breathless recital of examples of Vincent's "consuming,"[98] "ardent,"[99] "heroic"[100] charity "as a true pastor of souls"[101] serving the poor. "Here Messieurs, is the example of a charitable heart dedicated in the highest degree to a perfect charity (and prodigious generosity[102]) towards the neighbor in imitation of the heart of God, which is to say that he embraced everyone and refused no one."[103] The bishop also pointed out, "You know from the account of his actions, and the sentiments of his own heart, that God had created him to be poor only in order to serve the poor."[104] "Monsieur Vincent said, 'We are for the poor, and the poor are ours. Just as a hunter chases his game everywhere, wherever we find *les misérables* it is necessary for us to assist them at all costs.'"[105]

Vincent's charitable activities toward the poor were matched by his zeal, "the urgency of his love, [and] the tenderness of his compassion"[106] in addressing their spiritual poverties as well. According to Maupas du Tour "he courageously fed souls with the three excellent foods of the Church... Jesus Christ, the sacraments, and scripture."[107] It was through his pastoral zeal, and that of his followers:

> ...that millions of souls have been sanctified through the work of the parish missions... It was he who saved, from ultimate disaster those unfortunate souls, who by a deadly combination of a profound ignorance of our faith's sacred mysteries and of the Christian truths necessary for salvation, as well as shameful lives marked by crime and licentiousness, seemed destined never to know God except through the rigor of his judgments and the eternity of his punishments.[108]

For Maupas du Tour and his audience, the answers to the following rhetorical questions were obvious: "Was there ever an opportunity for helping the afflicted when he did not tenderly embrace them? When did he not run zealously to their aid?"[109]

Vincent de Paul saw evangelization and outreach to the poor as gospel hallmarks for the reform of the Church, especially parish life and the priesthood. Maupas du Tour and his audience fully appreciated Vincent's identity and activities as a Tridentine reformer.[110] In perhaps the most famous line from the *oraison funèbre*, the bishop noted: "Yes, Messieurs, it is necessary to tell you it was VINCENT DE PAUL who all but changed the face of the Church."[111] Vincent, in his zeal, was able to accomplish all of this because his "perfect love"[112] for the Church gave him a "heart... so vast, and so generous, that he refused to accept defeat in any of his Apostolic labors."[113]

His zeal to serve the Church included "the zeal he had to maintain the Purity of good doctrine."[114] With this, Maupas du Tour carefully laid out Vincent's opposition to the "doctrinal novelties"[115] of Jansenism, which he noted was "a vast subject."[116] He reminded his listeners that Vincent's opposition was first and foremost that of a theologian "who diligently studied theology in Toulouse, Rome, and Paris,"[117] and who was every bit the equal to any doctor of the Sorbonne, "the holiest and most knowledgeable School in the world."[118] As a theologian, Vincent "in perfect obedience... followed all the teachings and the doctrine of the Gospel, but only as they were interpreted by the Church,"[119] which is to say through "the authority of the Vicar of JESUS CHRIST in the person of him who is the successor of Saint Peter."[120]

The bishop described the Jansenists contemptuously, "You with your small minds; you who are rebels... you who are unnatural children and who scorn your holy Mother the Church.... learn from VINCENT DE PAUL.... This is an unjust quarrel against the Church who is the chaste Spouse of the Son of God, and the common Mother of all Christians. This same Church shares in Christ's authority since she is equally infallible today as she was in the time of the Apostles."[121] The French Church's internal struggles with Jansenism would last for more than 100 years, and would even play out dramatically during Vincent's canonization cause, as shall be seen.

NAME-DROPPING: "THE GREATEST FIGURES OF THE CHURCH, COURT, AND THE KING'S COUNCILS, ADMIRED HIS VIRTUE"[122]

There was a clear hierarchy to the appreciation and approval of Vincent de Paul that Maupas du Tour presented in his *oraison funèbre*. The most important seal to be publicized was that of the Crown, in the person of the regent, Anne of Austria: "I know that in the King's Council the Queen was able to observe first-hand the actions of the late Monsieur Vincent, Superior General of the Mission, and that she has spoken publicly about his virtues.... in bringing about peace, and the king's subsequent marriage."[123] "The most virtuous and the greatest queen in the world had the greatest admiration for his rare talents, grace and holiness."[124] The queen also demonstrated her approval through "her generous almsgiving"[125] in support of Vincent's efforts.

After the queen, it was important to establish Cardinal Jules Mazarin's admiration for Monsieur Vincent.[126] This was followed by documenting the approval of two other French cardinals (by this time deceased): Pierre de Bérulle[127] and François de la Rochefoucauld.[128] Another very important personal endorsement mentioned by Maupas du Tour was that of François de Sales. In his last visit to Paris in 1621, the bishop of Geneva had selected Vincent de Paul to serve as the ecclesiastical superior for the first monastery of the Visitation founded in the capital:[129] "In the preference to all others he chose the uniquely qualified Monsieur VINCENT who was an excellent copy of the perfect original."[130] It was perfect timing to recall the intimate connection between Vincent de Paul and François de Sales given the fact that the beatification of de Sales was then in the final stages of approval in Rome.[131]

Other contemporary figures mentioned by name included: Jean-Jacques Olier,[132] Marguerite de Gondi the Marquise de Maignelay,[133] Françoise-Marguerite de Silly,[134] and her husband Philippe-Emmanuel de Gondi.[135]

Contemporary portraits of Philippe-Emmanuel de Gondi; Françoise-Marguerite de Silly; and Marguerite de Gondi the Marquise de Maignelay.
Vincentian Studies Institute Collected Illustrations

VINCENT DE PAUL'S LAST GIFT TO FRANCE: PEACE

On 26 August 1660, the young Louis XIV made his triumphal entry into Paris with his new wife (and first-cousin) Marie-Thérèse d'Autriche, the Infanta of Spain.[136] The marriage had been arranged as part of the Peace of the Pyrenees negotiated by Cardinal Mazarin in 1659, finally bringing an end to a quarter century of warfare between the two kingdoms. In November of 1660, as Maupas du Tour delivered his *oraison funèbre*, the memories of these events would have been fresh in the minds of his listeners.

During Vincent's long lifetime there was not a single year in which France was at peace. The geo-political, economic, and other consequences of this constant warfare were considerable for the kingdom. Not the least of these consequences were famine, refugees, beggars, abandoned children and, in general, an unprecedented increase in the numbers of French subjects who were impoverished and living at the edge of disaster. Maupas du Tour described how Vincent came to the conclusion that "it was high time for the soldiers to be removed from the midst of our parishes, and time to declare a new war on behalf of the Gospel and the Faith."[137] Vincent therefore "resolved to offer himself to our Lord as a public victim in order to obtain peace."[138]

Vincent preaching, asking for support for the foundlings.
Nineteenth-century French print.
Courtesy Vincentian Studies Collection, Special Collections and Archives,
DePaul University, Chicago, Illinois

Maupas du Tour described how Vincent mobilized his missionaries at Saint-Lazare to undertake unceasing prayers for peace:

> He prayed to God for peace by means of an extraordinary novena. Every day for nine years the community of Saint-Lazare prayed for peace. Two or three confreres would receive communion for this special intention. Each day a priest from the community said Mass for this intention, and a brother took communion at this Mass that could appropriately be called a Mass for peace. The priest and the brother then spent the rest of the day fasting. There was a table inside the refectory where they sat which was called the fasting table. Monsieur Vincent... took his turn at this novena for peace with the only difference being that he took his turn twice as often as anyone else.... at the end of nine years, a general peace was concluded between the two crowns.[139]

Maupas du Tour commented on the efficacy of these prayers, noting that the queen "has said she has no doubts that the prayers of this great servant of God were instrumental both in bringing about peace, and the king's subsequent marriage."[140]

"VINCENT DE PAUL, WHO WE BELIEVE TODAY REIGNS IN HEAVEN..."[141]

The *oraison funèbre* ended with Maupas du Tour reiterating his personal belief that Vincent de Paul was a saint who now resided in heaven, and who from that place would continue to intercede on behalf of the Church, Cardinal Mazarin, the king and queen, each and every one of those who were in attendance at the memorial service, and indeed for the speaker himself.[142] Having finished his remarks the bishop invited his audience, in "the liberty of your own thoughts and judgments,"[143] to answer these rhetorical questions: "What can you say, Messieurs, about a man who was so humble, so full of abandonment, so forgetful of himself, so regular in all his actions? What can you say about a man who was so prudent that you could even say that he was wisdom personified, who decided nothing without consulting the will of God, and who accepted no work without an extraordinary indication from the Spirit of God?"[144] In essence, as the bishop implied in his rhetorical questions to his listeners: what can you say other than to agree that Vincent de Paul was a saint, and then to await the results of his miraculous intercession from heaven?

---

[1] See *Superna Hierusalem*, 40.

[2] Jean Couty served as Superior General of the Congregation of the Mission and the Company of

the Daughters of Charity from 11 March 1736 to 4 August 1746. Since the time of Vincent de Paul and Louise de Marillac, the Superior General of the Congregation of the Mission also serves as the Superior General of the Daughters of Charity. For a biographical sketch of Jean Couty see, *Recueil des Principales Circulaires des Supérieurs Généraux de la Congrégation de la Mission*, 3 vols. (Paris: Georges Chamerot, 1877-80), 1:515. Hereafter cited as *Circulaires*.

[3] See *Superna Hierusalem*, 40.

[4] For full details of the ceremony see *Ibid.*, 40-41. Vincent de Paul was canonized along with the Jesuit Jean-François Regis, Juliana Falconieri, and Caterina Fieschi Adorno.

[5] See "Relation de ce qui s'est passé à Saint-Lazare pendant l'octave solennelle de la Canonisation de saint Vincent de Paul," *Circulaires*, 1:769-776.

[6] See du Tour, *Funeral Oration*, p. 91.

[7] *Ibid.*

[8] For a short biographical sketch of Louis Abelly see John E. Rybolt, C.M., "Louis Abelly, his Life and Works," *Abelly*, 1:9-16.

[9] Abelly followed up on his massive 1664 biography with a much smaller condensed version, published in 1667. See Louis Abelly, *La vie du vénérable serviteur de Dieu Vincent de Paul, instituteur et première superior général de la Congrégation de la Mission* (Paris: Florentin Lambert, 1664 & 1667). See also *Abelly*.

[10] Both were well-known, well-connected, reform ecclesiastics (Maupas du Tour as a bishop, Abelly soon to be named a bishop). Both were best-selling authors (Maupas du Tour as the author of biographies of François de Sales and Jeanne de Chantal. Abelly as the author of numerous volumes of theology). Both also knew Vincent de Paul personally.

[11] Maupas du Tour was one of two bishops who gave the needed ecclesiastical approval for the publication of Abelly's biography of Vincent de Paul in 1664. See *Abelly*, 1:26-27.

[12] For example, Maupas du Tour's comment: "This is the miraculous genius of the great VINCENT DE PAUL whose grace, fidelity, and courage today is the object of our wonder, and who for countless centuries to come will receive the admiration of God's Church… whom you and I have often admired and considered to be a Saint." See du Tour, *Funeral Oration*, p. 105.

[13] As noted by Maupas du Tour: "Monsieur VINCENT was the instrument chosen by the greatest designs of Divine Providence to be involved in all the most important activities that have given glory to God, been advantageous to our religion, and brought honor to the state." See *Ibid.*, pp. 96-97.

[14] This meant of course that the Protestant minority in France would have to be marginalized. After their defeat in 1629 at the siege of La Rochelle, the days of a limited tolerance afforded to the Huguenots by the Edict of Nantes (1598) were numbered. In 1685 Louis XIV finally revoked the edict.

[15] As Abelly noted in the dedication of his biography to Anne of Austria:

> Should Your Majesty deign to give me audience I shall have the honor of recalling several matters which will without doubt confirm his reputation. They will console you greatly, for you will recognize the great things he accomplished for God and for the building up of the kingdom of Jesus Christ during the regency. These took place not only by your permission and support but even more so by your zeal, your concern and your generosity. What should be a source of joy for you is that all the great enterprises started by Monsieur Vincent still function, better than ever, under the wise guidance of our incomparable monarch who shines like the sun, vivifying all parts of his kingdom, who is very mindful to use all his strength of mind and inexhaustible zeal to preserve true religion and solid piety in all parts of the kingdom.

See *Abelly*, 1:22.

[16] One cost was incessant warfare: religious warfare with the Huguenot minority, the rebellions of the Fronde, the Thirty Years War, and the War with Spain.

[17] Contemporary architectural expressions of the self-confidence and self-perceived, self-ascribed

greatness of Louis XIV as "Ludovico Magno" include the triumphal victory arch at the Porte Saint-Denis, the Hôtel des Invalides, and, of course, the palace of Versailles.

[18] This brilliance was soon to be marred by the almost century-long internecine controversy over Jansenism which would split the French Church, have grave political consequences, and even affect Vincent de Paul's canonization cause, as will be seen in Chapter 3.

[19] Maupas du Tour also reminded his listeners of the impact of Vincent de Paul and his missionaries outside of France. See du Tour, *Funeral Oration*, **pp. 98-99, 102, 116, and 120.**

[20] See *Ibid.*, **pp. 96, 98, 118-120,** and **124-126.**

[21] As noted by Maupas du Tour, because of his "disinterested charity" Vincent de Paul also never took advantage of his access to power and privilege for any personal gain or personal favors that would have benefitted him or his communities. In the bishop's words: "Monsieur Vincent never said or did anything to acquire anything for himself.... even though he often had the opportunity to do [so]." This was worth noting as a heroic gesture because it was so unusual in a system which relied on patronage, power, and relationships to solicit and receive benefits. See *Ibid.*, **p. 114.**

[22] See *Ibid.*, **p. 93.**

[23] Vincent also required a corporate humility for the groups he founded. For example, "So, my dear confreres, let's humble ourselves to know that God has looked to this Little Company to serve His Church – if we can call a Company a fistful of men of lowly birth, learning, and virtue, the dregs, the sweepings, and the rejects of the world." Conference 2, "The Mission Preached In Folleville In 1617," n.d., *CCD*, 11:2.

[24] See, for example, Vincent's letter of 16 March 1644 to Bernard Codoing: "The rest will come in due time. Grace has its moments. Let us abandon ourselves to the Providence of God and be on our guard against anticipating it. If Our Lord is pleased to give any consolation in our vocation, it is this: I think it seems to me that we have tried to follow Divine Providence in all things and to put our feet only in the place It has marked out for us." Letter 704, "To Bernard Codoing, Superior, In Rome," Paris, 16 March 1644, *Ibid.*, 2:499.

[25] See, for example, Vincent's letter of 23 June 1656 to Jean Martin:

> If anyone in this world has a greater obligation to humble themselves, it is you and I (I include also those who are working with you): I, for my sins, and you, for the good God has been pleased to do through you; I, at seeing myself unable to assist souls, and you at seeing yourself chosen to contribute to the sanctification of an infinite number of them, and to do it so successfully. Profound humility is needed in order not to be complacent about such progress and public applause; a great but most necessary humility is required to refer to God all the glory from your work. Yes, Monsieur, you need a firm and vigorous humility to bear the weight of so many of God's graces, and a deep sentiment of gratitude to acknowledge the Author of them.

Letter 2085, "To Jean Marin, Superior, In Turin," Paris, 23 June 1656, *Ibid.*, 5:635.

[26] See, for example, the notes from the council meeting of the Daughters of Charity in February 1658:

> We first gave an account... of the thoughts God had given us concerning the grace His Goodness had granted us of preserving Most Honored Father from a serious accident.... We then remarked that God had used this means to make us realize that we hadn't made good use of the graces God had given our Little Company in his charitable guidance, his admirable concern, and his instructions on our obligations, given so often with such praiseworthy forbearance and gentleness.... we had all resolved, with God's grace, to be more attentive to the privilege we had of hearing Most Honored Father's word as the word of God pointing out His Will to us, and to be more faithful in putting it into practice.
>
> Most Honored Father in his great humility was very surprised at this; in his usual manner he began to speak in terms of very great disregard for himself,

saying, "I'm a miserable sinner who only spoils everything. If there's any fault in the Company, I'm the cause of it." Then he became very quiet, and his silence and recollection made us clearly understand that we had greatly embarrassed him. But, as usual, his forbearance kept him from reproving us for it.

Document 179, "Council Of February 29, 1658," *Ibid.*, 13b:359-360.

See also, for example, the letter of 14 September 1657 to Edme Jolly:

The illness of Messieurs Duport and Lejuge has distressed me deeply, especially that of the first-mentioned. Oh! What a loss, Monsieur, unless God performs a miracle to preserve him! We have great reason to fear that God may take them all, one after another, because of my sins, which alone bring upon the Company the trials God chooses to send it.

Letter 2377, "To Edme Jolly, Superior, In Rome," Paris, 14 September 1657, *Ibid.*, 6:482.

[27] See Letter 392, "To Mother De La Trinite, In Troyes," Saint-Lazare-lez-Paris, 28 August 1639, *Ibid.*, 1:570.

[28] See, for example, Vincent's conference of 20 August 1655: "Alas, wretch that I am! I humbly ask pardon of God.... O Savior, forgive this wretched sinner, who spoils all Your plans, who opposes and contradicts them everywhere..." Conference 134, "Method To Be Followed In Preaching," 20 August 1655, *Ibid.*, 11:247.

[29] A point that Abelly himself made in the introduction to his biography. See *Abelly*, 1:24.

[30] Most sources agree that an average lifespan for a man of his time was approximately 35 years of age.

[31] For example Vincent made no secret of his modest peasant origins and would constantly make reference to these as a counter-balance to any unwanted public attention he received. See du Tour, *Funeral Oration*, p. 137, n. 44.

[32] Maupas du Tour says that: "This is the only example we can find in his life of an exception to the candor of his soul.... He tolerated this violation of the usually inviolable laws of his honesty only because it was necessary that in this innocent quarrel between two of the most beautiful virtues, his humility should prevail..." *Ibid.*, p. 103. See also, Conference 198, "Seeking The Kingdom Of God," (Common Rules, Chap. II, Art. 2), 21 February 1659, *CCD*, 12:114; and Conference 210, "Moral Theology, Preaching, Catechizing, And Administration Of The Sacraments," 5 August 1659, *Ibid.*, 12:238. See also *Abelly*, 3:186.

[33] For a biographical sketch of Antoine Portail see Letter 26, "To Pope Urban VIII," [June 1628], *CCD*, 1:38-39, n. 2.

[34] For a biographical sketch of Louise de Marillac see Letter 12, "To Saint Louise De Marillac," 30 October 1626, *Ibid.*, 1:23-24, n. 1.

[35] For a biographical sketch of Philippe-Emmanuel de Gondi see Letter 6, "To Philippe-Emmanuel De Gondi, In Provence," [August or September 1617], *Ibid.*, 1:18, n. 1.

[36] In his *oraison funèbre* Maupas du Tour related an incident from Vincent's childhood: "Once, when he was a young boy he was carrying his father's grain from the mill to the granary when he distributed the wheat to the poor and then returned home." The source for this anecdote is unknown, although it was repeated with variations in subsequent biographies. See du Tour, *Funeral Oration*, pp. 112-113. See also *Coste*, 1:11-12.

[37] After the publication of the Abelly biography it became a universally recommended source for Lazarists and Daughters of Charity to reflect upon the example of their founder and better imitate his example. See, for example, "Moyens de conserver l'esprit primitif de la Congrégation, proposés en l'Assemblée générale de l'année 1668," *Circulaires*, 1:100.

[38] In 1657, Vincent's secretary, Brother Bertrand Ducournau composed a confidential memorandum advocating the documentation and preservation of "the holy discourses of Monsieur Vincent." He noted in part, "If the works he has accomplished are works of God, as they seem to be, God must have bestowed His Spirit on them in order to accomplish and maintain them; consequently, the advice and instruction employed to that end should be regarded as divine, and collected as a heavenly manna,

whose various flavors attracted so many different sorts of persons of both sexes and of every rank of life, who have associated themselves in various ways, on behalf of so many different enterprises, and who have been supported by his guidance...." Quoted in "Preface To The English Translation Of Father Coste's Work," *CCD*, 1:xix-xx.

[39] Abelly notes that in 1639 he took advantage of a trip to Gascony to visit Vincent's family in their home town and learn more about their famous relative. See *Abelly*, 1:24. See also du Tour, *Funeral Oration*, Chapter 2, notes 58 and 63.

[40] The Congregation of the Mission has two types of members: clerics and lay-brothers. Since the Congregation is not a religious order with solemn vows, its brothers have the canonical status of lay persons who join the Congregation to support its ministries and institutions by their labor. See General Curia of the Congregation of the Mission, *Constitutions and Rules*, English translation (Philadelphia, 1984), 28.

[41] For more information on Bertrand Ducournau see Stafford Poole, C.M., "Brother Bertrand Ducournau," *Vincentian Heritage* 6:2 (1985): 247-255. Hereafter *Ducournau*. For a biographical sketch of Brother Ducournau see "Introduction To The French Edition," *CCD*, 1:xxvi, n. 4.

[42] For a biographical sketch of Brother Robineau see *Ibid.*, 1:xxvi-xxvii, n. 5. Louis Robineau was the author of an extensive set of personal notes and observations about Vincent de Paul. See *Robineau*. These invaluable notes, and other information provided by Brother Ducournau, were essential resources for Louis Abelly's later biography.

[43] Once the Congregaton of the Mission received royal and papal approval (in 1627 and 1633 respectively), and became a legal and canonical entity, its corporate records, including those generated by Vincent de Paul as its superior general, were carefully preserved in the Congregation's archives. See Document 62, "Royal Letters Patent For The Approval Of The Congregation Of The Mission," [May 1627], *CCD*, 13a:226-227. See also Document 84a, "*Salvatoris Nostri*, Bull Of Erection Of The Congregation Of The Mission," [12 January 1633], *Ibid.*, 13a:296-304.

[44] See *Ducournau*, 252-253. It is interesting to note that the Daughters of Charity had long been preserving Vincent's conferences to them.

[45] Located in the present-day department of the Landes. See also *Ibid.*, 253-254.

[46] He was a canon of the cathedral chapter at Dax.

[47] For the texts of these two famous letters see: Letter 1, "To Monsieur De Comet, In Dax," Avignon, 24 July 1607, *CCD*, 1:1-11; and Letter 2, "To Monsieur De Comet, In Dax," Rome, 28 February 1608, *Ibid.*, 1:11-15.

[48] For more information on the extensive slave trade fostered by the Barbary pirates in the seventeenth century see, for example, Adam Tinniswood, *Pirates of Barbary: Corsairs, Conquests and Captivity in the Seventeenth-Century Mediterranean* (London: Riverhead Books, 2010).

[49] Vincent's letters to Monsieur de Comet were written not just to explain a two-year disappearance, but also to re-establish their patron/client relationship, so that the Dax lawyer might fulfill his request for assistance in acquiring and sending official copies of needed personal documents. See Letter 2, *CCD*, 1:13-15.

[50] For a brief biographical sketch of Jean Dehorgny, see Letter 26, *Ibid.*, 1:39, n. 6.

[51] For a brief biographical sketch of René Alméras (who would succeed Vincent de Paul as the superior general of the Congregation of the Mission and the Daughters of Charity in 1661), see Letter 368, "To Robert De Sergis, In Toulouse," Paris, 3 February 1639, *Ibid.*, 1:529, n. 7.

[52] For the full story of the provenance of these letters see Letter 1, *Ibid.*, 1:1-2, n. Letter 1.

[53] Letter 3101, "To Canon Jean De Saint-Martin, In Dax," 18 March 1660, *Ibid.*, 8:313.

[54] One of the ministries that Vincent de Paul and the Congregation of the Mission had undertaken was as French consuls in the Barbary states, to represent French interests there and, in particular, to minister to and assist in the ransom-release of French slaves. For more information see: *Abelly*, 2:84-126; and Coste, *Life*, 2:337-365.

[55] In this section of his letter, Brother Ducournau uses the content of one of the letters to construct a

metaphor summarizing Vincent's entire career. See the original of the letter referenced immediately below.

[56] See Appendix Letter 1, "Brother Ducournau To Canon De Saint-Martin," August 1658, *CCD*, 8:599-601.

[57] See du Tour, *Funeral Oration*, **p. 141**, n. 70, and **p. 146**, n. 120.

[58] The activities of Brothers Ducournau and Robineau in this process are key. André Dodin has commented:

> For more than ten years these two secretaries not only recorded what Father Vincent dictated to them. They listened to him, and carefully heard the tonalities of his voice. M. Vincent questioned them, and they in turn asked for his advice and counsel. He shared with them his impressions and his wishes. They were his primary confidants who witnessed his pains and his joys. The two secretaries did not hesitate to question their old master, to ask him what he thought about persons and events. Because of these two companions who shared a common life (with Vincent) we can better understand the atmosphere and presence that surrounded Vincent de Paul. Respectful and admiring observers they are the only ones who can aid us to better understand the passion which sustained his life....

See the "Introduction" to the original French publication of Louis Robineau, *André Dodin, C.M., présente Louis Robineau. Monsieur Vincent: Raconté par son secrétaire; Remarques sur les actes et paroles de feu Monsieur Vincent de Paul, notre Trés Honoré Père et Fondateur* (Paris: O.E.I.L., 1991), 10.

[59] See du Tour, *Funeral Oration*, **p. 93**.

[60] It is interesting to note, however, that Maupas du Tour admits that reverence for Vincent de Paul was not universal. Throughout his career, Vincent's public profile and activities placed him at odds with a variety of vested personal, political, economic, social, and religious interests, which led to some level of public criticism and even personal attacks. Maupas du Tour makes an oblique reference to such criticism in his *oraison funèbre*. See *Ibid.*, **pp. 116-117**. In addition, Maupas du Tour notes: "He suffered the most extreme slanders without ever trying to explain, or defend himself.... He chose instead to suffer, even if it meant his silence was interpreted as an admission of guilt." See *Ibid.*, **p. 122**. This issue is also addressed by Abelly and Robineau. See *Ibid.*, **p. 155**, n. 233.

[61] After attending Vincent's memorial service Jean Loret (the originator of the *gazette burlesque*) wrote in *Le Muse historique*: "En vérité, si c'etait moi le Pontifie de Rome, je canoniserais cet homme." Quoted in Coste, *Life*, 3:401. "Jean Loret (ca. 1600-1665) was a French writer and poet known for publishing the weekly news of Parisian society (including, initially, its pinnacle, the court of Louis XIV itself) from 1650 until 1665. He is sometimes referred to as the 'father of journalism' as a result of his topical writings." See *Wikipedia*, s.v. "Jean Loret," at: **http://en.wikipedia.org/wiki/Jean_Loret** (accessed 26 November 2012).

[62] See du Tour, *Funeral Oration*, **p. 105**.

[63] As Abelly noted, for example: "Some things I assert that I have seen with my own eyes, or heard with my ears, having had the good fortune of knowing and associating with Monsieur Vincent for many years." See *Abelly*, 1:24.

[64] See du Tour, *Funeral Oration*, **p. 98**.

[65] Maupas du Tour knew about this fine rhetorical line because of the difficulties he had encountered on this front in 1657 with the publication of his biography of François de Sales. For more information see notes 62 and 63 in chapter one, *supra*.

[66] See Lawrence S. Cunningham, *A Brief History of the Saints* (Malden, MA: Blackwell, 2005).

[67] 2 Cor. 8:18. All English language references to, or translations of portions of, Sacred Scripture are taken from *The New American Bible*, Saint Joseph Edition. Hereafter (NAB). All Latin language quotations from Sacred Scripture are taken from the Vulgate (Stuttgart edition) translation found at: **http://www.drbo.org/lvb/**.

[68] See du Tour, *Funeral Oration*, **p. 91**.

[69] *Ibid.*, p. 95.

[70] *Ibid.*, p. 99.

[71] *Ibid.*, p. 96.

[72] *Ibid.*, p. 98.

[73] *Ibid.*, pp. 96-97.

[74] *Ibid.*, p.93.

[75] *Ibid.*, pp. 93, 95.

[76] *Ibid.*, pp. 92, 128.

[77] *Ibid.*, p. 95.

[78] *Ibid.*, p. 97.

[79] *Ibid.*, pp. 95-96.

[80] *Ibid.*, p. 94.

[81] *Ibid.*, p. 105.

[82] *Ibid.*, p. 93.

[83] *Ibid.*, p. 100.

[84] *Ibid.*, pp. 98-99.

[85] *Ibid.*, p. 103.

[86] See, for example, Letter 3089, "To Sister Mathurine Guérin, Sister Servant, In La Fére," 3 March 1660, *CCD*, 8:298. "Indeed the great secret of the spiritual life is to abandon all that we love to Him by abandoning ourselves to all that He wishes, with perfect confidence that everything will turn out for the best."

[87] See du Tour, *Funeral Oration*, pp. 104-105.

[88] *Ibid.*, p. 99.

[89] *Ibid.*

[90] See, for example, Letter 1134, "To Brother Jacques Rivet," 5 September 1649, *CCD*, 3:476.

[91] See du Tour, *Funeral Oration*, p. 99.

[92] *Ibid.*, p. 100.

[93] *Ibid.*

[94] Maupas du Tour dedicated a section of the *oraison funèbre* to a discussion of Vincent's confidence in Divine Providence. See *Ibid.*, pp. 113-114.

[95] *Ibid.*, p. 100.

[96] *Ibid.*

[97] *Ibid.*, p. 98.

[98] *Ibid.*, pp. 110, 115.

[99] *Ibid.*, p. 112.

[100] *Ibid.*, pp. 118-121.

[101] *Ibid.*, p. 121.

[102] *Ibid.*, p. 112.

[103] *Ibid.*, p. 113.

[104] *Ibid.*, p. 113. Maupas du Tour was capable of making extreme and unsubstantiated statements. With respect to Vincent's youth spent on his family's farm, where he said over and over again he had tended to swine and livestock, the bishop noted: "he purposely described himself as being rooted in the earth, and even in the dung of the herds he often shepherded as a country youth, more as a practice of humility than because of the necessity of fortune." *Ibid.*, p. 102.

[105] *Ibid.*, p. 113.

[106] *Ibid.*, p. 108.

[107] *Ibid.*, p. 124.

[108] *Ibid.*, p. 96.

[109] *Ibid.*, p. 106.

[110] *Ibid.*, pp. 138-139, notes 50-56.

[111] *Ibid.*, p. 96.

112 *Ibid.*, p. 118.

113 *Ibid.*, p. 120.

114 *Ibid.*, p. 125.

115 *Ibid.*

116 *Ibid.*

117 *Ibid.*, p. 126.

118 *Ibid.*

119 *Ibid.*, pp. 126-127.

120 *Ibid.*, p. 126.

121 *Ibid.*, pp. 125-126.

122 *Ibid.*, p. 98.

123 *Ibid.*, pp. 86-87.

124 *Ibid.*, p. 98.

125 *Ibid.*, p. 109.

126 We have already seen in the first chapter the reasons that led Maupas du Tour to dedicate the published *oraison funèbre* to the cardinal. See also *Ibid.*, p. 131.

127 For a biographical sketch of Pierre de Bérulle, see Letter 7, "Madame De Gondi To Saint Vincent," [September 1617], *CCD*, 1:19-20, n. 3.

128 See du Tour, *Funeral Oration*, p. 125.

129 For more details on Vincent's relationships with François de Sales, Jeanne-Françoise de Chantal, and the monasteries of the Visitation in Paris, see *Ibid.*, p. 159, n. 275, and, n. 280.

130 See *Ibid.*, p. 128. Maupas du Tour's great emphasis on Vincent's relationship with François de Sales, Jeanne-Françoise de Chantal, and the Visitation is explained by his own close relationship with, and devotion to, them. He was the author of the first biographies of both figures, and preached the funeral oration in Paris for Jeanne-Françoise de Chantal.

131 The cause of the bishop of Geneva was under the patronage of the French Crown. François de Sales was beatified on 28 December 1661. Interestingly, the ceremony marked the first time a solemn beatification was held according to the new guidelines issued by Alexander VII. See, **http://www. vatican.va/roman_curia/congregations/csaints/documents/rc_con_csaints_doc_20050929_ saraiva-martins-beatif_en.html** (accessed 29 November 2012).

132 See du Tour, *Funeral Oration*, pp. 115-116.

133 For a biographical sketch of Charlotte-Marguerite de Gondi, the Marquise de Maignelay, see Letter 471, "The Marquise De Maignelay To Saint Vincent," Nanteuil, 21 August [1640], *CCD*, 2:109, n. 1. See also Marc de Bauduen, *La vie admirable de tres-haute, tres-puissante, tres-illustre, et tres vertueuse dame Charlote Marguerite de Gondy, marquise de Magnelais: où les ames fideles trouveront dequoy admirer & des vertus solides à imiter* (A Paris: Chez la veusve Nicolas Buon..., 1666).

134 For a biographical sketch of Françoise-Marguerite de Silly, see Letter 7, *CCD*, 1:19, n. 1.

135 For a biographical sketch of Philippe-Emmanuel de Gondi, see Letter 6, *Ibid.*, 1:18, n. 1. See also *Robineau*, 46-69.

136 See Jean Tronçon, *L'entrée trimphante de leurs majestez Louis XIV roy de France et de Nauarre, et Marie Therese d'Austriche son espouse: dans la ville de Paris capital de leurs royaumes, au retour de la signature de la paix generale et de leur hereux marriage* (Paris: chez Pierre Le petit...Thomas Ioly... et Louis Vilaine..., 1662). See also, Bernard Pujo, *Vincent de Paul: The Trailblazer* (Notre Dame: University of Notre Dame Press, 2003), ix.

137 See du Tour, *Funeral Oration*, p. 130.

138 *Ibid.*, p. 129

139 *Ibid.*, pp. 130-131.

140 *Ibid.*, p. 87.

141 *Ibid.*, p. 133.

142 *Ibid.*

143 *Ibid.*, p. 131.

144 *Ibid.*

Chapter 3

THE CANONIZATION OF VINCENT DE PAUL: "ANNUNTIO VOBIS GAUDIUM MAGNUM."[1]

If Maupas du Tour's *oraison funèbre* is to be recognized as the unofficial opening of Vincent de Paul's canonization cause, then the history of that cause from 1660 until its successful completion in 1737 is worthy of some study.

Louis Abelly's epic 1664 biography was the next stage in the pre-cause activity.[2] Like Maupas du Tour, Abelly also began with the presumption of Vincent's mature sanctity. He projected this assumption backwards and as he came to large gaps in the narrative of Vincent's early life he filled them in with a variety of mythic stories rooted in a greater, lesser, or non-existent degree of historicity.

Abelly's goal was to create a seamless and inspiring story of Vincent's sanctity from cradle to grave. For him the projection of sanctity backwards, and gap-filling, were eminently reasonable stratagems in service of an obvious conclusion and noble goal. Thus, where biography ran short, hagiography filled in and smoothed over. The resulting biography of Vincent de Paul proved to

Louis Abelly (1603–1691).
Vincentian Studies Institute Collected Illustrations

be tremendously popular, running into multiple editions. Most importantly it established a solid historical foundation for the close scrutiny of a canonization cause.[3]

In his 1748 post-canonization biography of Vincent de Paul, Pierre Collet, C.M., devotes his final chapter to the *"histoire de son culte"* in which he traces the full history of Vincent's road to canonization.[4] Of particular value in Collet's account are his detailed descriptions of the signs of the miraculous, which in his view were apparent in Vincent's life. Collet believed these were confirmed by the popular devotion of the faithful who, after Vincent's death, spontaneously turned to him seeking his intercession for their most pressing personal needs, especially healings. The news of extraordinary favors apparently granted through Vincent's intercession, particularly those that took place at his tomb at Saint-Lazare, created a continual popular buzz which had the effect of building the necessary momentum for the cause's eventual introduction. *Superna Hierusalem* describes these preparatory years thusly:

> Immediately after the death of this faithful servant, the reputation of his sanctity was diffused abroad in every place, and God deigned to confirm it by shining proofs and evident miracles, thus exciting, according to the admirable order of His Providence, in the hearts of the faithful a profound veneration for his inanimate remains, showing thereby, what glory his soul enjoyed in heaven, when in his body deprived of life, God manifested the signs of his power.[5]

One of the examples cited by Collet of a miraculous healing performed by Vincent during his lifetime was the spiritual healing of a Visitandine nun at the monastery in Troyes in 1637.[6] Another interesting instance Collet noted was a favor received by Henri de Maupas du Tour himself. According to Collet, a few years after Vincent's death Maupas du Tour was pressed to leave for Rome to work for the canonization of François de Sales (which would take place in 1665). However, he felt he could not depart without first finding someone to take over his responsibilities as *Grand Aumônier* to the aged Queen Mother, Anne of Austria; nor could he leave without arranging for his beloved niece's future. The bishop visited Vincent's tomb and "consulted him about these two concerns as he had been accustomed to do when he was still living." According to the bishop, he no sooner returned home that day when someone came and offered to see to his court responsibilities during his absence. The next day, the Comte de Coligny asked for the hand of his niece in marriage. According to Collet, the bishop "said he could not help but believe that his old friend had come to his assistance again."[7]

As Collet concluded: "these amazing events taking place continually since the death of the Servant of God over time naturally convinced his children to seek his beatification."[8] In October 1697, the General Assembly of the Congregation of the Mission met in Paris to elect a successor to the late superior general Edme Jolly. At the assembly's fifteenth session, held on October 18th, the delegates voted by acclamation to start their founder's cause.[9] There was a certain urgency behind their decision given the fact that the generation of those who could give personal testimony toward the cause was rapidly diminishing. The new superior general, Jean Pierron, sprang into action and began the preliminary steps.[10]

Under canonization rules then in effect there was a requirement of a fifty year waiting period following a person's death before the formal opening of his or her cause by the Holy See. The 1697 decision of the General Assembly to begin preparations to open Vincent's cause, thirteen years before the magic date of 1710, was not at all unusual. There was a tremendous amount of preparatory work to be done, and the Lazarists wanted everything to be ready when the moment arrived for the Holy See to act.

The official portraits of: Edme Jolly, C.M.; Jean Pierron, C.M.; and François Watel, C.M.
Vincentian Studies Institute Collected Illustrations

On 5 January 1705, Pierron's successor as superior general, François Watel,[11] assisted at the formal diocesan opening of Vincent's cause in the presence of Cardinal Louis-Antoine de Noailles, the archbishop of Paris.[12] It took only one year for sworn testimony to be recorded from 299 witnesses.[13] While the depositions were being taken in Paris and elsewhere, the archbishop conducted the process *de non cultu* to ascertain "that the honors paid to the Servant of God have not transgressed the limits authorized by the Church for those not yet officially beatified."[14] This included an official visitation of Saint-Lazare to inspect Vincent's tomb and his room.

The final stage of the initial preparation process in France consisted of the collection of postulatory letters. The canonization process required that the introduction of a cause "should be in response to a collective appeal, which the Church demands because She does not wish to examine a Cause until informed by a number of eminent personages... that the particular Cause is worthy of attention."[15] Vincent's file as forwarded to the Holy See contained seventy-two letters from prominent figures of Church and State, including most notably letters from Louis XIV, and James III of England (the Stuart "Old Pretender" who was living in exile in France). The General Assembly of the Clergy of France also sent a collective petition.[16] The cause was formally opened in Rome on 4 October 1709.[17]

Cardinal Louis-Antoine de Noailles (1651-1729), Archbishop of Paris.
Vincentian Studies Institute Collected Illustrations

The canonization process,[18] as reformed in the seventeenth century by Urban VIII and Alexander VII, was juridical in nature and designed to be long, complicated, adversarial, filled with red tape, ruinously expensive, and controlled tightly by the Holy See to emphasize the authority of the papacy.[19] International, local, and Roman politics, personalities, current and unforeseen events, also always influenced the pace and outcome of the process.

The Church's working assumption was that the candidate was not worthy of such an honor. After all, the Church and the pope were contemplating an infallible decision which would establish a person for time immemorial as a perfect example of Christian discipleship, a figure who could be counted on to provide a powerful heavenly intercession. Such a decision was not to be taken lightly. Thus, the famous role of the "devil's advocate," or the "Promoter of the Faith,"[20] was to protect the Church by methodically picking apart every candidacy, trying to find any reasonable doubt to delay or stop the cause either on evidentiary or procedural bases.[21]

In the case of Vincent's cause the most substantive *dubia* presented by the Promoter of the Faith was the nature of Vincent's early friendship with Jean du Vergier de Hauranne, the Abbé Saint-Cyran.[22] In 1668, Saint-Cryan's nephew Martin de Barcos had published a short book questioning Abelly's negative portrayal of Vincent de Paul's relationship with his uncle.[23] Jean Couty, the Lazarist representative in Rome, was able to clarify the facts of the relationship to the satisfaction of the Promoter of the Faith, Prospero Lambertini, and the other cause officials.[24] However, this exchange highlights the more important fact that Vincent's cause was unfolding against the backdrop of a renewed ecclesial and

---

Jean du Vergier de Hauranne, the Abbé Saint-Cyran (1581-1643).
Seventeenth-century etching by Jean Morin.
The Metropolitan Museum of Art. The Collection Online.
OASC via www.metmuseum.org

political crisis over Jansenism in France, which would reach a fever pitch after the issuance (at the request of Louis XIV) of the bull *Unigenitus* by Clement XI in 1713.[25]

"THE SHOCK WAVE OF UNIGENITUS…"[26]

On 1 January 1713, the Lazarist superior general, Jean Bonnet,[27] wrote in his New Year's circular letter to the community that he estimated Vincent's cause might only take five or six more years to complete.[28] His optimism proved unfounded. The dizzying stages of the process constantly moved attention and activity back and forth between Rome and Paris. Typically when some activity or report was due from the Lazarists, or had to take place in Paris, the response of the cause's supporters was quick. Just as typically, when the process or activity shifted back to Rome its pace was reduced to what the French perceived as a snail's pace, but which in reality was just Roman: unhurried.[29]

Prospero Lambertini's presentation of all his objections finally took place on 18 December 1717. These were ably answered by Jean Couty, and the French

Antoine Arnauld (1612-1694). Jansenist author of *De la fréquente Communion* (1643). *Courtesy Vincentian Studies Collection, Special Collections and Archives, DePaul University, Chicago, Illinois*

hoped that the pace of the cause would now quicken.[30] Instead, ten years passed. The Jansenist crisis in France intervened.

Historians and theologians have always had great difficulty in pinning down and explaining "Jansenism." Jean-Louis Quantin explains: "Jansenism... is a loose a polemical notion, which was redefined as the orthodoxy it was taken to oppose was itself refashioned. According to a well-known mechanism, condemnation and repression produced deviance at least as much as they responded to it. Anti-Jansenists, moreover, who had their own axe to grind, used the name to stigmatize ideas and practices that were never condemned by Church authorities."[31]

The papal bull *Unigenitus* of 1713 had been designed to put an end, once and for all, to the Jansenist controversies, but instead it radically politicized a theological debate — thus casting "a long baleful shadow over France throughout the eighteenth century."[32] The controversy became the most divisive political issue of the reign of Louis XV, spawning contentious debates about "political sovereignty and royal despotism."[33] These debates undermined "the judicial fictions that bound the *ancien régime* together: the identification of the corporate kingdom with the divinely ordained kingship and the conjunction of citizenship and Catholicity."[34] As Jacques Grès-Gayer noted, the bull created a theological crisis which "challenged papal authority, redefined Church doctrine, gave birth to 'ecclesiastical Gallicanism,' and sharpened the lines between orthodox Catholics and Jansenists."[35] Eventually, there were also elements of religious hysteria that came to the fore, including Jansenist claims of miraculous healings, ascetical self-torture, and the famous *convulsionnaires*.[36]

The Duc de Saint-Simon added his own predictably trenchant commentary on *Unigenitus* and the new controversies it engendered.[37] In his view the papal bull was "*si fatale à l'Église et à l'État, si honteuse à Rome, si funeste à la religion, si avantageuse aux jésuites, aux sulpiciens, aux untramontains, aux ignorants...*"[38] ("fatal to the Church and to the State, shameful to Rome, harmful to religion, advantageous to the Jesuits, Sulpicians, Ultramontanists, and the ignorant...").[39] He further commented: "Everything shines in it except the truth."[40] Then in 1714, Saint-Simon noted in his memoirs: "*Nous voici parvenus à l'époque... de la persécution qui a fait tant de milliers de confesseurs et quelques martyrs, dépeuplé les écoles et le places, introduit l'ignorance, le fanatisme et la dérèglement, couronné les vices, mis toutes les communautés dans la derniere confusion, le désordre partout, établi la plus arbitraire et les plus barbare inquisition.*"[41] ("We are now living... in a time of persecution, which has depopulated the schools, introduced ignorance, fanaticism, and disorder, crowned vice, thrown every community into the utmost confusion, with disorder everywhere, and established the most arbitrary and barbarous inquisition.")[42]

In his New Year's circular of 1715, Jean Bonnet wrote to his fellow Lazarists: "With respect to the present controversies in the Church, be extremely careful not to say or do anything outside of the bounds of Christian prudence, it is not enough for us as faithful Catholics to be far from all novel beliefs, and entirely submissive to our Holy Father the Pope and to our lords the Bishops. We are also required to be wise and prudent in our words and in our public conduct."[43] Bonnet struggled to maintain the Congregation's corporate silence in these very public disputes with danger in every direction.[44] He was still repeating this advice to his confreres in 1722.[45] His words had little effect, and the French members of the Congregation of the Mission became just as bitterly divided as the rest of the Gallican Church.[46]

The Lazarists in Italy and Poland were shocked by the divisions among their French confreres.[47] Given the prominence of the Lazarists in France, especially their pastoral role in royal foundations and in directing numerous diocesan seminaries, silence was not a sustainable strategy.[48] This stance also did nothing to advance the cause of Vincent de Paul, and even put the superior general himself under suspicion in Rome.[49]

On the eve of the Congregation's "turbulent" ninth General Assembly, held in Paris in August 1724, Jean Bonnet announced the expulsion from the community of two leading French Lazarists, Pierre Himbert (the superior general's first assistant)[50] and Antoine Philopald Delahaye.[51] They were accused of "trying to spread the fire of their revolt everywhere,"[52] by allegedly planning to challenge the general's authority at the coming General Assembly. After voting to confirm Himbert's deposition from his position as first assistant, there was considerable debate among the delegates about the exact phrasing to be used in the Congregation's public acceptance of *Unigenitus*.[53] The papal nuncio

Official portrait of Jean Bonnet, C.M.
Vincentian Studies Institute Collected Illustrations

became involved in the proceedings on 5 August.[54] He ordered that the Assembly move immediately to vote to adopt the papal bull, before conducting any other business.[55] Finally, after great struggles, wording was agreed upon which satisfied the nuncio and would signify a full acceptance of *Unigenitus* with only a minimum of reservation with respect to traditional Gallican liberties.[56] The language adopted said that the Congregation "accepted the *Unigenitus* bull and the other pontifical documents as 'published' by the bishops."[57]

The delegates supposedly "amidst perfect order, peace, and tranquility" unanimously affirmed "*sans gène et sans contrainte*" ("without trouble and without hesitation") the Congregation's full adherence to *Unigenitus*.[58] At the eleventh session of the Assembly held on 11 August, the delegates voted to require all priests, seminarians, and novices in the Congregation to indicate their acceptance of the bull. Those who refused were to be expelled from the community.[59] However, the king later said the corporate acceptance of the bull by the general assembly was sufficient. This leniency, however, did not apply to those French Lazarists who had publicly stated their opposition to the Bull. Those who refused to submit departed or were expelled from the Congregation.[60]

The Congregation of the Mission, its Superior General, and the French Lazarists were now unequivocally on record as being anti-Jansenist. The cause of Vincent de Paul was finally back on track in Rome.[61]

BEATIFICATION TO CANONIZATION

On 16 September 1727, in the presence of Benedict XIII, a general congregation of the Congregation of Rites "*déclarée, de voix unanime, avec toutes les marques de joie et d'applaudissement imaginables*" ("unanimously declared, with applause and every imaginable sign of joy") the decree establishing the heroic nature of the "theological and cardinal virtues" of Vincent de Paul.[62] As Pierre Coste noted:

> The most difficult stage was now over, but still the end of the journey had not been reached. Mortal men had been consulted, had borne witness, and all of them had proclaimed the holiness of Vincent de Paul. Another testimony remained to be studied, that of God Himself; it had been stated that He too had borne witness to the heroic virtue of His servant by working miracles. Rome was now to examine the truth of these statements.[63]

Luckily, the Lazarists had not allowed the controversies of the intervening years to stop them from collecting evidence of miracles that could be attributed to the intercession of Monsieur Vincent. There was a pool of twenty-one miracles ready to be presented. Since only three confirmed miracles were needed for the beatification of a founder of a religious community, only eight claims of instantaneous cures were brought forward.[64] Of these, four were rejected and four accepted.[65]

On 13 August 1729, Benedict XIII issued the brief for Vincent's beatification.[66] The elaborate beatification ceremony took place in St. Peter's basilica on the 21st of August. Appropriate ceremonies marking the occasion also took place the next month in Paris.[67] Even though the staggering costs of the beatification had tempted Jean Bonnet to delay moving forward with Vincent's canonization, he was persuaded otherwise.[68] The press for continuing the cause and certifying the final two miracles began immediately.

Meanwhile, back in Paris a Jansenist competitor to Blessed Vincent de Paul and his miracles emerged. As the Crown and orthodox French Catholics celebrated the beatification of the anti-Jansenist Monsieur Vincent, the Jansenists, for their part, found a holy figure for their intense counter-devotion: François de Pâris.

Born in 1690, as a young Jansenist cleric (he did not progress past ordination to the diaconate) François became famous in Paris (a heavily Jansenist city) as "Monsieur François." Living in one of the poorest sections of the city in the parish of Saint-Médard, his charity[69] and extreme public and private asceticism were renowned.[70] He died on 1 May 1727 as a result of what amounted to ascetical self-torture.[71] The crowds at his funeral desperately collected any relics they

Pope Benedict XIII (1650-1730).
Public Domain

could of "Blessed Pâris."[72] His tomb in the parish cemetery quickly became a site of pilgrimage. The posthumous publication of his eloquent profession of faith and devotional prayers reinforced both Jansenist theology and piety.[73] Biographies were rushed into print. Three appeared by 1731, and just as quickly were condemned.[74] There was also a flood of popular engravings.[75] One of these pointedly portrayed a number of Vincent de Paul's own *sœurs de la charité* attending Monsieur François during his illness.[76]

Throughout their struggles the Jansenists counted on miracles that would represent heavenly confirmation of their position. Claims of miraculous healings attributable to Monsieur François began with his funeral[77] and quickly escalated in subsequent years, finally leading to an outbreak of religious hysteria at his tomb among the famous *convulsionnaires*.[78] Thus, at one end of Paris at Saint-Lazare was the sedate tomb and popular pilgrimage site of the anti-Jansenist Blessed Vincent de Paul, who awaited the final two miracles needed for his canonization,[79] while at the other end of Paris at Saint-Médard was the not-so-sedate tomb of his Jansenist rival, awash in a sea of "miracles."[80]

Against this Parisian backdrop the final phase of Vincent de Paul's canonization began with another round of letters to the pope from Louis XV, James III, other European noble figures, and the General Assembly of the Clergy of France. The Lazarists were ready with seven possible miracles which had taken place since the beatification.[81] The officials of the Sacred Congregation of Rites met and considered each of these. Five of the seven were disallowed. If only one of the two remaining had been rejected the cause would have suffered a serious setback. One of these miracles would prove problematic: two healings experienced by a Benedictine nun, Sœur Marie-Therese de Saint-Basil from Montmirail in Brie.[82]

On 30 January 1736, the consideration of these last two miracles began.[83] The Promoter of the Faith and some of the Cardinals of the Congregation of Rites put forward strong opposition to the alleged healings of the nun. Opponents cited the rumor that she had sought a cure from the Jansenist Monsieur François. They also questioned whether a simple woman could give the type of polished testimony evident in her deposition.[84] The Lazarists and their supporters (now including Prospero Lambertini, who had been promoted to the cardinalate, and the see of Ancona) defended the authenticity of the miracle. After five months Clement XII decided to put an end to the debate. On 24 June 1736, he summoned the cause officials to his bedside at the Quirinal Palace (he was suffering from an attack of the gout) and accepted both proposed healings as miraculous.[85] The pontiff signed the final decree on 10 August.[86] Planning for the canonization ceremony could now begin.[87]

The superior general, Jean Couty, was still very conscious of the enormous expense of a canonization ceremony. He resolved, therefore, to wait for a number of other causes that were nearing completion to propose a single ceremony with shared expenses. All of these details were very complicated, but the date for the ceremony was finally set for 13 June 1737.

What had begun in November 1660 with Vincent's memorial service and the publication of Maupas du Tour's *oraison funèbre* would be completed with the canonization and publication of its accompanying papal bull, *Superna Hierusalem*. The anti-Jansenist rhetoric of the canonization bull was unmistakable:

> Now, it has pleased this God who has granted him the reward of eternal felicity in Heaven, this God who alone works miracles, to render him illustrious upon earth by miracles and prodigies, at a period especially in which by false and pretended miracles, innovators have endeavored in France, to diffuse their errors, to trouble the peace of the Church, and to separate simple souls from the apostolic See... Hence, conforming ourselves to the divine will, in order to animate the faithful to run in the way of salvation, to repress the wickedness of the perverse and to confound the malice of heretics, we this day decree, by our apostolic authority, that the servant of God, Vincent de Paul, may be venerated and honored with the worship and honor which are rendered to the Saints by all faithful people....[88]

The papal bull then presented the biography of Vincent de Paul not from the perspective of presumed sanctity, as Maupas du Tour and Louis Abelly had done, but of proven sanctity.[89] The biographical details in the bull are consistent with the foundational narratives of du Tour and Abelly. However, the impression given by the document is not so much that the patron of charity, evangelization, and Church reform was being canonized, but rather the zealous foe of Jansenism. Again the commentary on Vincent's opposition to Jansenism is unyielding:

> He was animated with a lively faith; hence he showed himself until his last sigh a valiant defender of the Church; and when heresy arose in France as a tempest, causing trouble and alarm every where, the servant of God sighed bitterly over it, because he saw that the error of Jansenism attacked faith at its foundation, that the heretics laid snares for simplicity, and allured the multitude into their impious belief.[90]

According to the bull, Vincent single-handedly rallied the bishops of France "to defend the sheep of the Lord which are confided to them from the rapacity of wolves."[91] This episcopal appeal to Innocent X had urged the pontiff:

...to condemn by his apostolic authority, these errors which contaminated people on every side, to the end that the Church, confirmed in its laws by a decisive decree, might close every entrance against its enemies, who, skillful in the perfidious art of deceiving, gave to their subtle reasonings the semblance of Catholic faith; and who, exhaling a mortal poison, perverted the most upright hearts, and endeavored to overturn all that faith teaches with regard to free will, to grace and the redemption of the human race, through the passion and death of JESUS CHRIST.[92]

Then Clement XII allowed his combative rhetoric to distort history. He noted that once Jansenism had been condemned by the Holy See, Vincent de Paul:

...ceased not to engage the King and Queen and their counselors, to use a just rigor in order to bring back the contumacious to obedience, and to banish even from every part of the kingdom, as a contagious evil, the most obstinate in their errors, in order that the severity of the civil laws might supply for the mildness of ecclesiastical discipline, which contenting itself with a sacerdotal judgment, abhors cruel vengeance, but nevertheless, makes use of the constitutions of Christian princes,

Pope Clement XII (1652-1740).
Public Domain

when the fear of corporal pain may lead to search for spiritual remedies.[93]

There is no evidence of any such activity by Vincent de Paul. In fact, this more closely describes the contemporary struggles of the papacy and their desire that Louis XV apply the full weight of his authority to silence Jansenism, and punish the Jansenists.

The celebrations in Paris honoring the new saint were only a few months past when the Jansenists tried a last ditch effort to stand up against papal authority. They were incensed by the pope's repeated descriptions in the bull of their cherished beliefs as heretical. They were equally angered by the direct attacks on the veracity of the miracles of François de Pâris. They bristled at the thought of intrusive papal calls for their punishment and extirpation by the king. They also were disturbed by what they perceived to be the selective historicism of the bull, which described Vincent de Paul's role in the condemnation of the famous five propositions,[94] but was silent on his opposition to moral laxism (which of course the Jansenists attributed to their enemies the Jesuits). The

---

The title page of *Augustinus* by Cornelius Jansen, published in 1640.
The text formed the basis of the Jansenist movement.
Public Domain

Nouvelles Ecclésiastiques was quick to confirm this assertion, pointing to Abelly's biography.[95] In his discussion of Vincent's opposition to Jansenism, Abelly accurately detailed:

> Although Monsieur Vincent was moved to true zeal against Jansenism and did all he could to oppose it, he was able to distinguish the condemned errors from laxism, which he never approved, as he showed on many occasions. He always recommended his confreres attach themselves strongly to a truly Christian morality, as taught in the Gospels and in the writings of the fathers and doctors of the Church. He highly praised the bishops and the Sorbonne who worked against moral laxity, just as much as against Jansenism. He accepted graciously what the Holy See taught on both the one and the other.[96]

On 4 January 1738, the Parlement of Paris issued an order suppressing the publication of the canonization bull, characterizing it as an ultramontane attack on the Gallican liberties.[97] The Parlement made it clear they were not opposing the canonization of Vincent de Paul, or the judgment of his holiness *per se*, only the ultramontane language of the bull and the underlying papal claims to supreme doctrinal and disciplinary authority over the Gallican Church. Pierre Coste quotes the Reporter General from Parlement saying:

> One cannot fail to recognize in the expressions employed (in the bull) the spirit of exaggerated partisans of the Court of Rome in regard to the plenary powers which they attribute to the said Court in ecclesiastical affairs, and especially, as far as doctrine is concerned, on the blind obedience which they wish should be paid to its decrees as soon as they are promulgated and on the rigorous penalties which the secular power cannot carry out sufficiently soon for their taste.[98]

At the same time, in January 1738, a group of twenty Jansenist pastors in Paris published their own challenge:

> The Bull...contains several other clauses which render it one of the most improper Bulls that have appeared in recent times. It would seem as if the canonization of the founder of the Mission was only a pretext, and that the real object proposed therein was a denial of our most holy maxims [the Gallican Liberties],[99] an insinuation of those most contrary to them, a direct attack on our holy liberties, a hateful suggestion of the state of France in the last century, and even an attempt to disturb it in this.[100]

For his part, Louis XV was in no mood to brook any further Jansenist opposition. In July of 1737 he had been surprised by Louis-Basile Carré de Montgeron, a Jansenist parlementaire, as he was leaving his prayers at the palace of Versailles. Montgeron presented the startled monarch with a copy of his multi-volume work defending the veracity of the miracles of the diâcre de Pâris.[101] Montgeron paid for his boldness and was imprisoned under a letter of cachet for the rest of his life.[102]

The king wisely chose to defuse the situation. Cardinal de Rohan[103] instructed the superior general, Jean Couty, to write to the king to defend the bull in light of the parlement's public criticisms.[104] The cardinal carefully instructed Couty as to how to present his arguments. On 22 January 1738, the monarch struck down the parlement's order as an over-reaction, stating that the customary protection of the Gallican liberties as maintained by royal authority was sufficient to prevent "a too rigorous interpretation of the document."[105] Parlement appealed to the king to reconsider. In August the monarch turned down their appeal: "I have taken steps to deal with the substance of your remonstrances... and will always show a similar attention to the maintenance of the laws of my Kingdom and the peace and tranquility of my realm."[106]

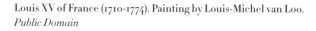

Louis XV of France (1710-1774). Painting by Louis-Michel van Loo.
Public Domain

POSTSCRIPT: VINCENT THE PERSON AND VINCENT THE SAINT

In the present Jansensim is but a dim memory, and the great political and theological controversies which surrounded it are largely impenetrable if not irrelevant to the modern mind. Vincent de Paul's own role during his lifetime in the first phase of these struggles, and how the memory of that opposition was re-framed and re-used as a theological and ideological weapon in much later phases, falls into the same category of memory.

More than two-hundred-and-seventy-five years have passed since Monsieur Vincent's canonization, and the image of the haloed saint holding foundlings tenderly in his arms speaks to the compelling popular vision of him today as charity's saint. This depiction, while true enough, has tended to turn him into a rather one-dimensional figure. Too little remains in the popular imagination of his compelling life-long struggle for conversion. Too little memory remains of his very human faults, and even his dark side. Too little memory remains of the pastoral zeal of the great priest and effective evangelizer. Too little memory remains of the hopeful ardency of the Church reformer. Too little memory remains of the brilliant, detail-oriented organizer and no-nonsense business man.

The great challenge of contemporary Vincentian historiography is the contextualized recovery and re-interpretation not of "Saint" Vincent de Paul, but rather of Vincent de Paul the person. This requires temporarily putting aside the title of "saint" and recapturing his life, as much as is possible, as it unfolded decision-by-decision, situation-by-situation within the complex realities of seventeenth-century France. The monumental recovery, translation, and annotation of the extant correspondence, conferences, and documents of Vincent de Paul is the essential beginning point of this effort. However, these letters, conferences, and documents themselves must also be critically contextualized as an essential part of their ongoing interpretation.

The value of Maupas du Tour's *oraison funèbre* is more than just the role it played in preparing the way for Louis Abelly and the eventual canonization of Vincent de Paul. Its wider value lies in being the first public reflection on his life and works, by those who knew and admired him, at the moment that he passed from the scene. Together with the notes of Brother Louis Robineau, the Abelly biography, and the Coste volumes, Maupas du Tour's *oraison funèbre* is a source which now, fully annotated, can contribute to the contextualization and re-interpretation of the life of Vincent de Paul.

---

[1] "Décret de la canonisation du Bienheureux Vincent de Paul," 16 July 1736, *Circulaires*, 1:531.

[2] For a discussion on questions concerning the exact nature of Abelly's authorship of the biography,

see Abelly, *Life*, 1:12-13.

[3] In fact, despite its hagiographic flaws it remains the cornerstone of Vincentian historiography.

[4] See Collet, *La Vie*, 2:511-593.

[5] *Superna Hierusalem*, 62-63.

[6] Collet, *La Vie*, 2:517.

[7] *Ibid.*, 2:520-521.

[8] *Ibid.*, 2:532.

[9] "Postea quæsitum fuit, utrum expediat jam nunc aliauid aggredi per ordinem at Beatificationem Rev. admosym in Christo Patris nostri piissima memoria D.D. Vincentii a Paulo venerabilis Institutori nostro ac primi Superioris Generalis. Omnes unanimi voce, concordantibus votis, cum veneratio tam insigni viro debita, singulari gaudio et maxima grati animi significatione propositioni tam acceptabili, tam jucunda acclamaverunt." See "Acta Sexti Conventus Generalis Congregationis Missionis (1697)," Minutes, GA: 1661-1697 (1967), *General Assemblies*. Paper 4:8-9, at: **http://via.library.depaul. edu/cm_ga/4.** (accessed 28 November 2012).

[10] Pierron noted:

> Our recent General Assembly expressed the ardent desire that we should... ascertain what would be the necessary steps for us to undertake the beatification of our venerable founder: M. Vincent. It charged me to study this question from two perspectives: the first regards evidence for the sanctity of his life, and what evidence there is for the apostolic and Christian heroicity of the virtues he practiced. And whether this evidence can be produced by irreproachable witnesses on oath before an ecclesiastical judge. Secondly, and this is of greater importance for Rome, whether there are miracles or other extraordinary events that took place before, or since his death. It is necessary that we have multiple testimonies to all of these matters provided as required by law. This is why I am now asking you confidentially to provide me with any information that you have whether coming from members of our Congregation, that of the Daughters of Charity, or from extern persons which would serve this purpose....

"Recherches des faits propres à de la béatification de M. Vincent, 26 October 1697," *Circulaires*, 1:274.

[11] For a biographical sketch of François Watel see *Ibid.*, 1:303.

[12] Louis-Antoine de Noailles was born 27 May 1651 into a family with close connections to the court of Louis XIV. He was ordained a priest on 8 June 1675, nominated to be bishop on 24 February 1679, and ordained on 18 June 1679 to serve the See of Cahors. On 21 June 1680 he became the Bishop-Count of Châlon-en-Champagne, where he entrusted his theological seminary to the Lazarists and founded a minor seminary. He was named to the position of archbishop of Paris and duc de Saint-Cloud on 19 August 1695, and was raised to the cardinalate on 21 June 1700. His position on the Jansenist controversy was confusing to many. Though he was among the bishops who condemned the propositions of the Jansenists, he also opposed the Jesuit tactics directed against them. In addition, he opposed the papal bull, *Unigenitus* up until the year before his death on 4 May 1729.

[13] From beginning-to-end the various French Lazarists who were appointed by the superior general to lead the cause in Rome were models of efficiency, patience, and zeal. One of them, Jean Couty, capped his long service to the cause by being elected superior general.

[14] Coste, *Life*, 3:404.

[15] *Ibid.*, 3:406.

[16] *Ibid.*, 3:406, n. 6: "*Epistolæ ad SS. D.N. Clementem, Papam, XI, pro promovenda Beatificatione et canonizatione V. Servi Dei Vincentii a Paulo*, Romæ, 1709."

[17] *Superna Hierusalem*, 63.

[18] There have been many changes to the canonization process since the time of Vincent's canonization. John Paul II, in his 1983 apostolic constitution *Divinus Perfectionis Magister*, made the most recent and

substantive changes.

[19] See, for example, *Circulaires*, 1:316, 359, 447-448, 469, 531, and 533-534.

[20] It is interesting to note that the initial Promoter of the Faith in Vincent's cause, Prospero Lambertini, was elected pope in 1740, taking the name Benedict XIV.

[21] Coste, *Life*, 3:408-409.

[22] For more background on the relationship between Vincent de Paul and Saint-Cyran see, for example, Document 32, "Testimony Concerning Abbé De Saint-Cyran," [31 March, 1 and 2 April 1639], *CCD*, 13a:104-110; and Document 33, "Interrogation of Abbé De Saint-Cyran," [14-31 May, 1639], *Ibid.*, 13a:110-136. See also, Coste, *Life*, 3:113-143.

[23] Martin de Barcos, *Defense de feu M. Vincent de Paul, Instituteur et Premier Superieur General de la Congregation de la Mission contres les faux discours du livre de sa vie publieé par M. Abelly, Ancien Evesque de Rodez, et contre les impostures de quelques autres ecrits sur ce sujet* (Paris, 1668).

In the introduction to the English translation of *Abelly*, John Rybolt notes:

> Abelly read his own strong anti-Jansenism into Vincent's life. The reality of Vincent's opposition to the Jansenist movement is far more complex than Abelly presents. This was especially true with regard to Vincent's relationship with the Abbe de Saint Cyran, which was generally close and amicable until 1644. After Saint Cyran's arrest, Vincent refused to testify against him or gave testimony so confusing that it was useless. Vincent's opposition to Jansenism after 1644 seems to have arisen from the question of frequent communion and especially the impact that Jansenist teaching on this subject had on the parish missions.

Abelly, 15.

[24] Coste, *Life*, 3:409-410.

[25] For an overview of the very long and complex Jansenist controversies, see Brian E. Strayer, *Suffering Saints. Jansenists and Convulsionnaires in France, 1640-1799* (Brighton: Sussex Academic Press, 2008). Hereafter, *Jansenists*.

[26] Catherine-Laurence Marie, *De la cause de Dieu à la cause de la Nation: Le Jansénisme au XVIIIᵉ siècle* (Paris: Editions Gallimard, 1998), 9.

[27] For a biographical sketch of Jean Bonnet, see *Circulaires*, 1:329-330.

[28] *Ibid.*, 1:360.

[29] See Coste, *Life*, 3:408-418.

[30] *Ibid.*, 418.

[31] Jean-Louis Quantin, "A Godly Fronde? Jansenism and the Mid-Seventeenth-Century Crisis of the French Monarchy," *French History* 25:4 (2011): 477.

[32] *Jansenists*, 162.

[33] See David Bell, *Lawyers and Citizens: The Making of a Political Elite in Old Regime France* (New York: Oxford University Press, 1994), 68-71. See also *Jansenists*, 162.

[34] Jeffrey W. Merrick, *The Desacralization of the French Monarchy in the Eighteenth Century* (Baton Rouge, LA: Louisiana State University, 1990), 49. See also *Jansenists*, 162.

[35] See Jacques M. Grès-Gayer, "The *Unigenitus* of Clement XI: A Fresh Look at the Issues," *Theological Studies* 49:2 (1988): 273-281. See also, *Jansenists*, 162.

[36] See "The Shaking of Jansenism: Miracle Cures and the *Convulsionnaires*, 1727-1740," in *Jansenists*, 236-265.

[37] Louis de Rouvroy, Duc de Saint-Simon (1675-1755), was a courtier at Versailles and the author of a set of memoirs about court life that are considered among the classics of French literature.

[38] Aimé Richardt, *Le Jansénisme de Jansénius à la mort de Louis XIV* (Paris: François-Xavier de Guibert, 2002), 145.

[39] *Jansenists*, 165.

[40] Prince Michael of Greece, *Louis XIV: The Other Side of the Sun*, trans. by Alan Sheridan (New York: Harper & Row, 1983), 386.

41 Louis de Rouvroy, duc de Saint Simon, *Mémoires complets et authentique de duc de Saint-Simon*, 20 vols. (Paris: Librairie Hachette et Cie, 1874), 10:129.

42 *Jansenists*, 165.

43 *Circulaires*, 1:372.

44 Luigi Mezzadri, C.M., *Fra Giansenisti e Antigiansenisti. Vincent de Paul e la Congregazione della Missione (1624-1737)* (Firenze: "La Nuova Italia" Editrice, 1977), 38. Hereafter, *Giansenisti*.

45 *Circulaires*, 1:419.

46 *Giansenisti*, 144-166. See also, Luigi Mezzadri, C.M., and Francesca Onnis, *The Vincentians: A General History of the Congregation of the Mission*, trans. by Robert Cummings, ed. by Joseph E. Dunn, Felicia Roşu, and John E. Rybolt, C.M., 6 vols. [vols. 4-6 forthcoming] (Hyde Park, New York: New City Press, 2009-2013), 2:77. Hereafter cited as Mezzadri, *Vincentians*.

47 *Giansenisti*, 149.

48 For a detailed history of the impact of the Jansenist controversies on the Congregation of the Mission see, Mezzadri, *Vincentians*, 2:55-86.

49 Coste, *Life*, 3:419.

50 In Himbert's case there is evidence that his expulsion was a long-time coming. In 1717, Jean Bonnet had informed the Congregation that Himbert was temporarily leaving Paris and his duties as an assistant general allegedly because of ill-health. In 1719, the general appointed a temporary replacement for Himbert in Paris. It seems a reasonable suspicion that Himbert's Jansenism may have been at least a contributing factor to his original departure, and his continued absence. See "Lettre Circulaire à toutes les maisons pour leur donner avis de raisons qui ont porté M. Himbert à souhaiter de sortir de la maison de Saint Lazare," 28 juillet 1717, *Circulaires*, 1:388.

51 *Giansenisti*, 151.

52 *Circulaires*, 1:429.

53 The delegates to the General Assembly included 27 French, 7 Italian, and 3 Polish confreres.

54 "Acti Noni Conventus Generalis Congregationis Missionis (1724): Sessio Quarta," Minutes, GA: 1703-1747" (1747), *General Assemblies*. Paper 3:4, at: **http://via.library.depaul.edu/cm_ga/3** (accessed 28 November 2012). Hereafter *Conventus Generalis*.

55 Mezzadri, *Vincentians*, 2:80.

56 *Giansenisti*, 154. Strictly speaking the final language required full acceptance of not only *Unigenitus Dei Filius*, but also the earlier *Vineam Domini Sabaoth*, as well as earlier condemnations issued by Innocent X and Alexander VII. See *Conventus Generalis*, 4.

57 Mezzadri, *Vincentians*, 2:81.

58 *Circulaires*, 1:431. See also "Sessio Quinta," *Conventus Generalis*, 5.

59 See "Sessio Undecima," *Conventus Generalis*, 8-9.

60 Mezzadri notes that *Nouvelles Ecclésiastiques* reported the departure of 84 missionaries, while the number expelled from the Congregation was another 40. Mezzadri, *Vincentians*, 2:82.

61 It must be acknowledged that other factors contributed to the various delays of Vincent's cause, including the slow nature of the process, the deaths of officials involved in the cause, and even the deaths of pontiffs. See, for example, Coste, *Life*, 3:420.

62 Jean Bonnet, "Déclaration de l'héroïcité des vertus de M. Vincent," 3 octobre 1727, *Circulaires*, 1:442. See also, *Superna Hierusalem*, 63.

63 Coste, *Life*, 3:420.

64 "Claude Joseph Compoin, ten years old, of blindness; Mary Ann Lhuillier, eight years old, of dumbness and paralysis from birth; Anthony Greffier, an infant of some months, of epilepsy, deafness and blindness; Geneviéve Catherine Marquette, four years old, of paralysis from birth; Sister Mathurine Guérin, Daughter of Charity, formerly a Sister Superior, of a cancerous ulcer in the leg; James Grou, thirty-nine years old, of hemorrhage; Michael Lepiné, forty years old, of ulcer of the liver; and Alexander Philip Le Grand, four year old of paralysis." See Coste, *Life*, 3:420.

[65] "Those of Compoin, Lhuillier, Le Grand and Sister Mathurine Guérin" were accepted. See *Ibid.*, 3:422. See also, "Décret de l'authenticité des miracles du venerable serviteur de Dieu Vincent de Paul," 22 septembre 1727, *Circulaires*, 1:759-760.

[66] "Servus Dei Vincentius a Paulo in Beatorum Numero Adscribitur," in *Acta Apostolica Bullæ, Brevia et Rescripta in gratiam Congregationis Missionis* (Parisiis: Typis Excudebat Georges Chamerot, 1876), 93-95. Hereafter cited as *Acta Apostolica*. See also, *Ristretto Cronologico della Vita, Virtù, e Miracoli del B. Vincenzo de Paoli Fondatore Della Congregazione della Missione, e delle Serve de' Poveri, dette le Figlie della Carità. Alla Santità di Nostro Signore Papa Benedetteo XIII* (Roma: Antonio de'Rossi, 1729).

[67] See "Récit de ce qui s'est passé dans la maison de Saint-Lazare à Paris, à l'occasion de la solennité de la beatification du bienheureux Vincent de Paul, instituteur et premier Supérieur général de la Congrégation de la Mission et de la Compagnie des filles de la Charité. Servantes des pauvres malades," 1 octobre 1729, *Circulaires*, 1:761-763.

[68] See Coste, *Life*, 3:424.

[69] See, for example, *M. de Pâris travaille de ses mains pour soulager plus abondamment les pauvres*, at: **http://gallica.bnf.fr/ark:/12148/btv1b8408685q.r=diacre+de+paris.langEN** (accessed 1 November 2012).

[70] The French Jansenists produced a clandestine newspaper, *Nouvelles Ecclésiastiques*, through which they proved themselves to be very effective communicators and propagandists.

[71] See, for example, *M. de Pâris afflige son corps par le jeûne, les veilles et les macérations*, at: **http://gallica.bnf.fr/ark:/12148/btv1b8408669m** (accessed 1 November 2012).

[72] See, for example, *Obsèques de Monsieur de Pâris*, at: **http://gallica.bnf.fr/ark:/12148/btv1b8408676r.r=diacre+de+paris.langEN** (accessed 1 November 2012).

[73] See, for example, *Testament de feu François de Pâris, diâcre cy devant supérieur des clercs de le paroisse to St. Cosme, lequel donne un just idée de ses mœurs comme de ses dernières volontez*, at: **http://gallica.bnf.fr/ark:/12148/btv1b8408660w.r=diacre+de+paris.langEN** (accessed 31 October 2012).

[74] Charles de Saint-Albin, *Mandement et Instruction Pastorale de Monseigneur l'Archevêque, Duc de Cambray, Portant Condamnation de trois Ecrits, dont le premiere a pour titre: Vie de M. de Pâris, Diacre, à Bruxelles, chez Foppens, à l'Enseigne du Saint Esprit, 1731. Le second: Vie de M. de Pâris, Diacre du Diocése de Paris, en France, 1731. Et le troisiéme: Vie de M. de Pâris, Diacre, 1731* (Paris: Marc Bordelet, 1732).

[75] The Biblotheque Nationale de France has a collection of fifty-five of these popular engravings. See: **http://gallica.bnf.fr/Search?ArianeWireIndex=index&f_typedoc=images&q=diacre+de+paris&lang=EN&n=15&p=2&pageNumber=4** (accessed 1 November 2012).

[76] See *M. de Pâris est pensé par les sœurs de la charité*, at: **http://gallica.bnf.fr/ark:/12148/btv1b84086723.r=Mr+de+Pâris+est+pensé+par+les+soeurs+de+la+charité.langEN** (accessed 31 October 2012).

[77] See, for example, *Epitaphe de M. de Pâris, mort en odeur de saintete de 1er may 1727, agé de 37 ans, enterrèe à St. Médard à Paris. Miracle de Mlle. Du Boier, opéré par l'intercession du Bienheureux Pâris le 26 juillet 1731*, at: **http://gallica.bnf.fr/ark:/12148/btv1b84087748.r=diacre+de+paris.langEN** (accessed 1 November 2012). See also, *Concours et Miracles au tombeau de Monsieur de Pâris*, at: **http://gallica.bnf.fr/ark:/12148/btv1b8408678k.r=diacre+de+paris.langEN** (accessed 1 November 2012).

[78] See, for example, *Le Tombeau du B. François de Pâris, Diacre de l'église de Paris, mort le 1er may 1727, illustré par des miracles sans nombre et des conversions éclatantes*, at: **http://gallica.bnf.fr/ark:/12148/btv1b84087763** (accessed 1 November 2012).

[79] From the time of his burial the tomb of Vincent de Paul had attracted pilgrims, and had also been the site of the various healings which would be presented as miracles in his cause. As Clement XII noted in *Superna Hierusalem*:

> Immediately after the death of this faithful servant, the reputation of his sanctity was diffused abroad in every place, and God deigned to confirm it by shining proofs and evident miracles, thus exciting, according to the admirable order of His

> Providence, in the hearts of the faithful a profound veneration for his inanimate
> remains, showing thereby, what glory his soul enjoyed in heaven, when in his body
> deprived of life, God manifested the signs of his power.

See *Superna Hierusalem*, 62-63. Vincent's tomb at Saint-Lazare was first opened in 1712 as part of the canonization process. For an account of the key role that the relics of his bodily remains played through the rest of the canonization process see, Coste, *Life*, 3:411-413, 422-423, 433-434.

[80] See *Jansenists*, 237-245.

[81] "*Positio super dubio: an et de quibus miraculis constet post indultam eiden Beato venerationem in casu...*" (Romæ, 1735); "*Consilia pro veritate seu Dissertationes medico physica Marci Angeli de Marcangelis super miraculis.*" See Coste, *Life*, 3:425, n. 27.

[82] See *Sacra Rituum Congregatione...Parisien. Canonizationis B. Vincentii A' Paulo, Fundatoris Congregationis Missionis, & Societatis Puellarum de Charitate. Positio Super Dubio. An, & de quibus Miraculis constet post indultam eidem Beato venerationem in casu etc.* (Romae, Typis Reverendæ Cameræ Apostolicæ, 1735).

[83] The other miracle was "the instantaneous cure of an inveterate and well characterized rupture in the person of François Richer." See *Superna Hierusalem*, 65.

[84] Coste, *Life*, 3:426.

[85] *Ibid.*

[86] The documentation for Vincent de Paul's cause from the *Congregazione dei Riti, Processus* in the Secret Vatican Archives, includes: *Congr. Riti, Processus* 2221-2222: versio processus ordinarii super fama (years 1705-1706), ff. 1856; *Congr. Riti, Processus* 2223: versio processus super virtutibus (years 1710-1711), f. 1062; *Congr. Riti, Processus* 2224: versio processus super virtutibus (years 1712-1713), ff. 1085; *Congr. Riti, Processus* 2225: versio processus super miris post beatificationem (years 1731-1733), ff. 1582; *Congr. Riti, Processus* 2226-2227: processus ordinarius super fama (1705-1706), ff. 1749; *Congr. Riti, Processus* 2228: processus apostolicus Parisien. super fama in gen (1709-1710), ff. 87+48; *Congr. Riti, Processus* 2229: processus ordinarius super non-cultu cum versione (1705-1706), ff. 178+39; *Congr. Riti, Processus* 2230: processus apostolicus super virtutibus (1711-1712), ff. 632; *Congr. Riti, Processus* 2231: processus apostolicus super virtutibus ne pereant... (1710-1711), ff. 358; *Congr. Riti, Processus* 2232: processus apostolicus Parisien. super miris post beatificationem (1731-1733), ff. 1030.

[87] There were still a number of secret and public consistories held to confirm the coming canonization. These were even being held within a month of the final ceremony. See *Superna Hierusalem*, 66-67.

[88] *Ibid.*, 44-45.

[89] *Ibid.*, 45-62.

[90] *Ibid.*, 61.

[91] *Ibid.*

[92] *Ibid.*

[93] *Ibid.*, 62.

[94] The condemnation (*Cum Occasione*) issued by Innocent X in 1653 of five statements said to be extracted from *Augustinus* and *On Frequent Communion*. Vincent lobbied the French bishops to request this condemnation. See Appendix Letter 1, "Letter Of The Bishops Of France To Pope Innocent X," [1651], *CCD*, 4:607-608.

[95] *Nouvelles Ecclésiastiques*, 12 (1739), 33-36.

[96] Abelly, 2:371.

[97] See "Arrêt de la Cour du parlement qui supprime un imprimé, intitule: *Canonisatio B. Vincentii a Paulo*, Parisiis, e typis Petri Simon, 1737, *Extrait des registres du Parlement*," *Circulaires*, 1:767-768.

[98] Coste, *Life*, 3:429.

[99] The so-called "Gallican Liberties" were longstanding ecclesial and state traditions which, while recognizing papal authority as essential for Catholic unity, minimized it with respect to the counter-balance of the rights of the French Church and the French king to govern the Church in France. These

attitudes were typically shared and enshrined by the other Catholic monarchs and kingdoms in Europe, at the expense of papal authority.

[100] Quoted in Coste, *Life*, 3:431.

[101] Louis-Basile Carré de Mongeron, *La Verité des miracles operés par l'intercession de M. de Pâris: demontrée contre M. l'Archevêque de Sens. Ouvrage dedié au roy* (Utretcht: chez les Libraires de la Compagnie, 1737).

[102] A "Letter of cachet" was an act of the king's sovereign legal authority by which he ordered the arrest and imprisonment of a subject. Neither the cause of the arrest, or the term of imprisonment were given.

[103] Armand-Gaston-Maximilien de Rohan (1674-1749) prince-bishop of Strasbourg and grand aumônier of France. See "Lettre du cardinal de Rohan à M. Couty, Supérieur général, relativement à arrêt du Parlement contre la bulle de canonisation," 15 janvier 1738, *Circulaires*, 1:768.

[104] *Ibid.*

[105] Coste, *Life*, 3:430. See also "Arrêt du conseil d'État du roi, au sujet de la bulle de canonisation de saint Vincent de Paul, du 22 janvier 1738," *Circulaires*, 1:769.

[106] Coste, *Life*, 3:430.

HENRI
DE MAUPAS
DU TOUR

✝

*The Funeral Oration
for Vincent de Paul*

23 November 1660

TO HIS EMINENCE[1]

MONSEIGNEUR,

Someone once observed that when the great and powerful exercise their authority they naturally inspire a certain fear in persons who are timid.[2] After their deaths, however, they no longer have the power to inhibit either the freedom of speech or of pens that can then attack their memory with impunity; publicly censuring their lives and actions!

As for myself, Monseigneur, I believe all reasonable people will acknowledge it was Heaven itself which raised you to the position of trust and glory you hold.[3] This fact will overcome the jealousy of the great, the passions of the populace, and the fickleness of the present age to establish an enduring respect and honor for your name. Envy will be forced to recognize the true merit of your conduct, so that even your harshest critics will have to acknowledge you as the most illustrious guardian of the public welfare. This will be so because you have always sacrificed your personal interests in order to end the war, establish Peace among the Nations, and restore Universal harmony.

It is well known, Monseigneur, that Your Eminence entered into office when the war was already under way, and that you have happily made our great Monarch victorious both in this armed struggle, and in the midst of great civil disturbances.[4] During the King's minority you upheld the Crown and the person of the King, marking the years awaiting his coming of age with victories.

It is also known that the late King, LOUIS THE JUST,[5] of most glorious memory, and his Minister the great Cardinal de Richelieu,[6] so greatly esteemed the powerful genius and rare talents of Your Eminence that they judged you worthy to be entrusted with the most precious interests of our Monarchy. Under your care, the most beautiful and whitest of lilies has blossomed; displaying a purity, innocence, and faith surpassing all our hopes and answering all our prayers.[7]

You have, Monseigneur, won victory Laurels for the King in war and Olive branches for him in Peace. You gave a glorious hint of what was to come on the famous day at Casale when, at the risk of your own life, you stopped two powerful armies from going into battle.[8] And it must be said, Your Eminence, that you continued this same generous conduct when you spared the lives of those who, possessing a less heroic virtue, had attacked you.[9]

Yet, you have done something even greater than this, Monseigneur. You have chosen to honor, with the favors at your disposal, those persons of a less heroic virtue whom you could have made the objects of your just anger. Making your magnanimity and courage complete, you repaid the injuries you received with acts of kindness; so the enemies you defeated have been forced to exchange their arms for sentiments of gratitude for your good deeds.

But above all, Monseigneur, Your Eminence should know that by bringing Peace to Europe you have, in one fell swoop, accomplished one of the greatest deeds possible thus making yourself the benefactor both of the people, and of the world's greatest Crowns.[10] It is because of all this, Monseigneur, that public opinion admires your Eminence's conduct. My vocation requires me to judge everything in light of the Gospel, and to refrain from praising any actions that do not conform to the Church's teachings. Thus, I want to add my own veneration of Your Eminence's actions, especially for those that are perhaps lesser known, and might even appear at first to be relatively insignificant.

Your Eminence, I know that in the King's Council the Queen was able to observe first-hand the actions of the late Monsieur Vincent, Superior General of the Mission, and that she has spoken publicly about his virtues.[11] After this great man's death, she promised to protect the members of his Congregation.

left Portrait of Maupas du Tour.
Courtesy Vincentian Studies Collection, Special Collections and Archives, DePaul University, Chicago, Illinois
right Jean-François-Paul de Gondi, Cardinal de Retz (1613-1679).
Public Domain

She has said she esteems the works of these good Priests. She also has said she has no doubt the prayers of this great Servant of God were instrumental both in bringing about Peace,[12] and the King's subsequent Marriage.[13]

I also recall, Monseigneur, on the day when I had the honor of being deputed by the Bishops to speak to Your Eminence concerning an affair of great importance for the Faith, you told me with such good grace that you would willingly shed your own blood in defense of the Church's interests.

Thus, Monseigneur, I dedicate this Funeral Oration to Your Eminence. Perhaps it will better reveal my motivations which are innocent, and in no way mercenary. My only motive is to acknowledge the debt I owe Your Eminence for your promise to protect my Diocese;[14] a promise you made in the presence of the Deputation of fourteen of our great Prelates who accompanied me to the Court at Fontainebleau in support of my rights; rights which are inherent to our shared episcopal office.[15]

It is true, Monseigneur, that Your Eminence has graciously offered me other Benefices, and I owe you the same obligation of gratitude[16] as if I had accepted them.[17] Since then, however, I have lost my nephew in military service of the King so that my family is almost extinct, leaving me nothing else.[18] Monseigneur, I believe it is by the action of God's Divine Providence that I have been reduced to this present state where I have nothing more to lose. Therefore, I will make good use of my disgraces so when I speak of the respect everyone should have for your great actions, the public will have reason to believe I am freely and faithfully offering you the dedication of my entire life.

MONSEIGNEUR,
I am your Eminence's most humble and obedient servant,

Henry, Bishop of Le Puy

FUNERAL ORATION
DEDICATED TO THE MEMORY
OF THE LATE MONSIEUR
VINCENT DE PAUL
INSTITUTOR,
FOUNDER,
AND SUPERIOR GENERAL
OF THE PRIESTS OF THE MISSION

delivered on the 23rd of November 1660, in the
Church of S. Germain l'Auxerrois,[19]
By Monseigneur the Illustrious and Most Reverend Bishop
and Count of Velay, the sole Lord of Le Puy,

HENRY DE MAUPAS DU TOUR

At Paris
Gaspar Meturas, ruë Saint-Jacques, à la Trinité
Jacques Langlois, Ordinary Printer to the King located on
Mont Sainte-Geneviéve, and at his store located in the
grand' Salle du Palais, at the Reyne de la Paix,
and
Emm. Langlois, ruë Saint-Jacques, à la Reyne du Clergé

M. DC. LXI.
With Royal Permission
License from the King[20]

By the Grace and Authorization of the King, permission is given to Messire HENRY
DE MAUPAS DU TOUR, Bishop and Sole Lord of Le Puy, Count of Velay, Ordinary
Councilor of the King in his Privy Council and Council of State, and first Chaplain to
the Queen Mother[21] to have printed a Book he has composed, entitled: *Funeral Oration
to the Memory of the Late Monsieur VINCENT DE PAUL, Institutor, Founder, and
Superior General of the Priests of the Mission.* Therefore all persons, of whatever quality
or condition, are forbidden from printing or having printed the said Book without the
consent of the said Lord, under the penalties prescribed by these Letters of Privilege,
given at Paris, 4 January 1661.

By the King in His Council, OLIER

The said Lord Bishop of Le Puy has given Permission to Gaspar Meturas, and James
and Emmanuël Langlois, to print the said book in accordance with the
agreement entered into between them on the sixth day of January 1661.

THE FUNERAL ORATION

Part One: His Humility[22]

"...cuius laus est in evangelio per omnes ecclesias."

("...[the brother] who is praised in all the churches for his preaching of the gospel.")[23]

The praise we give to the memory of the Just is a well-deserved tribute and offers a blameless homage, since the praise we give them is also part of the praise we are obliged to offer to God. Meanwhile, there are other venal and mercenary souls who merit only eternal scorn because they have no fear or sorrow for having prostituted their consciences to the attractions of sensual delights, and to the interests of mere worldly fortune and ambition. These people should be scorned because by rejecting grace, which is the solid foundation and the source of all true praise, they have dried up the spring at its very source.

In contrast to these people there are other generous souls who, unconcerned with these perverse activities, spend their lives concerned only with spiritual matters. Saint Bernard (of Clairvaux) described these persons as, *"qui cælistibus terrena mercantur."* ("those earthly inhabitants whose lives are heavenly.")[24] They merit true praise because of their virtue and discretion, and because they desire no other guide for their public and private lives than the Gospel, and no other foundation for their lives than that of grace. They especially rely on that grace which, in the words of the first of the Apostles, makes it possible for those souls who faithfully respond to its attraction to share in the Divine nature, as Saint Peter says: *"...divinæ consortes naturæ."* ("...to share in the divine nature.")[25] Strengthened by this grace, these chosen souls share in the praise of God, and their glory is thus made part of the praise that we must render to God for: *"...tunc laus erit unicuique a Deo."* ("...then everyone will receive praise from God.")[26]

Now, Messieurs, without further delay, I will place before you a vivid and lifelike portrait of the great VINCENT DE PAUL. I will tell you boldly and freely about the praise which is due to the story of his rare virtues, since it can be said of his very holy life and his very happy death that they were designed by grace, and crowned by the Gospel.

"...cuius laus est in evangelio per omnes ecclesias."

("...[the brother] who is praised in all the churches for his preaching of the gospel.")

For praise to be deserved it must be given only in recognition of good works. However, too often praise is corrupted by the mouths of those who offer it, and by the ears of those who listen to it. In this world, those who praise others out of weakness, selfishness, fear, or envy, are often listened to as if they were a voice speaking from Heaven. Yet, this "praise" quickly degenerates into discordant and meaningless sounds. Thus, the pleasing harmony which should result from the concord of all the virtues becomes instead nothing more than loud noise, caused by false notes sounding from an instrument of deception and envy.

However, in this case Messieurs, this is not what I am doing. If I praise the memory of the great VINCENT DE PAUL it is because, when I consider the profound humility and the perfect scorn this great man had for himself during his entire life I cannot say enough to imbue you with an esteem for his virtues.

HIS HUMILITY[27]

There once was a Philosopher who could not hide his vanity. He admitted that of all the songs he knew, he did not know of any he found to be more pleasing than those which sang his praises.[28] VINCENT DE PAUL, Messieurs, would not

---

Henri de Maupas du Tour. Detail of 1645 engraving by Michel Lasne.
Courtesy © Fitzwilliam Museum, Cambridge, United Kingdom

have had such profane thoughts. It was totally contrary to his modesty to say anything to his own advantage. In fact, anyone who said anything favorable about him cruelly tortured his humble soul. "*Qui me laudat, me flagellat.*" ("The one who praises me, scourges me.")[29]

Doubtlessly, this horror he had of being praised is difficult for us to understand. However, I can honestly testify before the most Sacred Altars, as I recall the conversations I had with him over the course of many years I always found him to be the most admirable and literal example of Christian humility. To have observed the gestures, speech, room, food, clothing, and everything else that surrounded the eminent VINCENT DE PAUL (who called himself a beggar, who I esteem as a Saint and whom you have so often admired), was to have encountered an example of perfect humility.[30]

"...cuius laus est in evangelio per omnes ecclesias."

("...[the brother] who is praised in all the churches for his preaching of the gospel.")

In this life, praise is all too often given to persons whose legacy is truly disgraceful, and whose lives are stained by the record of their crimes. Public opinion, however, soon turns on them after their deaths. Meanwhile, in another much longer life, their souls will be condemned to suffer agonies. "*Laudantur ubi non sunt, cruciantur ubi sunt.*" ("They are praised where they are not; they are tormented where they are.")[31] In this case, however, our feeble praise is justly given because both Heaven and public opinion have crowned his heroic virtues with Glory.

View of the Church of Saint-Germain-l'Auxerrois, Paris; site of the funeral oration.
Vincentian Studies Institute Collected Illustrations

Today praise is given to those who are considered to be the famous and great, more often because of the enormity of their vices, than because of the brilliance of their fortune and dignity. The pretext for this praise is an illusory virtue that hides the debaucheries and the extortions of an often tortured and scandalous life; a life which was dedicated to satisfying the most shameful passions, and which hides under pretenses, impostures, and flattery, the grievous truth which truly is worthy only of public scorn.

One example of this type of praise is the Funeral Harangues given for those unfaithful cheaters, whom the very great indulgence of the laws does not punish severely enough. These are the men who violate the rules governing coats of arms, debasing the laws of this heroic science by tracing false lines in their own genealogies.[32] These men steal coats of arms from the most illustrious families trying wrongly to have noble blood flow through their own obscure veins. Because of this behavior they have, in the past, merited the chastisements of the highest tribunals of Justice and the disfavor of our very great Monarchs and Sovereigns.

These men behave in this way because they want to be raised up from the dust of their lowly births even if it is at the expense of the tears, and by the cruel shedding of the blood of the poor. These persons invent fantastic myths to add legitimacy and luster to their illegal titles. Thus, they should be considered as nothing less than the hereditary enemies and opponents of true virtue. These persons put together a confusing blend of both history and fable in order to forge, and then to wear, the fraudulent ornaments and the false finery of an unworthy noble status. Thus, they find themselves simultaneously obligated to a double restitution both for the praise they unworthily receive, and for using their fraudulent honors to enrich themselves at the expense of widows.

Messieurs, let us sigh on behalf of these unfortunate creatures, and groan while we say together with the Prophet Isaiah: "*Væ qui trahitis iniquitatem in funiculis vanitatis.*" ("Woe to those who tug at guilt with cords of perversity.")[33] Avarice and pride serve as their unfaithful and bloodthirsty counselors inspiring both their contempt for the humility of the poor, as well as their own mistreatment of these unfortunates. Meanwhile, we have the completely different example of VINCENT DE PAUL who glorified his lowliness, and who made himself poor in order to enrich the poor.

Come you arrogant spirits who have nothing truly worthy of praise within you! You who are so full of vanity and a false sense of glory! Since you search in a quicksand of lies for your nobility learn from a Latin Poet who said: "*Nam genus et proavos, et quæ non fecimus ipsi, vix ea nostra voco.*" ("Birth and ancestry, and that which we have not ourselves achieved, we can scarcely call our own.")[34] Or perhaps it is even better to say; learn from the teaching of the great Saint Ambrose and from the virtuous example of the great VINCENT DE PAUL: "*Probati enim viri genus virtutis prosapia est.*" ("True nobility belongs to those whose genealogy is based only on the practice of the virtues.")[35]

VINCENT DE PAUL was a person of humble birth, but he was a person of eminent virtue who is to be admired because of his humility. He concealed these eminent virtues with all his might, while he publicly spoke only of the lowliness of his birth.

We honor the relics and the memory of Geneviève, a shepherdess, who guided her herds to the gates of Nanterre.[36] We honor the iron plough of Isidore, a farmer from Spain.[37] We recently have witnessed extraordinary public ceremonies honoring the relics of John of God, who in human eyes was an object of scorn.[38] But, I do not know if even these great souls welcomed scorn as much as VINCENT DE PAUL, who took great care always to live on this earth as the least among men.

Moses, the great Lawgiver of God's people, humbly took off his shoes and walked on the mountain in his bare feet. At the same time he covered himself with a veil that hid the splendor of the brilliant light that shone from his face.[39]

This is the same image, Messieurs, called to mind by VINCENT DE PAUL's rare humility.[40] He was entirely radiant, and his face shone with light like another

---

St. Vincent de Paul, man of virtue and humility.
Courtesy Vincentian Studies Collection, Special Collections and Archives,
DePaul University, Chicago, Illinois

Moses. Yet, he was the only one who could not see, or appreciate, the beauty of his own eminent virtues.[41] As the sacred Text says: "...*ignorabat quod cornuta esset facies sua ex consortio sermonis Dei.*" ("...he did not know that the skin of his face had become radiant while he conversed with the Lord.")[42] Or, as the learned Liranus also described them: "*radiis coruscans*" ("the glimmering rays.")[43]

Moses took off his shoes and walked in his bare feet in order to approach the mountain, and he covered the radiance of his face with a veil. VINCENT openly spoke of the lowliness of his birth. He wanted everyone to see the dirt that covered his peasant feet. He wanted everyone to know he was only the son of a farmer, and that in his youth he had tended flocks like another Moses.[44] However, when it was a question of also being considered as a Lawgiver like Moses, a man chosen by God's own hand to lead his people, this is when he covered his face in shame wishing only to remain unnoticed.[45]

Nevertheless, Messieurs, it is necessary that it be said freely and without any exaggeration that the hand of God chose VINCENT DE PAUL to bring the "tablets of the Law" to his people. It was through his admirable zeal, and that of his worthy children, that millions of souls have been sanctified through the work of the parish Missions.[46] It was he who procured the spiritual and temporal relief of entire provinces ruined by the evils of war.[47] It was he who rescued millions of people from the gates of death. It was he who saved, from ultimate disaster those unfortunate souls, who by a deadly combination of a profound ignorance of our faith's sacred mysteries and of the Christian truths necessary for salvation, as well as shameful lives marked by crime and licentiousness, seemed destined never to know God except through the rigor of his judgments and the eternity of his punishments.[48]

Yes, Messieurs, it is necessary to tell you it was VINCENT DE PAUL who all but changed the face of the Church by means of the formation given to ecclesiastics belonging to the Tuesday Conferences,[49] and by the numerous Seminaries he established.[50] It was he who, by means of the Ordination Exercises[51] and other spiritual Retreats,[52] reestablished the clerical state to the glory of its primitive splendor.[53] He lovingly opened his house, his heart, and his arms, to embrace all who came to him to benefit from being instructed in this holy school of true Ecclesiastical discipline.[54] It was he who rescued so many Ministers of the Altar who paid no attention to the rules of their vocation and who without fear, and for profane reasons, took part in sordid activities that reflected poorly on their sacred Ministries.

It was he who formed numerous important ecclesiastics to serve in many of our Dioceses as Vicars-General, Vice-regents, Promoters and other officials.[55] It was he who also provided numerous great Prelates for France.[56]

Monsieur VINCENT was the instrument chosen by the greatest designs of Divine Providence to be involved in all the most important activities that have given glory to God, been advantageous to our Religion, and brought honor to the State. Nevertheless, even though this great man deserved many glorious rewards for his actions, he kept his merits completely hidden from view under the veil of his humility.[57] In his fervent desire to be treated only as an object of the greatest contempt, he hid them under the cover of the darkest nights, and in the depths of the profound abyss that were his view of his own nothingness. It is this consuming humility, Messieurs, which merits our praise and the esteem of the Angels.

"...cuius laus est in evangelio per omnes ecclesias."

("...[the brother] who is praised in all the churches for his preaching of the gospel.")

Messieurs, you must not tolerate those petty, insolent spirits who are consumed by a vain concern for the advancement of their own fortune, and who want you to listen to them as if they were oracles. These are the same men who want even the most insignificant of their actions to be praised and held over the heads of others. But the most effective remedy for their vain ambition is to make them realize they amount to little more than the dust of the earth from which

---

The Apotheosis of Vincent de Paul.
Vincentian Studies Institute Collected Illustrations

they were made, and to which their mortal bodies will one day return in the decay of their tombs. As the Latin poet once observed: during the most beautiful and sunny days of the spring season when the flowers first come into sweet bloom bees leave the winter quarters of their hives and fly to find new sources of honey. Sometimes, they will also fly forth to do battle — for often discord accompanied by great agitation befalls two kings... they swarm densely, summoning the enemy with a great clamor. However, the tumult of passion and these overwhelming struggles are brought to rest, checked, by the tossing of a little dust.[58] *Hi motus animorum atque hæc tanta certamina, compressa jactu exigui pulveris, quiescent.*[59]

Here we find the puny remnants of human vanity. However, here we also find the beautiful remnants of the great VINCENT DE PAUL's humility. We could say of him, even though his modesty would never have allowed it, that all the flowers growing in all the most beautiful gardens have neither the variety, nor the beauty, of his virtues that were displayed for everyone to see.

The most virtuous and the greatest Queen in the world had the greatest admiration for his rare talents, grace, and holiness.[60] The greatest figures of the Church, Court, and King's Councils, admired his virtue. Both the Louvre and the Palace agree he did infinite good not only in Paris but also throughout the Kingdom, and indeed throughout the entire Church of God. The entire world was warmed by the holy zeal of his charity.[61] None of this, however, ever shook the constancy of his humility.

Louise de Marillac, co-founder of the Daughters of Charity.
Vincentian Studies Institute Collected Illustrations

To uncover the full extent of his zeal you would need to cross the seas and travel to the very limits of Christianity. You would also need to visit prisons, and the darkest dungeons.[62] You would need to visit all the places where the sick are to be found.[63] You would need to go to the great General Hospital.[64] You would need to see the tears of the afflicted that he wiped away, and the wounds he healed. You would need to see the indigent he clothed. You would need to see the five, six, or seven thousand people who, according to a reliable source, are assisted daily by the Confraternities of Charity he founded,[65] and the Sisters,[66] and the Ladies of Charity whom he also founded.[67] France, Savoy, Piedmont, Italy, Poland, and other faraway places all were the scenes of his charitable works and love.[68]

You would also need to descend into the galleys, as he did, to understand the compassion he had for these poor slaves. You would need to be chained yourself in order to be able to shatter their irons as he did, and be a slave yourself, as he was, in order to bring liberty to captives.[69] As he did, you would need to endure the cruelty of a Galley-master and to flinch under his lash. It would be necessary to have been a servant as he was, of an Alchemist, a Turk, and a Renegade, and to have spared no effort or risk in working for the salvation of a soul.[70] Thus, you would need to go to Tunis and Algiers in the heart of Barbary to discover the full extent of his zeal.[71] It would even be necessary to go as far as the Isles of Madagascar.[72]

To understand the zeal one must have for the extension of God's kingdom one could also travel to the Missions of Canada, Japan, China, Indochina, Laos, and Tonkin where the Fathers of the Company of Jesus have worked so worthily and so usefully, and where the people feel the effects of their charitable care and zeal.[73]

In accomplishing all of this, many of the principal members of his Congregation were exposed to the furor and the perfidy of the pagans, the plague and the plague-stricken, as well as a thousand other dangers. All this was necessary in order to extend the conquests of the Gospel by planting the standard of the Faith in countries lost to the Faith, and in previously unknown countries ravaged by Paganism. Again, you will see that nothing could shake the constancy of his humility. After this, Messieurs, allow me to tell you two things.

First, what I am telling you is not a myth, or mere ostentatious boasting, but rather it is a true account of an inexhaustible fountain of virtues. VINCENT DE PAUL's courage was above all the encouragement of hope against all fears.[74] The cloying flattery of the members of the Court, the approval of the great and the most powerful, the charm of the most charming, the passion of the most passionate, the violence of the most violent, all of these combined were incapable of disturbing VINCENT DE PAUL's generous heart. All of these did not affect the constancy of his humility in the least.[75]

In a word, he knew that human beings are always prone to seek that which is the sweetest, the most agreeable, the most innocent, the most prosperous, and the most advantageous to their own interests, even above the interests of God's glory. He also realized that giving in to these merely human concerns was a terrible danger that could threaten the entire ruin of his Congregation, and the true interests of God's glory.

Again, however, all these considerations were incapable of shaking the confidence of this great Soul, which was firmer than a rock amidst the waves of the sea because "...*fundata enim erat supra petram*" ("...because it had been built on rock") ...*petra autem erat Christus.*" ("...the rock was the Christ.")[76] It is this rock that saved him from the fury of the winds, the storms, and the anger of the waves. Thus, we can say of him what saint (John) Chrysostom said of the Apostles: "*Pulsata fluctibus rupe, firmius constiterunt.*" ("For when the waves of the world were beating against them... they stood firmer than a rock, and dispersed them all.")[77] For this was a man who had no other support for his cares, his conduct, and for all of the great works of God's Providence that were confided to him than the pure teachings of the Gospel which are incapable of either being evaded or defeated, by any earthly Crown or Empire.[78]

Everyone knows he had a profound respect for Bishops, at a time when the sacred Miters were often treated with scorn.[79] One day, speaking to a Bishop he said to him, "*Monseigneur, never betray the teaching of the Gospels.*"[80]

After hearing all of this, Messieurs, don't you agree that we have good reason to say: "...*cuius laus est in evangelio per omnes ecclesias*" ("...[the brother] who is praised in all the churches for his preaching of the Gospel") when we speak of an incomparable man who was so totally void of false wisdom, and instead filled so completely with the wisdom of the Gospel?

One day at Court, a great Noble of the Kingdom who had demanded a Benefice for one of his sons and who knew that Monsieur VINCENT, as a member of the Council (of Conscience), had opposed his request, reproached him in these words, "*Why, are you opposing me Monsieur VINCENT?*" Here is the response Monsieur VINCENT gave him; an answer filled with both a perfect meekness and firmness, "*Monseigneur, I know the respect that I owe to you, but by the grace of God you have no power over my conscience.*"[81] He discovered the perfect temperament by combining meekness and humility with a confidence that never gave way to merely human considerations.[82] He knew that if humility is not also accompanied by strength, it has only the appearance of virtue and none of its effects.

I know it is easy to be astonished by the success of all the activities he undertook in ways that were so totally contrary to the means which ordinarily would have been suggested by mere human prudence.[83] This great success came about because he carefully worked to strip himself of his human spirit, and to search for guidance only from the inspirations provided by God's spirit. God, for his part, draws near to those who search for him and he fills them with the light of his wisdom. He then brings about favorable conclusions to even the most difficult affairs having but the gloomiest prospects of success, which would ordinarily make even the most prudent spirits grow faint. "*Qui confidunt in Domino sicut mons Sion non commovebitur in aeternum qui habitat in Hierusalem [montes in circuitu eius]...*" ("Like Mount Zion are they who trust in the Lord, unshakable, forever enduring. As mountains surround Jerusalem...")[84]

On the contrary, worldly "Sages" are the enemies of Christian sincerity because they have strayed through their intrigues only to find that their wisdom is confounded. "*...declinantes autem in obligationes* (στραγγαλιὰς in the Greek text) *adducet Dominus cum operantibus iniquitatem...*" ("But those who turn aside to crooked ways may the Lord send down with the wicked.")[85]

The second thing I have to tell you, Messieurs, is that during his lifetime VINCENT DE PAUL was the only one who was blind to his heroic virtues. The more highly you praised him to the heavens, the more he humbled himself in the obscurity of his lowly birth.

Messieurs, don't we admire the modesty of the Patriarch Joseph and his brothers? Joseph was destined to rule over Egypt, yet he told his brothers to describe themselves as being only humble shepherds. This was an occupation that the Egyptians scorned considering it to be disgraceful, as can be seen in the Book of Genesis: "*...detestantur Ægyptii omnes pastores ovium.*" ("...all shepherds are abhorrent to the Egyptians.")[86] Yet were not Joseph and his brothers the Descendants of Abraham, and their ancestors in faith? Didn't they belong by

Detail of turn-of-the-twentieth-century postcard illustrating the birthplace of Vincent: Who, then, will this child be? The image alludes to his giving alms to a poor man.
Vincentian Studies Institute Collected Illustrations

blood to an illustrious lineage that had so often been singularly honored with God's blessings, receiving the fulfillment of the promises of their inheritance as the children of the Most High? Yet, in spite of all this he still sought scorn, because as Rupert notes: "*Scilicet quod hominibus non solum non placere, sed etiam displicere quæsierunt.*" ("Men are certainly not placed on the earth to seek to please, but rather they must seek to displease.")[87]

Likewise, when you speak of VINCENT DE PAUL, and all the marvelous things you have admired in him, you are testifying to the satisfaction and the esteem you have of his virtue. In your presence he purposely described himself as being rooted in the earth, and even in the dung of the herds he often shepherded as a country youth, more as a practice of humility than because of the necessity of fortune.[88]

Ah! Great man, who so many people consider to be another Abrech or another Joseph, who by relieving the extreme famine of Lorraine, Champagne, Picardy, and the frontiers of Luxembourg accomplished more than just relieving the famine of Egypt.[89] Ah! Great man you helped so many of the poor refugees from England, Scotland, and Ireland who suffered exile and the loss of their possessions because of the Faith. Yet, even in light of such holy actions he preferred to receive contempt rather than to receive praise.[90]

When he first came to Paris, he hid his surname because he feared the name "de PAUL," might be mistaken as a noble one.[91] He thought if he introduced himself simply as Monsieur VINCENT, as one might be informally introduced as "Monsieur Pierre" or "Monsieur Jean," he would then be assumed to be someone who was unimportant.[92] What could be a more direct proof of his humility than this innocent artifice? We know that when Caesar, Xenophon, Cato, Sylla, and Brutus wrote they did so using pseudonyms so as to hide their accomplishments.[93] But for someone to hide his name just because it is too beautiful, this is an example of rare modesty.

We know that the Emperor Justinian[94] wanted the Greek title for the office of the "Night Prefect" (νυκτέπαρκος in Book Thirteen of the Civil Code) to be changed because he thought it was too obscure and somber. When, in obedience to his order, this was done in the new law, the title of this Prefect was changed to the "People's Prefect."[95]

But you, VINCENT DE PAUL, why did you change your name by hiding its better half? Since you kept watch against the disorders of the night in order to put a stop to the crimes which take place in these shadows, doubtlessly you could have borne both of these names, one which is somber and belongs to the night, and the other which is brilliant and belongs to the day. This was so because through your practice of the works of the light you provided charitable relief for so many of the afflicted in the towns, countryside, and in the kingdom's great cities, "*nec est qui se abscondat a calore eius.*" ("...nothing escapes its heat.")[96] Thus, you were more useful to the public than the "People's Prefect" of ancient times.

Messieurs, do not think it is wrong to find the source of great deeds rooted in the illustrious names of those who perform them. According to Plato, Socrates said fathers should take particular care to give good names to their infants for the purpose of rooting them in the practice of virtue, and to make them grow in public esteem, and also so their agreeable names might gain them a freer access to Princes, from whom they could hope to receive favor and graces.[97] Doesn't it seem that the Poet had also studied these Laws when he said: "*convenient rebus nomina sepe suis*," ("everyone agrees that things often are what they are named,")[98] and since even the Jurisprudence we teach says proper names, "*rebus esse*." ("[be] appropriate to things.")[99]

Doesn't Saint Thomas (Aquinas), the master of the Sacred School, teach that names should be given with the intention of imparting the particular qualities associated with the chosen name?[100] I can cite a number of examples of this truth that are found in Scripture; in "Abram" and "Abraham," the father of the Nations and the father of all Believers;[101] in "Joseph," in whose name we find reflected both the progress of his fortunes and of his virtue.[102]

In order to testify to the plan that he had for saving the world, the Savior of our souls wanted to take the name of "JESUS," which signifies Savior: "...*ipse enim salvum faciet populum suum a peccatis eorum*." ("...because he will save his people from their sins.")[103]

Thus, shouldn't we conclude that it was by the singular action of Heavenly Providence, that VINCENT DE PAUL bore these two beautiful names of "VINCENT" and "de PAUL?" From this perspective, we can see that a part of his generous labors and his illustrious victories can be attributed to the name "VINCENT" and the rest to the name "de PAUL," in that he was the perfect imitator of the great Saint Paul's zeal?[104] Nevertheless, Messieurs, persevering in the practice of humility from which he never strayed, he wished to remain unnoticed, or as it is more accurate to say, he preferred to be thought of as being a man of no real importance.

When he spoke of his educational background he said he was only a "weak Fourth," but in fact he held a Bachelor's degree in Theology.[105] He said this so often that most of the members of his own Congregation mistakenly believed he had not been educated beyond the first classes of Grammar. This is the only example we can find in his life of an exception to the candor of his soul, which was whiter than snow and purer than the lilies. He tolerated this violation of the usually inviolable laws of his honesty only because it was necessary that in this innocent quarrel between two of the most beautiful virtues, his humility should prevail, so that under the veil of this customary humility the secrets of his most beautiful accomplishments would remain hidden.

Once, at the height of a life-threatening illness, a famous Jesuit Religious (it is to be noted how servants of God so often end up as friends) asked him during a visit, "Monsieur, what are you thinking about at this moment?"[106] This holy and humble servant of God immediately responded: "*In spiritu humilitatis et in animo contrito suscipiamur a te Domine.*" ("In a spirit of humility and with a contrite soul receive us, O Lord.")[107] How could it be said that this great soul, so disengaged from the corruption of sin, merited nothing but punishments?

In effect, Messieurs, wasn't it necessary that a soul so dedicated to self-abandonment, and which throughout every moment of life had sought nothing other than the glory of God, would have had to descend far into the deepest abyss to establish the source of its humility? And, Messieurs, what is this ultimate abyss at the bottom of the earth? It is hell, that sad, eternal, dwelling place for God's enemies "...*dura sicut inferus æmulatio...*" ("...its flames are a blazing fire...")[108]

This holy man, who was so full of God's spirit, was also filled with the spirit of abandonment so admirably described by the great saint Teresa (of Avila): "O Greatness, which speaks of the infinite grandeur of the essence of God. O great nothingness, which speaks of the infinite smallness of the creature when compared to the grandeur of God."[109] Messieurs, I dare to say that this great man, revealed what he honestly thought about himself when he said he was worse than the devil.

Vincent's death. "O God, Come to my assistance."
Late nineteenth-century French holy card.
Vincentian Studies Institute Collected Illustrations

He also encouraged the members of his Congregation to regard themselves as being more contemptible than even the damned, and to consider themselves as having a place even lower in creation than the devils. He noted:[110]

> The devils have only sinned once, while alas, how many are our offenses and how numerous are our sins? The devils have not had the example of the Son of God to humble them, as we have had, and they have not had the same opportunities to do penance that God has given us. Have we not had many opportunities that we have not taken advantage of to wipe away our faults? If the demons were again given the freedom and the grace that we have had to honor and serve the adorable Majesty of our God, they might well acquit themselves in a way that is superior to our efforts. By what can we be glorified? By our birth? Alas, don't the devils have a nobler heritage than we do? What about our knowledge? Ha, the least of the devils has more than all people put together. All the Libraries, and all the Universities of the world, have nothing to compare to the knowledge possessed by the lost spirits. What then, is there that we can make the subject of our vanity besides our good words? O my God! Who can do anything by himself? You alone, Oh my God, are the Author of all that is good; and the one who attributes this honor to himself, Messieurs, serves as the servant of the devil, and the enemy of his Creator, by taking away the glory which belongs only to God. '*Gloriam meam alteri non dabo.*'[111] (My glory I give to no other.)[112]

Messieurs, it is not my mere words that now move your hearts; rather it is the spirit of VINCENT DE PAUL, a spirit which through the expression of its charity and humility ascended to the highest Heavens from the depths of the greatest abysses. This was astonishing to witness, Messieurs, because through his incredible humility he was able to compartmentalize his heart. On the one hand he could feel the fires of hell. Simultaneously, however, because of the ardor of his zealous charity he could also feel those very different flames which resemble the innocent flames of the Seraphim that burn in Heaven.[113]

This is the miraculous genius of the great VINCENT DE PAUL whose abundant grace, fidelity, and invincible courage today is the object of our wonder, and who for countless centuries to come will receive the admiration of God's Church. While awaiting the full story of his life to be written, it is here that we must cut our discourse short, not saying anything more about the practices of his humility because it is now necessary to pass to a recital of some of the effects of his love and charity. This will form the second and last Part of the discourse.

The Second Part: His Charity[114]

Yes, Messieurs, we must say that VINCENT DE PAUL has given us reason to see that his purpose in life was to imitate the great saint Paul's zeal. This worthy Superior General of the Mission was a true imitator of the great Apostle, and often repeated with him: *"Quis nos separabit a caritate Christi?...certus sum enim quia necque mors, necque vita etc..."* ("What will separate us from the love of Christ?...For I am convinced that neither death nor life etc...").[115] Or as saint John Chrysostom said: *"O animam furentem insania sed quæ sobrietatem pariat!"*[116] ("Indeed one may see he was always enflamed with a wonderful love for the faithful!")

VINCENT DE PAUL, what was said about the Apostle can also be said about you. Didn't he also say with the Apostle: *"Quis infirmatur, et non infirmor?"* ("Who is weak and I am not weak?")[117] Was there ever an opportunity for helping the afflicted, when he did not tenderly embrace them? When did he not run zealously to their aid? One can say of him, without any exaggeration, what saint Jerome said of Fabiola: *"Morbos in tanta miserorum oblectamenta commutavit, ut multi*

St. Vincent de Paul. The father and friend of the poor and weak. "...He is the father of the orphans. The beloved of God and of men whose memory is blessed."
Mid-nineteenth-century French holy card.
Vincentian Studies Institute Collected Illustrations

sani languentibus reviderent." ("She so wonderfully relieved the diseases of the suffering poor that many of the healthy began to envy the sick.")[118] I won't even mention the three or four hospitals he established in Paris, or those that he established in the Provinces, or this discourse would go on forever.[119]

With regard to the galleys, there are just two things about him that I am going to mention. Once while he was on a sea voyage, he was taken captive by Pirates and put in chains along with many other persons who were with him on the same vessel. They were then taken to Tunis where this young slave joined with the others who were to be companions in his punishment, but not in his virtue. However, among the many captives, there were some who were able to appreciate the modesty, the sweetness, the patience, and the thousand other admirable qualities which were found in the person of VINCENT DE PAUL.[120]

While the others complained of the rigors they endured, VINCENT DE PAUL recognized them as being nothing other than their destiny under the direction of Divine Providence to which he yielded with love. While the others complained and sighed in the midst of their many sufferings; totally to the contrary, he found delight in his captivity, since it was God's will.

One could hear in their cries and sobs evidence of the bitterness and sorrow that afflicted their hearts. Meanwhile, however, VINCENT DE PAUL sang the Canticles of Sion in the middle of this Babylon. His Master's wife listened to him chanting the Psalms of David, and her heart was touched. She then spoke with her husband. Instead of carrying the infection of sin, as the words of Eve our first Mother did in carrying original sin to the first humans, her words led him to choose a better, happier, life. Instead of approving his apostasy, she reproached her husband for his crime. At the same time she pointed to the example of the constancy and piety of this amiable captive.

By his prayers and works of charity, VINCENT DE PAUL so influenced his Master and some others of his household that the Master arranged for them to escape to Avignon. Here he renounced the Koran, and was received back into the bosom of the Church. Here is one of the first conquests of VINCENT DE PAUL. Here we find the prelude to the great conquests that one day he would achieve through the Missions, where he saved so many souls from being shipwrecked and lost to slavery, in order to gain them for God.

Secondly, I will consider the concern that he had for the sufferings of the convicts in the Galleys at Marseille.[121] He could not witness their miseries, nor could he tell their story to the charitable women whom he sent to help them, without being bathed in tears.[122] Mesdames, he opened your eyes to their pitiful condition; being covered with vermin and maggots. Thus, he could say together with Job: "*...putredini dixi pater meus...et soror mea vermibus...*" ("If I must call corruption 'my father,' and the maggot... 'my sister'...")[123] Despite the vermin and maggots, he embraced these poor people as if they were his brothers.

Can't you still see him giving his always fervent exhortations or spiritual conferences that were filled with the fire of his charity, which given his good natured heart he could not restrain?[124] Was it the urgency of his love, or the tenderness of his compassion, he wanted to be silent about, but which he only rendered even more eloquent by his efforts to mute them?

O Divine Mercy of the chaste heart of my Savior JESUS CHRIST that set fire to the heart of VINCENT DE PAUL, explain these mysteries to us![125] Words failed him, and tears fell from his eyes as he was moved by his love and the pain of seeing the sight of the miseries of his neighbor, who was dearer to him than life itself, for *"interdum lachrymæ pondera vocis habent."* ("tears on occasion carry the weight of speech.")[126] His eyes expressed themselves eloquently even without his having to speak; for, Mesdames, you will agree that it took only one sigh from him requesting ten pistoles for the poor, and you would generously open your purses.[127] His tears gave birth to yours. You then joined the sentiments of your good hearts with your own compassion. And thus, Messieurs, isn't it natural to expect that a mixture that was both so innocent and so divine would produce so much fire, as well as so many tears?

Saint Vincent de Paul. A man of prayer. Early nineteenth-century French holy card. *Vincentian Studies Collection, Special Collections and Archives, DePaul University, Chicago, Illinois*

St VINCENT DE PAUL.

I will not speak of the role that our great Queen, the Mother of our great King, played through her generous almsgiving on these occasions. Her own modesty in this matter causes me to remain silent.[128] But I must tell you that one brother from Monsieur VINCENT's House made fifty-three trips to Lorraine carrying a total of almost 150,000 livres, without ever being captured.[129] He passed right through the midst of the soldiers without ever losing anything. Sometimes he carried 20,000 livres, and often even greater sums, even though he had no other escort than the prayers and the charity with which he had been sent.

I am not going to tell you at any length about the quantities of cloth and clothing that he sent to Lorraine, in order to help clothe so many honest women and so many good Religious who suffered because of their extreme poverty.[130]

Saint Vincent de Paul receiving the last rites. Banner carried by the angels: "O God. Come to my assistance." Quotation from Psalm 40 (41): "Blessed the one concerned for the poor; on a day of misfortune the Lord delivers him."
Late nineteenth-century French holy card.
Vincentian Studies Institute Collected Illustrations

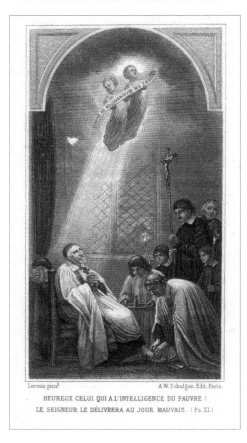

Thus these women found themselves wearing wedding gowns, since they were wearing the clothing of charity, the spouse of holy souls and the Queen of all the virtues. Should you not be told, Messieurs, that one of the subjects of this great Missionary transported more than 8,000 pieces of clothing to yet another province? Or that still another brought more than 500,000 livres of relief to yet another province?[131] No, no, Messieurs, we should no longer be silent about these events. On the contrary, you should know about them.[132]

You should know it was Monsieur VINCENT who provided the man power and the funds to clean up the manure heaps, the cesspools, and the bodies of dead horses which were the cause of the deadly plague in the city of Etampes.[133] He also did this after the battle of Rethel, when he arranged for the burial of 1200 to 1500 bodies which were beginning to cause an unbearable stench, as well as an epidemic which brought about the entire ruin of these sad regions.[134]

But, Messieurs, the charity of this worthy Founder and First General of the Mission was a consuming charity, like that of the great saint Paul whose name he bore. He was never satisfied with his zeal, even if he had given all that he had to help the afflicted. He wanted to be able to say what saint Paul had written to the Corinthians: "*Os nostrum patet ad vos o Corinthii cor nostrum dilatatum est...*" ("We have spoken frankly to you, Corinthians; our heart is open wide.")[135] Or as the same apostle said in chapter 12: "*Nec enim debent filii parentibus thesaurizare sed parentes filiis ego autem libentissime inpendam et superinpendar.*" ("Children

Vincent delivering bread to victims of the flood.
Early nineteenth-century French engraving.
Vincentian Studies Institute Collected Illustrations

ought not to save for their parents, but parents for their children. I will most gladly spend and be utterly spent for your sakes.")[136]

Messieurs, you witnessed the great flood which brought a deluge to the gates of Paris and which in the countryside reduced entire villages to famine, but you did not see what was carefully hidden from you until now. Yes, Messieurs, it is necessary to tell you that Monsieur VINCENT opened the granaries of his own House of saint-Lazare, even though what was stored there was needed to feed the numerous members of his own family. With this grain he had a great amount of bread made to relieve the people's hunger. This was distributed by boat; a ladder being used to carry the bread to the windows of the higher floors of their homes where the poor had taken refuge, suffering both from the floodwaters and their hunger. He risked the lives of his own good servants, who in their desire to save others often found themselves in danger of drowning.[137]

I cannot but tell you that in the city of Toul these good Missionaries, animated by the spirit of their General, never used for themselves any part of the alms that were to be distributed to the poor.[138] But didn't they, Messieurs, deserve twice as much? "*Dignus operarius mercede sua.*" ("A worker deserves his pay.")[139] After all, isn't it only fair that he who serves at the Altar should be supported from the income of his priestly ministry?

Yes, Messieurs, such a course of action undoubtedly would be blameless since these laws of recompense are legitimate, but the zealous impulses of the

The Church of Saint-Lazare, Paris.
Vincentian Studies Institute Collected Illustrations

ardent charity of VINCENT DE PAUL followed even higher principles: "*Ego autem libentissime inpendam et superimpendar.*" ("I will most gladly spend and be utterly spent for your sakes.")[140] This was said by the incomparable saint Paul, and was said again in our day by the incomparable VINCENT DE PAUL. You have seen his works in Paris,[141] and I have seen them in my own Diocese.[142] I had never before seen, nor have I ever seen since, such prodigious generosity, even more than could be expected from a father, as evidenced in the order given by Monsieur VINCENT to distribute the grain stores of Saint-Lazare in such profusion.

VINCENT DE PAUL your own Family was so numerous, and you had put it into debt by the alms that your prudence and charity already had given! But this did not matter to him, Messieurs, for he saw how much his granaries could furnish, and his charity was more abundant than the contents of all these warehouses combined. For three months he distributed armfuls of bread daily at the doors of saint-Lazare to feed two thousand poor people, and sometimes as many as three thousand or three thousand five hundred. "*Dispersit, dedit pauperibus, iustitia eius manet in sæculum sæculi.*" ("Lavishly they give to the poor; their prosperity shall endure forever.")[143] He did so much good when the harvest failed, that he was able to help keep the public peace.

Oh, Adorable Providence of my God, by which you hold in your hands both abundance and famine! By this same Providence you, in your justice, mete out both the punishments that lead to the gates of death and the favors of your mercy that rescues from the tomb. It seems clear you wanted to honor the virtue of the great VINCENT DE PAUL by repeating the miracles performed by the great Prophet Elijah. A charitable widow nourished the Prophet with a little oil and a little wheat, and in order to repay this generosity which appeared to be so insignificant, she heard Elijah pronounce these wonderful words of blessing on behalf of God: "*Hæc autem dicit Dominus Deus Israhel hydria farinæ non deficiet nec lecythus olei minuetur usque ad diem in qua daturus est Dominus pluviam super faciem terræ.*" ("For the Lord, the God of Israel says: 'The jar of flour shall not go empty, nor the jug of oil run dry, until the day when the Lord sends rain upon the earth.'")[144]

Doesn't it seem, Messieurs, that the same thing could be said about the charitable VINCENT DE PAUL? Come daring and charitable Father of the poor.[145] Open your granaries, and from your house of saint-Lazare feed the two thousand to three thousand five hundred of the hungry every day for months since, "*Hydria farinæ non deficiet, nec lecythus olei minuetur.*" ("The jar of flour shall not go empty, nor the jug of oil run dry.")[146] The contents of your warehouses were nothing compared to the merit of your prayers, your alms, and your penances. These brought an end to all the troubles in Paris, bringing abundance to this great City and the blessing of Heaven on all those who belong to your family.

Were there not, Messieurs, early signs of his generosity? Once, when he was a young boy he was carrying his father's grain from the mill to the granary when he distributed the wheat to the poor and then returned home.[147] As saint (Peter) Chrysologus said: "O the lovable prodigal!"[148] If a father could find in his heart the love necessary to forgive a prodigal son who had been lost in debauchery, what can we expect for a holy prodigal who lived on earth for almost a century as if he was living in exile in a foreign land, and who has now, as we hope, finally returned to Heaven to live in his celestial homeland and receive a loving embrace from the Father of the human family? "...*cito proferte stolam primam et induite illum...*" ("...quickly bring the finest robe and put it on him...")[149]

Doubtlessly he could say of his youth, what was said by Job, that God was "...*ab infantia mea crevit mecum miseratio...*" ("...guiding me even from my mother's womb...")[150] You know from the account of his actions, and the sentiments of his own heart, that God had created him to be poor only in order to serve the poor.[151] Monsieur VINCENT said, "We are for the poor, the poor are ours. Just as a hunter chases his game everywhere, wherever we find *les misérables* it is necessary for us to assist them at all costs."[152]

Here, Messieurs, is the example of a charitable heart dedicated in the highest degree to a perfect charity towards the neighbor in imitation of the heart of God, which is to say that he embraced everyone and refused no one. "*Estote ergo misericordes sicut et Pater vester misericors est.*" ("Be merciful just as [also] your Father is merciful.")[153] It is true to say that his charitable rule of being concerned first for the needs of strangers rather than for the members of his own community, at times threatened them with having to depend on alms. But no, Messieurs, not even these threats could stop the outpouring of his charity; for the person who gives out of fear is less courageous than the person who gives with hope and delights in what he is doing. As he said: "*Let us take care of the affairs of God, and God without doubt will take good care of ours.*"[154] "*What difference does it make whether we become beggars ourselves if we are happy to be able to relieve the poor?*"[155]

HIS CONFIDENCE IN DIVINE PROVIDENCE[156]

One evening he was told that there wasn't enough food in the refectory stores to provide for the community's dinner the next day. "Ah, my brother!" he said, "What happy news since it gives us the opportunity to place our confidence solely on God."[157] "*Iacta super Dominum curam tuam et ipse te enutriet.*" ("Cast your cares upon the Lord, who will give you support.")[158] His confidence was not in vain, for that same night someone made a considerable donation.

Imagine a man who not only was responsible for a large Community, and who freely gave extraordinary spiritual and physical nourishment to twenty or thirty persons each day during the course of the year, but who also at the same time had many others residing in his house making their Spiritual Exercises, Retreats and preparing for their general Confessions.[159] I have seen around 100 or 120 young men prayerfully undertaking ten-day spiritual retreats led by the late Monsieur VINCENT. I have given these Ordination Retreats to those who were preparing to receive Orders.[160] All these men are received freely at the cost of the House of saint-Lazare which has no endowment to support this charitable work.[161]

Monsieur VINCENT, and these good Messieurs of saint-Lazare gladly welcomed Messieurs the Ordinands as if they were receiving treasures. These men came from everywhere to receive help from this charitable Father's heart. One could attribute to him, as a most appropriate description, what Valerian the Great said of Gillias: "*His house resembled a bountiful store. It seemed that he was not mortal for his kind heart understood well people's needs.*"[162]

HIS DISINTERESTED CHARITY[163]

Is there a more disinterested charity, "*Non quærit quæ sua sunt?*" ("which does not seek its own interests?")[164] Monsieur VINCENT never said, or did, anything to acquire anything for himself. He never thought of trying to procure even the smallest benefice for one of his own, even though he often had the opportunity to do this. One day he said, "*I will not take any steps, or do anything to procure any advantages for us.*"[165] He would rather have put his own house in debt than miss an opportunity to perform a good work. "*...[Q]ui post aurum non abiit nec speravit in pecunia et thesauris quis est hic et laudabimus eum...*" ("Happy the rich man who is found without fault, who turns not aside after gain! Who is he, that we may praise him?")[166]

The Charity of Jesus Christ urges me! (St. Paul)
Apostolic Spirit.
St. Vincent evangelist and evangelizer of the poor.
Mid-nineteenth-century French holy card.
Vincentian Studies Institute Collected Illustrations

If I had the time there are more edifying stories that I could tell you, especially concerning the charitable assistance that he gave to those poor sick whose flesh was consumed by ulcers and decay. He gathered them in his little carriage (that in his humility he remarkably called his "ignominy") in order to carry them to the hospital.[167] *"Hii in curribus et hii in equis nos autem in nomine Domini Dei nostri invocabimus."* ("Some rely on chariots, others on horses, but we on the name of the Lord our God.")[168]

His was a consuming charity that was without limits. His heart was like a vast sea. *"...omnia flumina intrant mare, et mare non redundant..."* ("All rivers go to the sea, yet never does the sea become full.")[169] Everyone who entered into the sea of his charity was received there. All sorts of persons: the Barbarian and the Scythian, the Jew, the Infidel, the just, and the sinner all found themselves immersed in the flood of his good works.

I have known many Servants of God, but I have never known any that were the equal of the two great servants of God, the late Monsieur l'Abbé Olier and the late Monsieur VINCENT. Because of the eminence of their virtues, they were perfectly united by the sacred ties of a holy and perfect friendship. Monsieur VINCENT and Monsieur Olier were both heavily burdened with many important affairs which they had undertaken for the glory of God, yet if you had any extraordinary spiritual or physical pain and you asked for their help they would drop whatever they were doing in order to console your heart in its affliction. Thus, I will say of them what saint Anselm and Theophylactus

Portrait of Marie Madeleine de Vignerot du Pont de Courlay, Duchesse d'Aiguillon (1604-1675). In his infirmity, she provided Vincent a carriage and horses — a luxury he decried as his 'ignominy.'
Courtesy Vincentian Studies Collection, Special Collections and Archives, DePaul University, Chicago, Illinois

both said about saint Paul: "*Patitur suas et simul aliorum infirmitates tolerat et solatur: tolerat infirmitates singulorum, et simul de communi salte et de toto orbe solicitus est.*" ("He suffered his own pains, while at the same time he relieved those of everyone else.")[170]

How many times after conversing with them did you say: "*...nonne cor nostrum ardens erat in nobis dum loqueretur in via...?*" ("Were not our hearts burning within us as he spoke to us on the way...?")[171] How many times have you said in adoring the infinite goodness of our God, "Oh how good is God's heart!" or "Oh, how loving is God's heart, since he is the source of such courageous actions, since he has put such good hearts into the chests of men!" One was to be the spiritual son, and the other was to be the spiritual father.

Monsieur VINCENT was the first spiritual Director of Monsieur l'Abbé Olier, and it was because of this relationship that Monsieur Olier called him his "Father." Later, Father (Charles) de Condren, the General of the Fathers of the Oratory (of Jesus), was also the director of this young Abbé.[172] Thus, he had two of the greatest masters of the spiritual life to form him and make him capable of reaching the highest levels of perfection. In time, this direction bore fruit as Divine Providence destined him to establish the beautiful Seminary of saint-Sulpice and he became the Father and Teacher of many virtuous Ecclesiastics. As I speak, these priests are working in our Dioceses with an abundance of graces and blessings.

One can say that Monsieur VINCENT was, in a manner of speaking, the first to have sown the seeds of these rich priestly harvests with the establishment of Seminaries at the Collège des Bons-Enfants, near Saint Victor's gate, of Saint-Charles near saint-Lazare for younger seminarians, also the Seminary of Annecy in Savoy for the examination of Ordinands, and of so many other establishments, some very small and others very large, some for youngsters and others for young men.[173] He established all of these through his zeal and his charity.

HIS PARDON OF INJURIES[174]

His charity had no limits. He generously gave his blessings, just as he willingly suffered injuries and always returned good for evil. One day, in the presence of the late Madame the Marquise de Maignelay, of most blessed memory, he exhorted a certain young Lady to reform her life.[175] This creature did not want to pay any attention to his holy advice and, instead of being grateful for her benefactor's charity, threw a chair at his head. Monsieur VINCENT received this attack with a smile, and he continued his conversation as if nothing had happened.[176]

On another occasion, a noble who correctly assumed that Monsieur VINCENT had opposed his request for a benefice publicly upbraided him with atrocious insults which he accepted with a heroic meekness. The Queen Mother was informed of this incident and wanted to banish the offending noble from

Court. However, Monsieur VINCENT knelt before Her Majesty to obtain his pardon.[177]

One day, because of the great weakness in his legs,[178] he was riding through the streets on his miserable twenty-four year old horse.[179] A man who was drunk saw him and yelled furious insults at him. Monsieur VINCENT got off his horse, knelt before this angry man, and asked his pardon with such civility that the next morning the man sought him out and admitted that what he had done was wrong. He stayed to make a Retreat at saint-Lazare as Monsieur Vincent's guest, and made a good Confession which changed his dissolute life. He became a penitent and changed man.[180]

HIS GRATITUDE[181]

If he showed such love for his enemies, what great charity could he then have been expected to show towards the least of his children, or for those who helped him in some way? He was always filled with the spirit and wisdom of the Son of God, and he always wanted to be faithful to the words of the Savior of our souls: "...*quamdiu fecistis uni de his fratribus meis minimis mihi fecistis.*" ("... whatever you did for one of these least brothers of mine, you did for me.")[182]

It made no difference to him whether he received either the least offense, or the least favor from you. In either case you became the master of his heart, of his person, and of all that he had or might have. It would take a separate volume filled with remarkable accounts to tell the full story of his famous generosity and the everlasting sentiments of gratitude that he always preserved for his benefactors.

The Church of Saint-Médard on the rue Mouffetard in the Latin Quarter. The Mouffetard District was once considered the roughest, most impoverished neighborhood in Paris.
Vincentian Studies Institute Collected Illustrations

As he said: "*We cannot have enough gratitude for our benefactors.*"[183] This was a thought he put into words, into writing, and into practice.

In one of his Letters he wrote:

> *God has recently given us the grace of offering to the Founder of one of our Houses, who seemed to me to now be in need, the same generosity that he had once given us. I feel that if he accepts this offer I will be greatly consoled because the measure of the divine goodness that we had originally received would then be totally returned to our benefactor with nothing remaining of it for us. And if this should happen wouldn't it be an honor, Monsieur, to become poor in order to help him who had helped us? May God give us the grace of being consumed in this way! I am always consoled when I think of this, in a way that I don't know how to explain to you.*[184]

HIS HEROIC CHARITY[185]

Lastly, God in his Providence had grand plans for this great man, which required a heroic charity from him in order that he might become a pastor of souls. The Son of God wanted to confide the care of his Church to Saint Peter and so he asked him: "*Simon Iohannis diligis me plus his?*" ("Simon, son of John, do you love me more than these?")[186] Do you love me more than Thomas, more than Nathaniel, more than James and John, and more than the other two Disciples who also were fishermen? You know that the Son of God asked this question twice more, and you know the answer that the Prince of the Apostles gave: "Lord you know that I love you." You also know the response of the Son of God who said to him: "Feed my lambs...Feed my sheep."[187]

Here, Messieurs, is the example of the most perfect love that we can have for the Son of God, which is to love his flock, to love his Church. Why is this, Messieurs? This is so because it was the Lord himself who above all else became the most beloved Pastor of our souls. Saint Gregory Naziazus (in his prayer #41) called the Lord: "...τοῦ ἀληθινοῦ καί πρώτου ποιμένος ..." ("...the true and first pastor...").[188] Saint Isidore called him "ποιμαντίκης ἡγεμών" ("the captain of the pastoral art"),[189] while Saint Clement of Alexandria described him, "Ποιμὴν ἀρνῶν βασιλικῶν." ("Shepherd of the royal sheep.")[190] Saint Peter called him "*pastorem et episcopum animarum vestrarum*" ("the shepherd and guardian of your souls"),[191] and in Chapter 5 "*princeps pastorum.*" ("the chief Shepherd.")[192] Saint Paul in his letter to the Hebrews (Chapter 13:20), described him as "*pastorem magnum ovium.*" ("the great shepherd of the sheep.")[193] The Son of God, as quoted by saint John (Chapter 10), described himself, "*ego sum pastor bonus.*" ("I am the good shepherd.")[194]

If you were to ask, "What is the chief characteristic of someone who serves as a Pastor of souls?" The answer is Charity. In the words of saint John Climacus,

"Pastorem verum ostendit charitas, quæ principem pastorum in crucem egit," ("The true pastor demonstrated his love by being crucified,")[195] or as saint Basil also said, *"Scire satis tibi est, bonus pastorem esse, animam suam pro ovibus posuisse. Cognitio Dei continetur his finibus."* ("One knows that the pastor is good because he offered himself for his sheep, and because this is the divine purpose of his mission.")[196]

It is at this point, Messieurs, where we must again say that the praise we give to the memory of Monsieur VINCENT is worthy and legitimate since he devoted himself with such zeal to meeting all the needs of God's Church. *"...cuius laus est in evangelio per omnes ecclesias."* ("...[the brother] who is praised in all the churches for his preaching of the gospel.")

It has been said, Messieurs, that there was nothing that could bring greater sadness or joy to his great heart than the Church's good fortune or its misfortunes. As saint Thomas Aquinas fervently prayed each day to God, *"De nullo gaudeam vel doleam, nisi quod ducat ad te, vel abducat a te."* ("May I not be unduly lifted up by the one, nor unduly cast down by the other.")[197] The same can be said of VINCENT DE PAUL, for he was devoted to the interests of God's Church. Saint

Vincent preaching in his cassock and surplice. Nineteenth-century color-engraving. *Courtesy Vincentian Studies Collection, Special Collections and Archives, DePaul University, Chicago, Illinois*

Paul described the tension he experienced in his own life, "...*instantia mea cotidiana sollicitudo omnium ecclesiarum.*" ("...there is the daily pressure upon me of my anxiety for all the churches.")[198] This was also true of VINCENT DE PAUL. Saint Augustine, speaking of the great apostle described his "*incursus in me quotidianus.*" ("daily struggle.")[199] Saint Ambrose described his "*urgentes omnium Ecclesiarum curæ.*" ("urgent care of all the churches.")[200] Although he was chained in prison, Saint Paul sent his Disciples to care for all of the Churches: Crescens to Galatia, Titus to Crete and Dalmatia, Tychichus to Ephesus, as well as Mark and others to different destinations.[201]

VINCENT DE PAUL sent members of his community to the province of Lorraine, to Champagne, Picardy, and to Barbary and Poland as well.[202] At other times he sent Priests to Madagascar, where six of them had already died. Three others left for these Isles, but no sooner had the ship departed than it was wrecked in a storm not far from port. Four years later other missionaries departed, only to have their ship captured by the Spanish. Did he lose courage after these deaths, after so many shipwrecks, after so much bad luck? On the contrary, his Apostolic zeal proved to be stronger than those trials that would have dissuaded someone with less courage.[203] He recalled that the universal Church had been established by the Death of the Son of God, and strengthened by the deaths of the Apostles, the Popes, and of the Martyr-Bishops, and it had spread throughout the world through persecution and the blood of martyrs, which according to Tertullian is the "seed of Christians."[204]

He had been assured that many of the people of these isles were favorably disposed to receive the light of the Gospel. In fact, a great number had already received Baptism through the zeal of the one Missionary God had preserved there after the deaths of all the others.[205] Do you think, Messieurs, he could abandon this Priest when he asked for help? Do you think that he could abandon these people who had opened their arms in order to be instructed, and who had already opened their hearts and ears in order to hear the words of life? No, no, Messieurs, we have nothing to fear, for he could not abandon these souls: "*Da mihi animas cetera tolle tibi.*" ("Give me the people; the goods you may keep.")[206] His heart was so vast, and so generous, that he refused to accept defeat in any of his Apostolic labors. He was determined, therefore, to overcome all obstacles. So, at the beginning of 1660, he sent five more of his confreres to this far away island.

Concerning his zeal, Messieurs, we will comment on three things.[207] The first is that whenever there was a question of a particular Mission, a work, or establishment he saw as useful and honorable, if he discovered there was someone else interested in doing that work, he always deferred to them. He preferred they take on the work and receive all of its benefits and glory.[208] O, what other beautiful stories must we pass by in silence on this occasion?

Secondly, he never sent any missionaries to Barbary, or into any other perils, who had not volunteered enthusiastically to undertake such a mission.[209]

Thirdly, with regards to the missions, he was personally filled with the spirit of martyrdom. For his part, he wanted at least in spirit, to fully share in the work of those whom he sent. He wanted to do all that he could to relieve their sufferings, even at the cost of his own blood and life.[210]

It seems to me that we must apply to him the words of a Father of the Church in speaking about saint Felicity, whose feast we are celebrating today. The mother of seven martyrs, she endured martyrdom seven times, witnessing the successive martyrdoms of each of her children before finally enduring her own.[211] Should we also not say of him what the holy Church says of the glorious saint Martin: "*O sanctissima anima quam si gladius perfecutoris non abstulit: palmam tamen martyrii non amisit.*" ("O, Most holy soul! Even though you sought the sword it did not take you. However, in the end you were not to lose the palm of the martyrs.")[212]

I would like at this point, Messieurs, to be able to say something about the great qualities possessed by this true Pastor of souls, this very worthy Superior General of the Priests of the Mission. But what can one say in such a short period of time when there is so much that could be said? I have told you, so very briefly, of the love he had for his own, but you should also be told of the patience, vigilance, and the constancy he had in the midst of his wearisome labors.

HIS PATIENCE[213]

You should be told about his admirable patience in both the practice of mortification, and in service of his neighbor.[214] You should be told of his personal austerity, which went beyond what is ordinarily considered to be even the most rigorous penitence. He took more than 100 blows of the discipline every morning from the time he was a young ecclesiastic, to the time that he was more than eighty years old.[215] Whether he was healthy or ill, he never desired or sought the least delicacy in his nourishment. On the contrary, he always asked that he be fed with the scraps left over from the community's table.[216]

I know about these admirable stories, because I have seen them with my own eyes. He slept on a pallet even when he was ill,[217] and never failed to make his Mental Prayer even when consumed by fever. He could thus say in two very different ways, both through the fire of his fever and through the fire of his devotion, "*in meditatione mea exardescet ignis.*" ("in my thoughts a fire blazed up.")[218] Every morning he spent three hours on his knees in Church praying, never paying any attention to the pains in his legs.[219]

He appeared at the King's Council poorly dressed in wretched clothing.[220] This was unprecedented, and our great Cardinal seeing this remarked to those at the Court: "*Qui mollibus vestiuntur in domibus regum sunt.*" ("Those who wear fine clothing are in royal palaces.")[221] VINCENT DE PAUL, yours was not an ordinary spirit of penitence and poverty. As Saint Gregory of Nyssa said so well: "in order for a Superior to establish his authority, he must be willing to do more than all the others." ["Δεῖ γὰρ ἐν τῇ ἐπιστασίᾳ μείζονα μὲν τῶν ἄλλων τοὺς προεστῶτας πονεῖν..."][222] One cannot reproach this worthy Superior General of the Mission with the words of saint Leo (the Great): "*Bestiæ irruunt, et ovium septa non claudunt.*" ("The beasts are attacking and the [seven] sheep are not protected.")[223] While the Brother-Porter was eating he took the keys and minded the front door himself. If you think performing this task was one that was below the dignity of a General, he would also then go to the kitchen and wash dishes and perform other such duties.[224]

HIS PENITENCE ON BEHALF OF OTHERS[225]

He did penance not only on behalf of those whom he knew, but also for strangers. He once asked our Lord to hear his prayers and relieve one of his penitents laboring under a violent temptation, which he was then attacked by for many years.[226] He once told someone confidentially that whenever he came to know the sins of someone else, he would undertake harsh bodily penances on their behalf.[227]

Where else can one find such a rare example of virtue? Where else can one find Pastors animated with this same zeal? Without a doubt he could say, following the example of the sovereign Pastor of our souls, "*Quæ non rapui tunc exsolvebam?*" ("Must I now restore what I did not steal?")[228] This was an apostolic man, a true imitator of Saint Paul, who was willing to be cursed on behalf of his brothers.[229] "*Bonus pastor animam suam dat pro ovibus.*" ("A good shepherd lays down his life for the sheep.")[230]

HIS CARE FOR HIS NEIGHBOR[231]

What can we say about his care for his neighbor? There once was someone who demanded Monsieur VINCENT grant him some favor he had refused him as a matter of conscience. What did this man do then, Messieurs? He continued to bother Monsieur VINCENT with frequent and useless visits. Monsieur VINCENT always received him with no show of dismay, and without ever being disturbed by such an extreme importunity which seemed so unbearable to everyone else but him.[232]

HIS SUFFERING FROM CALUMNIES[233]

He suffered the most extreme slanders without ever trying to explain, or defend himself, "*Sicut mutus...habens in ore suo redargutiones.*" ("...like the dumb, saying nothing.")[234] He chose instead to suffer, even if it meant his silence was interpreted as an admission of guilt. O rigorous modesty! O necessary silence! I respect your Laws even though they seem to me to be cruel in this instance. I will move on, Messieurs, without attempting to defend Monsieur VINCENT's innocence.

The heart of a Pastor's task is to be vigilant. In his *Third Homily* Saint Antiochus gives this beautiful description: "Ὀφείλει οὖν ὁ ποιμὴν ὅλος νοῦς καὶ ὀφθαλμὸς εἶναι." ("A Pastor must be both all spirit and all eye.")[235] Ah, Messieurs, we can also say this of our General of the Mission: "*Ecce, non dormitabit neque dormiet qui custodit Israhel.*" ("Truly, the guardian of Israel never slumbers nor sleeps.")[236] Or even better, what was said by another Prophet: "*Virgam vigilantem ego video.*" ("I see a branch of the watching-tree.")[237] Yes, without a doubt he could also say of himself what Jacob said while tending the herds of his father-in-law Laban: "*Die noctuque æstu urebar et gelu fugiebat somnus ab oculis meis!*" ("How often the scorching heat ravaged me by day, and the frost by night, while sleep fled from my eyes!")[238] For it is true that he arose every day at four o'clock, and yet every day went to bed later than everyone else. He denied himself sleep, using those precious moments to care for his dear flock.[239]

HIS STRENGTH AND CONSTANCY[240]

His strength and his constancy are worthy of a new discussion here. Virtue is praised whenever it is found, but it is extraordinary to find a person whose long life of eighty-five years (almost a century) was consumed, without any relaxation

The apotheosis of Vincent de Paul. Late nineteenth-century French engraving. *Courtesy Vincentian Studies Collection, Special Collections and Archives, DePaul University, Chicago, Illinois*

or interruption, by the exercise of virtue. His virtue was only finally hidden from our view by the veil of death. *"Imperatorem, ait, statem mori oportere."* ("For it is proper that the Emperor should die standing.")[241] What soul is so cold that it would not be warmed by such a beautiful sentiment?

Before finishing this Discourse, it is necessary that you recognize how he courageously fed souls with the three excellent foods of the Church spoken of by saint Ambrose: JESUS CHRIST, the Sacraments, and Scripture.[242] When he first started the Missions (coincidentally and most appropriately, on the feast of the Conversion of Saint Paul), he began on the lands of the late Madame Françoise Marguerite de Silly, the wife of Monsieur the Count of Joigny, Knight of the Orders of the King, General of the Galleys of France, and at present a Priest of the Oratory (of Jesus).[243] This holy and virtuous lady had Monsieur VINCENT as her Confessor and (spiritual) Director, and she made him promise that he would not leave her until her death. By commissioning these Missions, to be held on all her lands, she thus became the first Founder of the Mission.[244]

Oh what a beautiful sight! The Conversion of sinners gives birth to the joy of the Angels. You have seen Monsieur VINCENT in the pulpit completely filled with zeal for the salvation of souls. He preached with a holy vehemence, and was filled with God's spirit. He brought tears to the eyes, and touched the hearts, of all those who heard him. You have seen a deluge of tears come both from the Preacher and from his Listeners. At this first mission, the people came to him from everywhere. Everyone approached him. All the inhabitants of the Parish made their general Confession.[245] All the other villages followed this example, and the people went to Confession and availed themselves of the Sacraments and the Word of God. There were many Conversions and changes in lifestyle among even the most indifferent. All this astonished even those who were most skeptical. Monsieur VINCENT was indefatigable in his work which had no other goal than that of conforming hearts to JESUS CHRIST, *"donec formetur Christus in vobis."* ("...until Christ be formed in you.")[246]

He brought about a great blessing in God's Church by promoting the practice of making general Confessions, at a time when the practice had scarcely ever been known before. He rescued many people from a most profound ignorance of the mysteries of our faith. He taught many worthy Ecclesiastics and great Religious how to teach the Faithful effectively. He wanted them to preach and administer the sacraments in a simple and familiar, yet strong and powerful manner that would also be respectful of the Word of God.[247] In establishing Seminaries to form a Clergy capable of carrying the weight and dignity of their sacred ministry, he participated in this great work that the holy Council of Trent called *"Opus... tam pium, et tam sanctum."* ("A pious and holy work.")[248]

He had a marvelous respect for Priests,[249] and he wanted his confreres to be considered the least among them.[250] He also had a profound veneration for all the Orders of the Clergy, for the religious in their Cloisters, and for the Hierarchy.[251]

He had a well-known esteem for all the holy and famous congregations including the Company of JESUS,[252] and the Oratory of JESUS.[253] Concerning this, then, I have said enough.

Of all the relationships he had with great Servants of God whom he knew in his lifetime, the most important were with the two great lights of the Church, the Cardinals de la Rochefoucauld[254] and de Bérulle.[255] These prelates were renowned as much by the eminence of their piety, as by that of their sacred purple. They both had a very high esteem for the rare merits of the late VINCENT DE PAUL. They both spoke of the important role played by Monsieur VINCENT in the great works of this century; for most of which he laid the first foundations.

There is not enough time here to tell you of the zeal that he had to maintain the Purity of good doctrine, for it is such a vast subject.[256] One can only say that his conduct in this matter imitated that of the Apostles. His censure of all doctrinal novelties was based on his respect for the sacred Councils and for the holy Canons.[257] Saint Leo the Great excellently called these "...*Canones spiritu Dei conditos, et totius mundi reverentia consecratos*." ("The canons formed by the Spirit of God that the whole world reverently receives.")[258] The Council of Attiniaco called them "*Firmatus spiritu Dei Canones*." ("The canons established by the Spirit of God.")[259] The Councils themselves refer to them as "*Divinos Canones*." ("the sacred canons.")[260]

You with your small minds; you who are rebels against these most holy Laws; you who are unnatural children and who scorn your Mother the holy Church, learn from saint Augustine[261] who repeated what saint Cyprian had first said:

Pierre de Bérulle (1575-1629).
Courtesy Vincentian Studies Collection, Special Collections and Archives,
DePaul University, Chicago, Illinois

"*They will never have God for a Father, who also do not have the Church for their Mother.*"[262] Learn from VINCENT DE PAUL, who diligently studied Theology in Toulouse, Rome, and Paris. This is an unjust quarrel against the Church, who is the chaste Spouse of the Son of God, and the common Mother of all Christians. The same Church shares in Christ's authority since she is equally infallible today as she was in the time of the Apostles. "*Ecce vobiscum sum omnibus diebus usque ad consummationem sæculi.*" ("And behold, I am with you always, until the end of the age.")[263] The word of our Divine Master is found in the Church, for it is his Spouse. He loves it, and throughout the centuries he animates it always through his Spirit.

Didn't he also have respect for the authority of our holy Father?[264] VINCENT DE PAUL, you told us that you were only a "weak Fourth." You hid your studies. You hid the brilliance of your learning, and your spirit, with an unparalleled exercise of humility.[265] He was a Preacher, a Missionary, and a General of a Congregation. All these positions require a praiseworthy reputation, and an ability to teach and to preach, or else they would be without effect. Nevertheless, he wanted it believed that he was an uneducated person. But I, Messieurs, I know very well the truth in this matter. He was not in the least inferior even to the Sorbonne, the holiest and most knowledgeable School in the world.[266]

He always submitted himself in perfect obedience to the orders of the holy See. He recognized with a sincere submission of spirit the authority of the Vicar of JESUS CHRIST in the person of him who is the successor of Saint Peter.[267] How many of the sovereign Pontiffs have explained this in the past? Among others there were Luke, Mark, Felix, Agathon, Nicholas I, Leo IX, Innocent III, and above all saint Leo the Great.

How many of the Councils have spoken in the same way? All of the Faithful have acknowledged the Successors of Saint Peter, and have honored them with the beautiful titles of "*Teacher of the Faith,*" "*Head of the Church,*" "*Universal Pastor,*" "*Judge of Controversies,*" and "*Doctor of the World.*" Philip, the Legate of (pope) saint Celestine, at the Council of Ephesus was approved by all the Fathers of this holy and illustrious Assembly when he said that it was Saint Peter who judged matters of the Faith in the person of his successors, among whom he is still living and will always live.[268] Saint Jerome, one of the greatest men in the world, submitted himself blindly to the decision of the Pope when he settled the obscure and difficult controversy of the first centuries of the Church's history concerning the hypostasis.[269] Saint Augustine, after the Pope had pronounced on the error of the Pelagians, accepting the decrees of the two African councils even though they were not ecumenical, concluded that the controversy was thus over, "*Causa finita est....*" ("The matter is ended....")[270]

This was a doctrine, Messieurs, which delighted Monsieur VINCENT's heart because he was submissive to the Church, to our holy Father, and to the Nuncios of the pope. Whenever he was in need of immediate advice on certain theological matters he consulted the greatest men of the Sorbonne, and followed their advice. He also followed all the teachings and the doctrine of the Gospel, but only as they were interpreted by the Church and not by a spirit of personal ambition or of vanity. He perfectly understood these words of Saint Augustine: "*Ego vero Evangelio non crederem, nisi me catholicæ Ecclesiæ commoveret auctoritas.*" ("I truly would not believe the Gospel, unless the Church commanded it by its authority.")[271]

After all this, Messieurs, isn't it necessary for us to recognize, "*...cuius laus est in evangelio per omnes ecclesias*" (...[the brother] who is praised in all the Churches for his preaching of the gospel)? All the churches honor the great memory of VINCENT DE PAUL because it can be said of him that he honored and served all the Churches. Messieurs, haven't all the great Pastors of Paris, who are so celebrated for their doctrine and their virtue, testified to the respect they have for the memory of the great VINCENT DE PAUL? They have held memorial Services for him in their parishes, and others are planning to do the same thing. Together they have given praise to heaven because of the merits of his life.

Pico de la Mirandola once said, "*Æqua enim laus a laudatis laudari et improbari ab improbis.*" ("To be praised by the good, and blamed by the bad, is equal praise.")[272] This is one of the things that I have not done, and this is because if it is indeed true that public opinion is a good and faithful judge of the merit of the greatest of men, then what reasonable and unprejudiced man could find the least blemish in a sun as beautiful as Monsieur VINCENT? Messieurs of saint-Germain, worthy members of this Royal Church, you have done well to display

St. Francis de Sales (1567-1622). Bishop and Prince of Geneva.
Eighteenth-century engraving.
Vincentian Studies Institute Collected Illustrations

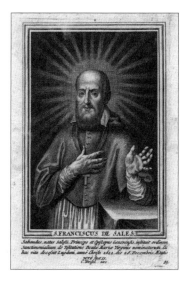

your own virtue by the esteem that you have for Monsieur VINCENT. You have proven your good grace by the desire you had that your church be the one chosen, among so many others that offered, to be the site for what we do as we gather here today.

But, Messieurs, can we leave this Pulpit and hide from you a fact that is as important as the one I am about to tell you? The Son of God who ardently loved both his Church and his Mother had two apostles who were very dear to him: Saint Peter and Saint John.[273] Having confided the care of his Church to Saint Peter, he confided to Saint John the care of his most holy Mother, whom the Greeks rightly call the παναγία ("All Holy.")[274] We have had in our days a Prelate of eminent sanctity, the great Francis de Sales, the Bishop and Prince of Geneva.[275] If God blesses our ardent prayers and our own small efforts we hope for his imminent canonization.[276] He held in his hands two treasures that were most dear to him, his Church and his Visitation; not his mother like the Son of God, but his good and holy daughters.[277]

In all of his affairs, Francis de Sales prayed to heaven in order to discern God's will. He needed to find two men who were worthy, to be confided with the care and direction of his two great treasures. He placed the Diocese of Geneva in very worthy hands, and I need not speak here of the qualities of the man who would take his place there.[278] Then, he chose a Spiritual Father for the worthy daughters of the Visitation in Paris, the first and most beautiful city of the world. In preference to all others he chose the uniquely qualified Monsieur VINCENT, who was an excellent copy of the perfect Original.[279] He chose a man who was filled with his teachings and the spirit of the Visitation; which is to say that he was filled with the spirit of all the virtues and in particular the most heroic virtues of humility, the purity of a perfect self-abandonment, a perfect scorn of self, a spirit of Prayer and of Retreat, the spirit of the hidden life of JESUS CHRIST in God, and of a sincere, cordial, pure union with God and his neighbor.

Ah! My dear Visitation, I know the holiness of your rare virtues. I have ever lasting obligations to the Father of your holy Institute, to your worthy Mother de Chantal, and to so many other excellent subjects of your holy Order.[280] "*Adhereat lingua mea faucibus meis si non meminero tui si non præposuero Hierusalem in principio lætitiæ meæ.*" ("May my tongue stick to my palate if I do not remember you. If I do not exalt Jerusalem beyond all my delights.")[281] And may we praise the choice of VINCENT DE PAUL, who governed you with holiness for so many years, and who has shared in your glory and your achievements. Saint Cyprian said Virgins are an illustrious part of the Lord's flock, and those of the Visitation have been a notable part of the charitable works of VINCENT DE PAUL, this worthy Pastor of souls.[282]

Finally, since a spiritual Father must Persevere in serving the interests of the Church, we are again obliged to say of our Superior General of the Mission, "... *cuius laus est in evangelio per omnes ecclesias.*" ("...[the brother] who is praised in all the churches for his preaching of the gospel.") He fervently embraced the interests of the holy Church. He often reflected, in the presence of God, that the true spirit of the Church is the spirit of peace, and that Christ, the true peaceful Solomon,[283] entered the world in order to found his Church, and to bring to an end all the wars that had for such a long time agitated the Roman Empire. It was for this reason that at his birth the Angels chanted a Canticle of peace, "*Pax hominibus bonæ voluntatis.*" ("...on earth peace to those on whom his favor rests.")[284]

Monsieur VINCENT continually resolved to offer himself to our Lord as a public victim in order to obtain peace. As he knelt in prayer before the Altar he sighed over the evils that wars caused in the world. He thought it always ill-advised to take up arms, since this could not be done without doing violence to virtue. He saw that war very often has the effect of giving victories to sin, while at the same time ruining piety and doing harm to the worship of God. He knew that the practices of Christianity are often destroyed in the heat of battle, the Sacraments are despised, Altars profaned, and Priests very nearly prevented from performing the holy functions of their sacred ministry.[285] "*Filii matris meæ pugnaverunt contra me.*" ("My brothers have been angry with me.")[286]

Who is it that fulfilled the role of the good Samaritan?[287] Who would shed his tears? Who would apply oil and wine to the wounds of the holy Church, which

---

Jeanne François de Chantal (1572-1641).
Foundress of the Order of the Visitation.
Vincentian Studies Institute Collected Illustrations

were even more grievous than those of the poor man languishing on the road to Jericho? He is here, Messieurs. It is VINCENT DE PAUL. Through the successful Missions held throughout the Kingdom, he knew that the ignorance of the people and the sins of Christians were daily growing greater because of the effects of warfare. He came to believe it was high time for the soldiers to be removed from the midst of our Parishes, and time to declare a new war on behalf of the Gospel and the Faith.[288]

He prayed to God for peace by means of an extraordinary novena.[289] Every day for nine years the community of saint-Lazare prayed for Peace. Two or three confreres would receive communion for this special intention. Each day a Priest from the community said Mass for this intention, and a Brother took communion at this Mass that thus could properly be called a Mass for Peace. The Priest and the Brother then spent the rest of the day fasting. There was a table inside the refectory where they sat called the fasting table.

Monsieur VINCENT, as general of his Congregation, took care of its

---

Saint Vincent de Paul. For God and the Poor.
Courtesy Vincentian Studies Collection, Special Collections and Archives, DePaul University, Chicago, Illinois

business, its meetings, and its correspondence. Even when he was burdened by old age, by pains and infirmities, he never dispensed himself from anything.[290] He faithfully followed the same rules as the rest of the community. He took his turn at this novena for peace, the only difference being that he took his turn twice as often as anyone else. Finally, at the end of nine years, a general peace was concluded between the two Crowns. After this, it was proposed to Monsieur VINCENT that this practice should now be ended, since it was a heavy obligation on a Community with many other obligations, and since without doubt it could be replaced by other good works. He replied in this way, *"No, Messieurs and my brothers, let us continue persevering to the end looking forward to the final establishment of peace, and praying that it will never again depart from us."* [291]

What can you say, Messieurs, about a man who was so humble, so full of abandonment, so forgetful of himself, so regular in all his actions? What can you say about a man who was so prudent that you could even say he was Wisdom personified, who decided nothing without consulting the will of God, and who accepted no work without an extraordinary indication from the spirit of God? This question, I will not answer, but I leave you to the liberty of your own thoughts and judgments.

But you must admit, Messieurs, that the praise given by our great Cardinal to Monsieur VINCENT is well-deserved.[292] As Saint Ambrose said, "...*prolixa laudatio est, quæ non quæritur, sed tenetur.*" ("True praise is that which is not sought, but that which is freely given.")[293] In a few words we have witnessed the life of Monsieur VINCENT, and we cannot remain silent. We have the evidence clearly before us so there is no need for us to search for anything further, let alone create proof. What we find here is true reason for giving great praise.

Yes, Messieurs, the general Peace that has been the glory of our Monarchy, the relief of Spain, and the consolation of all Europe, is the work of the Advice, the Prayers, and the Generous Labors of our incomparable Minister, who regardless of the costs to his health wanted to end the suffering and poverty endured by so many of the poor. It was he who forged this Peace by the sacred ties of the most beautiful, and the greatest Marriage that one could desire in this world. By the force of his prudent advice he has joined, not only in an alliance but in friendship, the two greatest Kings of the earth: the Most Christian King, the eldest son of the Church, and the Most Catholic King.[294] He then had this friendship sealed with an oath so holily sworn, and which I, by the Providence of God, was one of the Bishops who served as witness.[295]

Without a doubt this achievement justly merits praise, since these great actions comprise one of the greatest, most beautiful, chapters of History. What must attract the respect of the Crowns, and the veneration of all the Monarchies, is that these glorious designs have been formed on the basis of Christian principles. When one is considering the sacred interests of Religion, merely Political considerations are nothing more than an abomination before God's eyes.[296] A long time before the present Peace was concluded, in speaking to a prelate with whom he was very familiar, this praiseworthy Prince of the Church said that peace must be the work of Heaven because, "*Quam mundus dare non potest pacem.*" ("...that peace which the world cannot give.")[297]

Last June, on the day when our young Queen was crowned in the city of Saint Jean-de-Luz,[298] I said to His Eminence that after such hard work the day must have been an illustrious and glorious one for him.[299] After I said this, he responded to me, "*Monsieur, I have had nothing at all to do with this. It is God who has done it all.*"[300] In a word, he was inspired by Faith, and supported by the vows of VINCENT DE PAUL to be inspired to advise our Great Monarch to conclude a Peace.

May you, great Prince of the Church, after such glorious actions, continue to provide an example of the zeal and ardor with which the most precious interests of the Church must be embraced now more than ever! May you be able to make the Peace fruitful by the force of good works. May you now be able to repair the breaches that Christianity has suffered during the horror of war.[301]

Etching of Vincent's statue in Saint Peter's Basilica, Vatican City.
Courtesy Vincentian Studies Collection, Special Collections and Archives, DePaul University, Chicago, Illinois

And you, VINCENT DE PAUL, who we believe today reigns in Heaven; obtain for this incomparable Minister of State, for the sacred persons of Their Majesties whom you have so dearly loved and whom you have always served with such fidelity;[302] for all of these devout Listeners, who have so much respect for your memory and who have heard with such patience this weak recital of only a partial account of your admirable virtues; obtain, I ask, the help of the graces that are necessary for them to renounce earthly wisdom to follow the obligations of our holy Baptisms, to better regulate their conduct and all the movements of their hearts according to the laws of the Son of God, so that finally they will not falter nor be surprised by the false esteem of men; but that in imitating you, their praise for now and for all eternity may be established by all the Churches through the Gospel.

As for me, while you were here on earth I loved you as much as myself or my own family because you so often relieved my pains and my needs, as well as the greatest public needs of my office and my Diocese. Since you have obligated me by so many charitable services, make me feel today the trust that you now have before God. Finish in me what you began. Obtain for me the share that I desire of the most abundant blessings of Heaven. This is also what I desire for you, Messieurs, from the bottom of my heart, as much as I do for myself.

SOLI DEO HONOR ET GLORIA!
HONOR AND GLORY TO GOD ALONE![303]

THE END

---

[1] In an attempt to convey something of the contemporary feel of the *oraison funèbre* I have kept the capitalization and emphases that appear in the original published text. In addition, the original publication of the *oraison funèbre* contained marginal notes citing quotations from Scripture and the writings of the Fathers of the Church, as well as designating sections of the text. Where these appear in the original text, they will be identified as Marginal Note: followed by the wording of the note as it appeared in the original printed edition.

[2] This is a possible allusion to Machiavelli's work *The Prince*. See, for example, Chapter 17 of that work at: **http://www.gutenberg.org/files/1232/1232-h/1232-h.htm.**

[3] Louis XIV was only five years old at the death of his father Louis XIII in 1643. The country was ruled by a regency under the Queen Mother, Anne of Austria, assisted by Cardinal Mazarin. Even after the declaration of his majority in September 1651, at the age of thirteen, Louis XIV did not fully rule until after the death of Mazarin in March 1661.

[4] In actuality, Anne of Austria acted quickly to have parlement overturn the regency plans set out by Louis XIII in his will.

[5] Louis XIII (1601-1643) was the son of Henry IV and Marie de Medici. He ascended to the throne in 1610 upon his father's assassination in the streets of Paris. His mother served as regent until 1614 when his majority was declared. In 1615 he married Anne of Austria, the daughter of the Philip III of Spain. After years of childlessness the dauphin was born in 1638. He succeeded as Louis XIV in 1643.

[6] Armand Jean du Plessis, Cardinal-Duc de Richelieu et de Fronsac (1585-1642). The powerful Chief Minister of Louis XIII from 1624 until his death in 1642. He defeated the Queen-Mother Marie de Medici and her party in a bitter power struggle on the famous "Day of Dupes" in November 1630.

[7] Referring to the young king, Louis XIV.

[8] One phase of the Thirty Years War (1618-1648) was over the succession to the duchy of Mantua in northern Italy (1628-1631). While serving as a papal diplomat trying to mediate this conflict, Mazarin rode between the two armies who were drawing up for battle at Casale in Monferrato. His shouted cries of "Peace, peace!" stopped the battle from taking place although, in fact, a formal peace still had not been negotiated. A settlement was only reached by the Treaty of Cherasco, signed almost a year later on 19 June 1631.

[9] A reference to Mazarin's policy after the royal victories in the Fronde not to exacerbate national tensions by seeking retribution from his defeated enemies in the Paris parlement and nobility. Personal attacks on Mazarin and the queen during the Fronde had been particularly salacious and vicious, and at one point the court had been forced to flee from Paris. For a taste of the stridency of printed materials as political propaganda see, Jeffrey Merrick, "The Cardinal and the Queen: Sexual and Political Disorders in the Mazarinades," *French Historical Studies* 18:3 (Spring 1994): 667-699. During this period there was even a rumor in Paris that the queen and cardinal had been secretly married by Vincent de Paul. (Mazarin was a lay cardinal, and not in holy orders.) Vincent indignantly denied this rumor saying, "This is as false as the devil." See *Robineau*, 36, 97.

[10] Mazarin followed up the peace with Spain negotiated in the Peace of the Pyrenees on 7 November 1659 with the so-called "northern peace," represented by the treaties of Oliva and Copenhagen and signed, respectively, on 3 May and 27 May 1660. Finally, the Treaty of Paris, negotiated by Mazarin and signed on 28 February 1661, returned control of the Lorraine to its ducal family.

[11] If Anne of Austria had a deep appreciation for Vincent and his work, Cardinal Mazarin had more mixed feelings. In a letter to Vincent de Paul dated 7 September 1646, Mazarin wrote "I shall tell you that I have only praise for the zeal you manifest in all that regards the glory of God and the good of His Church." See Letter 854, "Cardinal Mazarin To Saint Vincent," Fontainebleau, 7 September 1646, *CCD*, 3:49-50. Mazarin undermined the role of the Council of Conscience and knew well that during the Fronde Vincent had counseled the queen to put him aside, at least temporarily, to help restore peace. Vincent's personal loyalty to the Gondi family also put him in Mazarin's bad graces, especially once the arch-conspirator Cardinal de Retz was received by papal command at the Lazarist house in Rome after his escape from captivity in France. See *Robineau*, 69, 98, 105. See also Coste, *Life*, 2:7-13.

[12] A reference to the peace with Spain. On Vincent's prayers for peace see, for example, Conference 125, "Repetition of Prayer," 24 July 1655, *CCD*, 11:189-190. See also *Abelly*, 1:220; and Coste, *Life*, 2:398.

[13] A provision of the Peace of the Pyrenees provided for the marriage of Louis XIV to his first cousin Marie-Thérèse, the daughter of Philip IV of Spain.

[14] For a discussion of the patron/client system undergirding societal relationships in *Ancien Régime* France see, Sharon Kettering, *Patrons, Brokers, and Clients in Seventeenth-Century France* (New York: Oxford University Press, 1986).

[15] This refers to Maupas du Tour's appeal as bishop of Le Puy for royal support in his bitter struggle with the Prince de Polignac to preserve the temporal authority he enjoyed as the Count of Velay. See *Rocher, le Blanc*, and *Arnaud* in Chapter One, notes 75 and 76, *supra*. See also the letter of 11 June 1658 from Maupas du Tour to Cardinal Mazarin, *Papiers de MAZARIN et de COLBERT. – Lettres originales adressées à Mazarin (1643-1660); correspondence de Benjamini Priolo (1656 et 1661-1664; notes diverses de Mazarin, datant de son exil à Brühl, en 1651* (Bibliothèque Nationale de France), 193.

[16] In 1653, the king awarded Maupas du Tour the commendatory abbacy of the Abbaye de l'Ile-Chauvet in the diocese of Montluçon. See *Chalendard*, 181.

[17] In 1664, a few years after Mazarin's death, Maupas du Tour would accept Louis XIV's offer

of another see (that of Évreux) to compensate him for his defeat in the Velay power struggle. See *Chaumiel*, 49. See also Bergin, *Episcopate*, 131.

[18] Maupas du Tour had ceded his seniority rights to his brother Jean-Baptiste, Baron du Tour et lieutenant-colonel of the Régiment de la Cavalerie de la Meilleraye. Jean-Baptiste married Marie de Morillon and had two children, Charles-Armand, killed at the siege of Dunkirk in 1658, and Anne who would marry Jean Saligny, Comte de Coligny, a lieutenant general of the Armies of the King. See *Chalendard*, 176. See also **http://gw3.geneanet. org/pierfit?lang=en;p=jean+baptiste;n=cauchon+de+maupas.** Also, the letter of Maupas du Tour to Cardinal Mazarin dated 20 January 1661, in *Recueil de pieces, et principalement lettres et billets orig., addresses pour la plupart à MAZARIN. (1651, 1659, 1660 et 1661.)* (Bibliothèque Nationale de France), 331-332.

[19] The Church of Saint-Germain l'Auxerrois, the parish church for the Louvre Palace in Paris.

[20] All books published in France needed to be licensed by the government before publication.

[21] Anne of Austria (1601-1666), daughter of Philip III of Spain, wife of Louis XIII and mother of Louis XIV. Regent from 1643 to 1651. She was a great patroness of Vincent de Paul. See Chantal Grell, ed., *Anne d'Autriche: Infante d' Espagne et reine de France* (Versailles: Centre de recherché du château de Versailles, 2009). See also Philippe Alexandre and Béatrix de L'Aulnoit, *Pour mon fils, pour mon roi: la reine Anne, mère de Louis XIV* (Paris: R. Laffont, 2009).

[22] For a discussion of Vincent's humility see *Abelly*, 1:113-118; and 3:180-204. See also Coste, *Life*, 3:358-360. Also, Luigi Mezzadri, C.M., "Humility in St. Vincent's Apostolic Dynamism," *Vincentian Heritage* 1 (1980): 3-30. Also *Robineau*, 29-50.

[23] 2 Cor. 8:18 (NAB).

[24] S. Bernardi, Claræ-Vallensis Abbatis Primi, Epistola CCIX, "Ad Eumdem, prædicat regiam ejus munificentiam in suscipiendis et fovendis Religiosis a se missis," in J.P. Migne, ed., *Patrologiæ Cursus Completus, Series Latina*, 221 vols. (Paris: Garnier Frères, 1844-1890), 182:376A. Hereafter cited as *PL*. The original Latin text reads: "*Et hæc quidem terena sunt, sed cœlestia mercantur.*"

[25] 2 Pt 1:4 (NAB).

[26] 1 Cor 4:5 (NAB). Marginal Note: "*1.Cor.4.*"

[27] Marginal Note: "*Son humilité.*"

[28] Xenophon, "Hiero," *Scripta Minora*, E. Capps, T.E. Page, W.H.D. Rouse, eds., E.C. Marchant, trans. (London: William Heinemann, 1925), 1:14. The Greek text reads, "...ἐπεὶ τοῦ μὲν ἡδίστου ἀκροάματος, ἐπαίνου, οὔποτε σπανίζετε..."

[29] S.P.N. Ignatii, Episcopi Antiocheni, Epistolæ cum genuinæ tum dubiæ et supposititiæ, "Ad Trallianos: IV, Humilitate et mansuetudine mihi opus est" in J.P. Migne, ed., *Patrologiæ Cursus Completus, Series Græca*, 161 vols. (Paris: Bibliothecæ Cleri Universæ, 1857-1891), 5:678B. Hereafter, *PG*. The Greek text reads, "*Οἱ γὰρ λέγοντές μοι μαστιγοῦσίν με.*" *PG*, 5:677B.

[30] See *Abelly*, 1:102; 2:180-204, 210, 223, 273, 360, and 373.

[31] This quotation is traditionally attributed to Saint Augustine, but it does not appear in this form in the Augustinian corpus.

[32] This section of the oration reflects a contemporary controversy over the attempts of many among the rising bourgeoisie class to lay claim to a privileged tax-free noble status through purchases and other stratagems. Indeed, one of the fund-raising strategies of the monarchy was the sale of noble offices and titles. Since it was difficult to criticize the monarchy directly, criticism was directed toward the perceived venality of those seeking to purchase noble status. For more details see, Roland Mousnier, *The Institutions of France under the Absolute Monarchy, 1598-1798* (Chicago: University of Chicago Press, 1979), 2:115, 159. See also Jay M. Smith, "'Our Sovereign's Gaze': Kings, Nobles, and State Formation in Seventeenth-Century France," *French Historical Studies* 18:2 (Fall 1993): 396-415.

[33] Is 5:18 (NAB).

[34] Ovid, *Metamorphoses*, 13:140-141. For a complete Latin text of *Metamorphoses* see: **http://ovid. lib.virginia.edu/.**

[35] Sancti Ambrosii, Mediolanensis Episcopi, *De Noe et Arca Liber Unus*, "Caput IV: Gigantibus qui vixerunt ætate Noe, etc.," *PL*, 14.1:386B. The full Latin text reads, "*Probati enim viri genus virtutis prosapia est; sicut hominum genus homines, ita animarum genus virtutes sunt.*" Marginal Note: "*lib. de Noë & Arca. c. 4.*"

[36] Sainte-Geneviève (c. 422-500). Born at Nanterre, near Paris, as a child she was acquainted with Saint Germain l'Auxerrois. Becoming a nun at the age of fifteen, she lived a life of penance and charity. When Paris was occupied by the Franks, and later when it was threatened by Attila and the Huns, she encouraged the people to defend the city. She is the patroness of the city of Paris. For Vincent's discussion of Sainte Geneviève as a role model for the Daughters of Charity see, Conference 13, "Imitating The Virtues Of Village Girls," 25 January 1643, *CCD*, 9:66-77. See also Document 194, "Perseverance In Good Works," *Ibid.*, 13b:420. Also, Document 197, "Report On The Work Of The Foundlings," *Ibid.*, 13b:426.

[37] Saint Isidore the Farmer (1070-1130). A native of Madrid and a peasant, he spent his life working in the fields of an estate just outside the city. Canonized in 1622 with the great Spanish saints of the Catholic Reformation: Ignatius Loyola, Francis Xavier, and Teresa of Avila; he is the patron of the city of Madrid and of farmers.

[38] Saint John of God (1495-1550), was the Spanish founder of the Brothers Hospitallers. In 1601, at the invitation of Marie de Medici, the first Italian brothers came to Paris to establish a hospital near Saint-Germain-des-Prés. This hospital was followed by several other foundations in France. The beatification of John of God in 1638 was celebrated in Paris with great solemnity. When the brothers in Paris asked for a relic of their founder, Anne of Austria promised her help. When peace between France and Spain was finally restored in 1659, it was sealed with the marriage of the Spanish Infanta to her first cousin Louis XIV. Anne took advantage of the occasion to ask her brother, Philip IV, the King of Spain, for a relic of Blessed John of God as "a precious guarantee of the peace which has just been signed." The Spanish King obliged his sister and a relic was dispatched. On 14 November 1659, the relic was officially transferred, with fitting public celebration, to the hospital chapel of the Brothers in Paris. See Norbert McMahon, O.S.J.D., *The Story of the Hospitallers of Saint John of God* (Philadelphia: Newman Press, 1959), 62-63. See also Jean de Loyac, *Le Triomphe de la Charité en la vie du Bienheureux Jean de Dieu. Institution et Progez de son Ordre Religieux. Avec les Ceremonies de sa Béatification, & de la Translation solmnelle de sa Relique, enuoyee a La Reyne Mère par le Roy d'Espagne* (Paris: Antoine Chrestien, 1659). Also, Alison Forrestal, "Vincent de Paul: The Making of a Catholic *Dévot*," in *Politics and Religion in Early Bourbon France*, ed. by Alison Forrestal and Eric Nelson (Basingstoke, U.K.: Palgrave Macmillan, 2009), 191.

[39] See Ex 3:5; 34:29-35 (NAB).

[40] In his biography Louis Abelly uses this same comparison between Moses and Vincent de Paul. See *Abelly*, 3:61:

> The primary and most excellent fruits of his mental prayer are unknown to us, for he drew a veil of silence over them all. We would have to be resigned to this lack of knowledge were it not that he sometimes appeared like another Moses, if not totally radiant. He at least had the same fervor and love as Moses when he came from his encounter with the divine majesty.

See also *Robineau*, 77:

> I often saw him praying before the Blessed Sacrament. His devotion was solid, humble and respectful. He knelt in such a way that suggested that he would have willingly put himself in the depths of the earth if he could have found a way to descend there. His attitude was so respectful that one could not doubt that Jesus Christ, God and Man, was present in the Eucharist, since his countenance showed it, and I affirm before God that I was often touched and edified by it.

See also 2 Cor 3:7-18 (NAB).

[41] See *Abelly*, 3:14:

He alone was unaware of his own goodness, for his humility seemed to be a veil
hiding this from his own eyes... Here was a person who truly possessed a treasure in
his virtues, and this treasure was even more secure in that it was hidden from him.

[42] Ex 34:29 (NAB). Hebrew Scripture describes the skin of Moses' face as רוֹע, "shiny." See Jay P.
Green, Sr., ed. and trans., *The Interlinear Hebrew-Aramaic Old Testament*, 3 vols. (Peabody, MA:
Hendrickson Publishers, 1993), 1:237. Marginal Note: "*Exod.34.*"

[43] Nicholas of Lyra (Nicolas de Lyre ; also Nicholaus Lyranus or Liranus) (c. 1270-October 1349), a
Franciscan friar and one of the outstanding pre-Reformation scripture scholars. He was the author of
the first printed commentary on the Bible, the 50 volume *Postillæ Perpetuæ in Universam S. Scripturam.*
See Nicholas de Lyre, "Pentateuch et Joshua," *Postillæ Perpetuæ in Universam S. Scripturam*, 50 vols.,
4:83.d, at: **http://bdh.bne.es/bnesearch/** (accessed 22 June 2012). Note: The digitized copy of
the Liranus manuscript shows he uses the words "*Radii miri splendoris apredentes*" (appearing as
wonderful shining rays) rather than "*radiis coruscans*" as quoted by Bishop du Tour.

[44] Abelly describes Vincent's peasant origins this way: "His parents were poor in worldly goods and
lived from their work... They owned a house and some small pieces of property they had inherited,
which they developed with the help of their six children." *Abelly*, 1:35. Maupas du Tour describes
Vincent as being the son of a *laboureur*. Owning their own land would have put Vincent's family a step
ahead of many of their neighbors, who would have been reduced to tenant farming. Although the life
of a peasant *laboureur* was a difficult one, at least, as Victor Tapié points out, "the peasant who ran
a small farm and owned some livestock, carts, and agricultural implements was relatively fortunate.
Prosperity or the hope of it was not beyond the reach of the *laboureur* who possessed his own
team and plough." See Victor L. Tapié, *France in the age of Louis XIII and Richelieu*, D. McN. Lockie,
trans. (Cambridge: Cambridge University Press, 1984), 28. See also John Lough, *An Introduction to
Seventeenth-Century France* (New York: Longmans, Green and Co, 1954), 4-5, 21-22.

Abelly cites numerous examples of Vincent's comments concerning his humble origins.
A typical quotation:

Once, Monsieur Vincent accompanied a priest to the door at Saint Lazare, where
a poor woman called out, "My lord, an alms, please." Monsieur Vincent replied,
"My poor woman, you do not know me well. I am a poor pig farmer, the son of a
poor villager." Another time he was met by a woman at the door as he bade farewell
to some noble visitors. She begged an alms and said she had been formerly the
servant of Madame his mother. Monsieur Vincent replied, in the presence of his
guests, "My good woman, you mistake me for someone else. My mother never had
a servant, but was a servant herself, being the wife, and I the son, of a peasant."

See *Abelly*, 3:186.

See also *Superna Hierusalem*, 45. "Vincent de Paul was born in a humble village called Pouy, in the
diocese of Acqs, of very poor but virtuous parents; from his childhood he was employed in the care of
sheep." For more of Vincent's references to his humble origins see: Letter 418, "To Louis Abelly, Vicar
General Of Bayonne," 14 January 1640, *CCD*, 2:5; Letter 524, "To Monsieur Perriquet, In Bayonne,"
Paris, Easter Sunday, 1641, *Ibid.*, 2:193; Letter 891, "To Michel Alix, In Aumone," Paris, 12 November
[1646], *Ibid.*, 3:121; Letter 1372, "To François De Saint-Remy, in Châlons," Paris, 21 June 1651, *Ibid.*,
4:219; Letter 1887, "To Antoine Chabre," n.d., *Ibid.*, 5:398; Letter 3153, "To François Fouquet,
Archbishop of Narbonne," [1660], *Ibid.*, 8:383; Appendix Letter 1, "Brother Ducournau To Canon
De Saint-Martin," *Ibid.*, 8:600; Conference 57, "How To Act When Away From The Motherhouse," 1
January 1654, *Ibid.*, 9:525; and Conference 85, "Service Of The Sick And Care Of One's Own Health
(Common Rules, Arts. 12-16)," 11 November 1657, *Ibid.*, 10:275.

For Vincent's references to himself as a "swineherd" see: Letter 418, *Ibid.*; Letter 524, *Ibid.*; Letter
1372, *Ibid.*; Letter 3153, *Ibid.*; Appendix Letter 1, *Ibid*. See also Conference 2, "The Vocation Of A
Daughter Of Charity," 5 July 1640, *Ibid.*, 9:13; and Conference 182, "Detachment From The Goods
Of This World," 8 June 1658, *Ibid.*, 12:19. Also, *Robineau*, 86, 99.

[45] See *Abelly*, 1:240.

> After all of this, gentlemen, what remains for me? I must imitate Moses, who gave
> the Law of God to the people and then promised all sorts of blessings for those
> who observed it.... Just so, gentlemen and my brothers, we must hope for all sorts
> of graces and blessings for those who observe these rules which he has given you....

[46] For information on the apostolate of the country missions for Vincent and the Congregation of
the Mission see, *Abelly*, 2:13-84. See also Coste, *Life*, 3:20-64. Also James E. Smith, C.M., "The
Vincentian Mission, 1625-1660," *Vincentian Heritage* 4:2 (1983): 40-60.

[47] For almost the entire span of Vincent's life, France was involved in a variety of destructive, draining
wars (civil, religious, and foreign). Most of the battles were fought on French soil. For his relief work
in the war-torn provinces see, *Abelly*, 1:185-189, 204-205; 2:316-345. In Coste, *Life*, see 2:366-491.
See also *Robineau*, 92, 95-96, 107, 110, 124-126.

[48] See *Abelly*, 2:28, speaking of the fruits of the country missions:

> Who can count the number of persons in blameworthy ignorance of the truths
> of salvation who were instructed in the truths they were obliged to know? How
> many others had lived their entire lives in a state of sin, from which they were freed
> through a good general confession? How many sacrileges committed by receiving
> the sacraments unworthily have been redeemed? How many enmities and hatreds
> and causes of usury have ended? How many bad marriages and other scandals
> have been rectified? How many pious practices and charitable enterprises have
> been encouraged? How many good works and virtues have been begun in places
> where they had scarcely been known? How many souls were sanctified and saved,
> who now glorify God in heaven? Without the help they received in the missions
> they might otherwise have died in their sin, and might now be blaspheming and
> cursing God with the demons in hell. God alone knows the extent and number of
> all the good his grace effected through his faithful servants, and which will one day
> be revealed to his own greater glory.

[49] For a description of the famous "Tuesday Conferences of Ecclesiastics," see *Abelly*, 1:144-147;
2:210-218, 225-228; and Coste, *Life*, 2:118-149. See also Forrestal, *Venues*.

[50] For a description of Vincent's role in the establishment of Tridentine-style seminaries in France see,
Abelly, 1:164-166; 2:249-258. See also Coste, *Life*, 2:170-191; and Letter 570, "To Bernard Codoing,
Superior, In Annecy," Saint-Lazare, 9 February 1642, *CCD*, 2:254-258.

[51] For a description of the "Ordination Exercises" established by Vincent see, *Abelly*, 1:138-140;
2:183-209. See also Coste, *Life*, 2:150-169. Also *Robineau*, 31, 114.

[52] For a description of the establishment of "Spiritual Retreats for Ecclesiastics" see, *Abelly*, 2:229,
241-248; and Coste, *Life*, 2:192-196.

[53] For a description of the general state of the French clergy and the French Church in the first years
of the seventeenth century see, *Abelly*, 1:31-34. See also Coste, *Life*, 1:243-267. Also, Joseph Bergin,
Church, Society and Religious Change in France, 1580-1730 (New Haven: Yale University Press, 2009).

[54] For a description of the variety of persons making retreats at Saint-Lazare see, *Abelly*, 2:232-233:

> With a wholly impartial charity, he opened the doors of his heart and his home to
> all those who wished to share in this good work. He would receive them kindly and
> paternally, with no distinction of persons. In this he was imitating the father of the
> family in the Gospel who accepted to his banquet all those who came: the poor,
> blind, lame, and the crippled, and sending out to the streets and squares of the
> cities, and even to the fields and most isolated areas, to invite and even compel all
> to attend.
>
> We must admit that in our day this great servant of God did something
> similar to the astonishment and edification of all. In the refectory at Saint Lazare
> many other persons could be seen among the missionaries. They were of all ages

and conditions, from city and country, poor and rich, young and old, students and doctors, priests and holders of benefices, ecclesiastics and prelates, gentlemen, counts, marquis, attorneys, lawyers and councillors, presidents, receivers of petitions and other officers of justice, merchants, artisans, soldiers, pages, and lackeys. All were received, lodged, and fed in this great hospice of charity to make their retreat, to find the remedy for their spiritual infirmities, or the help necessary to set them securely on the path of salvation.

Also, for information on the ancient priory of Saint-Lazare in Paris as the mother house of the Congregation of the Mission see, *Abelly*, 1:119-126; and Coste, *Life*, 1:160-176.

[55] See, for example, *Abelly*, 2:215-216, speaking of the success of the Tuesday Conferences:

...(God) brought to light the works it accomplished. Besides, his Providence allowed twenty-two prelates to be members, both archbishops and bishops for the benefit of their dioceses. We should add that the membership included vicars general, canonical judges of the dioceses, archdeacons, pastors, canons, seminary directors, superiors, and visitators and confessors of religious, all of whom as members of the Company spread everywhere the good odor of Jesus Christ through the example of their virtues.

[56] See Pierre Blet, S.J., "Saint Vincent and the Episcopate of France," *Vincentian Heritage* 10:2 (1989): 102-135.

[57] Abelly comments in his dedication, "...Monsieur Vincent during his life had taken every care to hide the marvelous graces he had received from God..." *Abelly*, 1:22.

[58] Janet Lembke, *Virgil's Georgics: A new verse translation* (New Haven, Yale University Press, 2005), 62-63.

[59] Levi Hart, V.R. Osborn, eds. and trans., *The Works of P. Virgilius Maro* (New York: David McKay Co., 1952), 111.

[60] The regent, Queen Anne of Austria. Abelly, in his dedication (1:22-23), comments:

The favorable reception Your Majesty always gave to Monsieur Vincent during his lifetime and the kindness with which you have honored his memory since his death gives me hope that you would accept this work... The innocence and sanctity of him whose life we write, Madame, assure us that he is in heaven with his God. We believe that he is imploring unceasingly God's goodness to shower his blessings upon our great prince, Your Majesty, and all the royal household. What particularly obliges him to this intercession is his recognition of the favors he received from your hands, and continues to receive in the person of the priests of his Congregation.

See also *Abelly*, 3:109, where he writes:

He was particularly noted for his open profession of sincere affection and his faithful service to the king, going so far as to risk the welfare of his community and even his own life to support the interests of His Majesty. A member of the nobility testified to this one day in the presence of the queen mother during the regency:

I know of few people attached with such a sincere fidelity, constancy, and disinterestedness to the service of the king as Monsieur Vincent. Your Majesty knows well how during the troubles in Paris he risked the pillage of his house at Saint Lazare, and risked even his own life, when he gave refuge to your chancellor on his way to Pontoise to find the king. You are aware of how he endured slander and the hatred of some by the firm and faithful way he handled the pious wishes of Your Majesty, as you had directed him, particularly in the administration of ecclesiastical goods.

The queen acknowledged this tribute and said that it was true.

[61] Abelly quotes Vincent in this regard, "How happy is the Missionary who has no limit in this world

on where he can go to preach the Gospel. Why then do we hesitate and set limits, since God has given us the whole world to satisfy our zeal?" See *Abelly*, 2:84.

[62] For Vincent's work with the galley-slaves/convicts see, *Ibid.*, 1:84-86, 148-151. See also Coste, *Life*, 1:115-118, and 2:315-336. For example:

> The convicts among whom I lived reacted the same way. When I spoke to them impersonally I spoiled everything. On the other hand, I began to praise them for their resignation, sympathize with their sufferings, and pointed out how fortunate they were to be making their purgatory in this life. I also kissed their chains, shared their sorrows, and spoke against their bad treatment. After that, they began to listen to me, give glory to God, and enter upon the road of salvation.

Abelly, 3:168.

[63] For Vincent's involvement with contemporary health care, see *Abelly*, 1:152-159. In addition, see Coste, *Life*, 1:232-242, 278-335, and 2:492-493.

[64] For further details on the nature and scope of poverty in seventeenth-century France see, Paul Christophe, *Les pauvres et la pauvreté, II éme partie, du XVIe siècle à nos jours*, Bibliothèque d'histoire du Christianisme, no. 7 (Paris: Desclée, 1987), 41-42, n. 12. The General Hospitals were institutions mandated by the Crown. They were an attempt to enforce a solution to the endemic problems and expenses associated with the vast number of beggars and wretched poor throughout the country, particularly in cities such as Paris. The government's policy favored forced committals of such poor persons to these institutions, and it outlawed begging which had been their only previous means of support and survival. Once committed to these institutions the poor were cared for and fed, but they were expected to live and work under close supervision. Vincent generally opposed the forced internment of the poor in these institutions. The Hôpital Général was established in Paris in 1653. See *Abelly*, 1:224-229; 2:218-220. See also Coste, *Life*, 2:280-304. Also, *Robineau*, 129-130. And, Edward R. Udovic, C.M., "Caritas Christi Urget Nos": The Urgent Challenges of Charity in Seventeenth Century France," *Vincentian Heritage* 12:2 (1991): 85-104. See also *Hôpital Général de Paris, L'Hospital General de Paris* (A Paris: chez François Muguet, 1676); and *Abelly*, 3:127:

> Hundreds of these poor would always come for help, and sometimes the number reached five or six hundred. He did have to stop distributing soup two or three years before his death, because after the establishment of the general hospital for the poor of Paris he was forbidden to do so. When the poor would complain to him, "Father, did not God direct that alms should be given to the poor," he would reply, "Yes, it is true, my friends, but God has also commanded that we should obey the magistrates." Despite these prohibitions, on the occasion of a particularly severe winter which brought many poor families to the brink of disaster, he would distribute soup and bread each day.

[65] For more information on the Confraternities of Charity see *Abelly*, 1:72-73, 127-132; 2:285-290. See also Coste, *Life*, 1:81-88, 95-102, 205-223, 232-242, and 268-277. Also, Jean-Pierre Renouard, C.M., "Châtillon: Les Charités," *Vincentiana* 31:4-6 (1987): 629-649.

[66] The Daughters (or Sisters) of Charity were founded in Paris by Vincent de Paul and Louise de Marillac on 29 November 1633. It is remarkable that there is only this passing reference to Vincent's involvement with the Daughters. Maupas du Tour also fails to mention Vincent's relationship with Louise de Marillac. He mentions most of the other important women in Vincent's life: Madame de Gondi, Jeanne-Françoise de Chantal, and the Marquise de Maignelay. Thus, the omission of *any* mention of Louise is very curious. For extensive discussions of Vincent's relationship with Louise and the Daughters of Charity see, *Abelly*, 1:127-137. See also Coste, *Life*, 1:177-232, 278-291, 297-298, 336-468; 2:255-279, 284-288, 319-323; 3:65-69, 281, 346, 365, 374.

[67] For more information on the Ladies of Charity see *Abelly*, 1:152-159; 2:303-315. See also Coste, *Life*, 1:232-242, 278-335. Also Collette Padberg and Daniel Hannefin, D.C., "Saint Vincent's First Foundation: The Ladies of Charity," *Vincentian Heritage* 3 (1982): 105-130.

[68] For Vincent's activities in France see: *Abelly*, 1:84-89, 148-151, 185-189, 204-205, 208-212, 224-229, 242-244; 2:30-55; 3:111-130; in Italy: *Ibid.*, 2:55-83; in Poland: *Ibid.*, 2:163-172. See also Coste, *Life*, for Vincent's work in France: 1:95-114, 511-608; 2:366-491; 3:20-47; in Italy: *Ibid.*, 2:1-30; 3:47-64; in Poland: *Ibid.*, 2:41-50.

[69] In this section, Maupas du Tour is speaking of the pious legend of Vincent's attempt to voluntarily substitute himself for a galley convict in the galleys of Marseille. For Abelly's account of this incident see, *Abelly*, 3:112-113. This account was uncritically accepted by subsequent biographers until definitively refuted by Pierre Coste, C.M. For details see Coste, *Life*, 1:124-131. See also Charles Lalore, *L'opinion de M. de Boulogne, évêque de Troyes: touchant la captivité volontaire de Saint Vincent de Paul sur les galères de Marseille* (Troyes: Dufour-Bouquot, 1875), 11.

[70] This is Maupas du Tour's first mention of Vincent's legendary "Tunisian Captivity." For more details see note 120, *infra*.

[71] For Vincent's involvement in Tunis and Algiers in Barbary see, *Abelly*, 2:84-126. See also Coste, *Life*, 2:337-365.

[72] For Vincent's involvement in the mission to Madagascar see, *Abelly*, 2:134-163. See also Coste, *Life*, 2:51-117. See also *Robineau*, 116. Also, Gerard van Winsen, C.M., "Saint Vincent and Foreign Missions," Jacqueline Kilar, D.C., trans., *Vincentian Heritage* 3 (1982): 3-42. And, Nivoelisoa Galibert, *À l'angle de la grande maison: les lazaristes de Madagascar: correspondance avec Vincent de Paul, 1648-1661* (Paris: PUPS, 2007).

[73] See *Abelly*, 2:84-85:

> [Vincent] showed a special veneration for Saint Francis Xavier, who had carried the Gospel all the way to the Indies with such courage and blessings. He appreciated the religious of his order, and all others who worked on the foreign missions. When any of them returned and had occasion to visit Saint-Lazare, he would assemble the entire household to hear of their work, with the hope of inspiring his own Missionaries to imitate their zeal. He would have their printed accounts read in the refectory, and did what he could to help their missions in foreign lands...

[74] See *Ibid.*, 3:21:

> If we say that the faith of Monsieur Vincent was great, we must also add that his hope was no less perfect. In imitation of the Father of all believers he often hoped against hope itself, by which we mean that he hoped in God, when according to all human expectations he ought to have despaired. Just as his faith was simple and pure, founded on the truth of God alone, so his hope was not based on considerations and reasonings of human nature but solely on the mercy and goodness of God.

[75] See *Ibid.*, 1:193:

> The Court was a sort of theatre where the virtues of this faithful servant of God appeared in full light. His humility won out over the vain plaudits of the courtiers. His patience was proof against their losses, troubles, and the vices of envy and malice. His constancy supported the interests of God and the Church, and there he showed himself free from all fear and human respect. On this stage he bore witness to his inviolable fidelity and constant affection for Their Majesties, his respect and submission to the prelates of the Church, the esteem and charity he preserved in his heart for all orders of the Church, and for all ecclesiastical and religious communities.

[76] Lk 6:48, and 1 Cor 10:4 (NAB). Marginal Notes: *"Luc 6. 48."* and *"1. Cor. 10."*

[77] See S.P.N. Joannis Chrysostomi, Archiepiscopi Constantinopolitani, Commentarius in *Sanctum Matthæum Evangelistam*, "Homilia XXIV al. XXV," *PG*, 57:324. Bishop du Tour may have paraphrased the Latin translation from the original Greek. The Latin reads: *"...testificari possunt et apostoli, qui omnibus orbis fluctibus in se irrumpentibus, populis item, tyrannis, domesticis et alienis, dæmonibus, diabolo, omnique admota machina, his solutis omnibus, petra firmiores sieterunt."* The Greek text reads:

"μαρτυρήσειαν δ᾽ ἂν καὶ οἱ ἀπόστολοι, τῶν κυμάτων τῆς οἰκουμένης προσρηγνυμένων αὐτοῖς, καὶ δήμων καὶ τυράννων, καὶ οἰκείων καὶ ἀλλοτρίων, καὶ διαμόνων καὶ διαβόλου, καὶ πάσης μηχανῆς κινηθείσης, πέτρας στεορότερον στάντες, καὶ ταῦτα πάντα διαλύσαντες."

[78] See *Abelly*, 3:293:

> To achieve this, his main and nearly universal method was to conform himself entirely to the example of Jesus Christ. He knew very well that he could not walk nor lead others on a surer path than that traveled by the Word and Wisdom of God. He had engraved his words and actions upon his own mind, modeling himself in all he did and said upon the prototype of all virtue and sanctity. His holy Gospel was etched in his heart. He carried it in his hand like a great light, so he could say with the prophet: "Your word, O Lord, is like a lamp unto my feet, to enlighten my path which leads to you...." He had learned from the Gospel that it profits us nothing if we gain the whole world but lose our own soul.

See also Warren Dicharry, C.M., "Saint Vincent and Sacred Scripture," *Vincentian Heritage* 10:2 (1989): 136-148. Also, André Dodin, C.M., "M. Vincent de Paul et la Bible," under the direction of Jean-Robert Armogathe, *Le Grand Siècle et la Bible. La Collection Bible de Tous les Temps*, 8 vols. (Paris: Éditions Beauchesne, 1989), 6:627-642.

[79] For a discussion of Vincent's respect for bishops see *Abelly*, 1:192-194; 2:373-384; 3:130-139. See also Coste, *Life*, 2:226-236. Also, *Robineau*, 53, 68. For example, *Abelly*, 3:109:

> [Charity] inspired him with sentiments of love and reverence for all the bishops of the Church... He showed them every kindness and submission that he possibly could. He supported their plans, promoted their wishes, and maintained their authority. He wanted and did all that he could that the clergy and people might regard their sacred persons highly, and deferred humbly and promptly to their directions.

[80] A unique reference found in no other source.

[81] While this incident is not exactly recounted by Abelly, the following narrative is very reminiscent of it. See *Abelly*, 3:280-281:

> A highly placed magistrate of a sovereign court once met him on the street. He attempted to persuade him to do something in his personal interest which Monsieur Vincent did not believe to be right in the sight of God. He therefore excused himself as politely as he could, and could not be swayed, no matter how much he was urged. The judge became angry and spoke most unbecomingly to him, but Monsieur Vincent remained serene. He showed no emotion except to say, "Monsieur, I am convinced you try to do your duty as worthily as you possibly can. I must try to do the same in my position."

There is another, similar account in *Ibid.*, 3:247:

> While Monsieur Vincent was on the Council for Ecclesiastical Affairs, one of the leading magistrates of the kingdom, a man of great authority, asked, through a priest of the Congregation of the Mission, that an abbey be given to one of his sons who did not have the requisite qualities. This gentleman promised that, if the abbey were given, he would see to it that the house of Saint-Lazare would regain some lands and revenues that had been lost. He was well informed of how to bring this about, with no involvement of the priests of the Congregation in this issue. Monsieur Vincent was urged to seize the opportunity while he was in office, since this was a common practice with several other orders, which the priest named. When Monsieur Vincent received this proposal, he responded: "Not for all the goods of the world would I do anything against God or my conscience...."

[82] For the virtue of meekness in Vincent see *Ibid.*, 3:163-179. See also Coste, *Life*, 3:308-309. See, for example, *Abelly*, 3:165:

There is a big difference between true and false meekness. Meekness which is so only in appearance is soft, cowardly, and indulgent. True meekness is not foreign to firmness in doing good. It is always a part of it, for true virtues are all interrelated. On this subject Monsieur Vincent said:

> No one is more constant or more firm in the good than the person who is meek and well-mannered. On the contrary, those given to anger and the passion of the irascible appetite are usually most inconstant, for they act by fits and starts. They are like raging torrents which have power only when bursting down the stream, but quiet down as soon as the flow of water stops. Rivers represent milder persons, without noise or show, flowing on without pause.

[83] For Vincent's prudence see *Abelly*, 3:222-232. See also Coste, *Life*, 3:326, 369-373. See, for example, *Abelly*, 3:225:

> This then, is the way Monsieur Vincent looked upon the virtue of prudence, and the way he practiced it. When there was a question of deliberating upon some matter or of giving an opinion or decision, he would raise his mind to God to implore his light and grace before opening his mouth to speak, and even before considering the question at hand. He would be seen to raise his eyes to heaven, and then keep them closed as though he were consulting God himself on what to reply. If it were a matter of some moment he would take time to pray, and to invoke the help of the Holy Spirit. Since he relied solely on this divine wisdom and not on his own personal insight, he received grace and light from heaven. This enabled him to discern things which the unaided human spirit could never have known. He used to say, "where human prudence begins to diminish, there the light of divine wisdom dawns."

Also, *Ibid.*, 3:21:

> Should one of his confreres, through a lack of hope and trust or because of human prudence sometimes point out the difficulty or even impossibility of achieving the purpose of the project, he would usually say, "Let us leave that to our Lord, for it is his work. It pleased him to begin it, so we must be sure that he will bring it to fruition in the way he deems best."

[84] Ps 125:1-2 (NAB). [Vulgate, Ps 124:1-2.] Note: The numbering of Psalms in the Hebrew Scripture and that found in the Septuagint vary. In some instances, the same can be said for the name assigned to a particular book of the Bible. In such cases, the book's name or the psalm numbering found in the NAB will be presented first and a notation showing where the quoted text is found in the Vulgate will follow in brackets. The NAB numbering of Psalms follows that found in the Hebrew Scriptures (150 psalms), and that found in the Vulgate is based on the system employed by the Septuagint (151 psalms).

[85] Ps 125:5 (NAB). [Vulgate, Ps 124:5.]

[86] Gn 46:34 (NAB). Marginal Note: "*c. 46. 34,*"

[87] R.D.D. Ruperti, Abbatis Monasterii S. Heriberti Tuitiensis, *De Trinitate et operibus ejus: Libri XLII*, "Commentariorum in Genesim, Liber Nonus, Caput XVIII: De patrum humilitate qua se coram Pharaone pastores ovium et peregrinos professi sunt," *PL*, 167:543B. The full Latin text reads: "*Sanctum peregrinorum stadium, Deo peregrinantium Scripturæ locus exprimit, scilicet quod hominibus non solum non placere, sed etiam displicere quæsierunt, et quod vere non hic manentem habentes civitatem, futuram et manentem inquirere studuerunt. (Hebr. XIII).*" Marginal Note: "*lib. 9. in Genesim. c. 18.*"

[88] Maupas du Tour provides an extreme, inaccurate interpretation of Vincent's humility on this point. Given their status as peasant '*laboureurs*,' Vincent's family would certainly have had to work quite diligently to sustain their always tenuous prosperity, thus Vincent's herd-tending was clearly out of necessity, rather than a sense of humility. Contrast this to the view expressed in: *Abelly*, 1:35; and Coste, *Life*, 1:8-9.

[89] A reference to Genesis 41:39-44:

> So Pharaoh said to Joseph: "Since God has made all this known to you, no one can be as wise and discerning as you are. You shall be in charge of my palace, and all my people shall dart at your command. Only in respect to the throne shall I outrank you. Herewith," Pharaoh told Joseph, "I place you in charge of the whole land of Egypt." With that, Pharaoh took off his signet ring and put it on Joseph's finger. He had him dressed in robes of fine linen and put a gold chain about his neck. He then had him ride in the chariot of his vizier, and they shouted "Abrek!" before him. Thus was Joseph installed over the whole land of Egypt. "I, Pharaoh, proclaim," he told Joseph, "that without your approval no one shall move hand or foot in all the land of Egypt."

The term, Abrek or Abrech (Hebrew: דרבא "to bend the knee"), appears only once in the Hebrew Scriptures. It is the cry of runners announcing the approach of Joseph in his chariot. Whether its origin is Egyptian or Semitic remains controversial. Some Jewish scholars read it as a hiphil form of the verb meaning "to *cause* to bend the knee." It may also derive from *abarakku*, an Assyrian word denoting a titled person. Rabbinic literature suggests both the meanings "father of wisdom who is young in years," from בא (*father*) and דר (*tender*), and "Alabarchos," the title given the leader of the Jews in Egypt. Palestinian and Babylonian scholars concluded it means "father of the king." Both Origen and Jerome preferred the *tender father* interpretation, though Origen believed a literal translation should be γονατιζειν ("bending of the knee"). See "Abrech" at: **http://www.jewishencyclopedia.com/articles/634-abrech** (accessed 13 July 2012).

[90] For Vincent's efforts to relieve Catholic refugees from England, Scotland, and Ireland see, *Abelly*, 1:188; 2:340-341; 3:144. See also Coste, *Life*, 2:497-500. Maupas du Tour does not mention the missionary efforts undertaken by the Congregation under Vincent's direction to Scotland, the Hebrides, and Ireland. For details on these see, *Abelly*, 2:126-134, 173-182. See also Coste, *Life*, 2:30-40.

[91] See *Abelly*, 3:182: "When he went to Paris, he never said that he was called 'de Paul,' lest this usage give the impression he belonged to some notable family. He called himself simply Monsieur Vincent, his baptismal name, as one would say Monsieur Pierre or Monsieur Jacques." See also *Robineau*, 30.

[92] All of Vincent's extant signatures are in the form: "Depaul."

[93] Caesar, Xenophon, Cato, Sylla, and Brutus were all classical authors who wrote under pseudonyms.

[94] Emperor Justinian (482-565 A.D.), one of the greatest of the Eastern Roman emperors.

[95] See Rudolfus Scheoll, "De Prætoribus Plebis," *Corpus juris civilis, Novellæ, XIII De Prætoribus Populi* (Berolini: Weidmannos, 1912), 3:100. The Greek term νυκτέπαρκος was changed to πραίτωρες δήμων, or *prætores populorum* in Latin.

[96] Ps 19:7 (NAB). [Vulgate, Ps 18:7.] Marginal Note: "*Psal. 18.*"

[97] Reminiscent of the content of Plato's Dialogues "Cratylus." See also S.A. Farmer, "Conclusions on the doctrine of Plato," *Syncretism in the West: Pico's 900 Theses (1486): The evolution of traditional religious and philosophical systems* (Tempe, Arizona: Medieval & Renaissance Texts & Studies, 1998), 167:454-455. "The opinion of the *Cratylus* on names should be understood this way: not that names are like that, but that they must be if they are to be correct."

[98] Richardus Venusinus, "De Paulino et Polla," in *Commedie latine del XII e XIII secolo* (Genova: Istituto di Filologia Classica e Medievale: 1986), 148.

[99] Thomas Collett Sandars, "Liber II, Tit. VII, *De Donationibus*," *The Institutes of Justinian: With English Introduction, Translation, and Notes* (London, 1883), 151. The full text reads: "*[s]ed nos plenissimo fini tradere sanctiones cupientes et consequentia nomina rebus esse studentes...*" (Wishing, therefore, to perfect the law on the subject and to make names appropriate to things...) Marginal Note: "*§ 3. instit. de donatio.*"

[100] This is found in Saint Thomas Aquinas' *Summa Theologica*, Part 3, Question 37, Article 2: "*nomina debent proprietatibus rerum respondere*" (a name should answer to the nature of a thing). See:

http://www.corpusthomisticum.org/sth4027.html for the Latin translation; and http://www.
newadvent.org/summa/4037.htm for the English translation (each accessed 17 July 2012).

[101] See Gn 17:5 (NAB). Vulgate: "*quia patrem multarum gentium constitui te.*"

[102] Names for men in Hebrew often are theophanic, reflecting a prayer for example. The name Joseph,
יוֹסֵף, is a form of the prayer יֹסֵף meaning "may He (יהוה) add." Thus, an interpretation of the name in
Genesis may be stated as: "May the Lord add another son (to Jacob's sons); and this one (is) to me,"
Gn 30:24. Bishop du Tour's comment on Joseph's name may also reflect a passage from the writings
of Saint Rupert: "*Post filios et parentum ponenda sunt nomina: Lia interpretatur laborans, Rachel ovis,
cujus filios Joseph, ab eo quod sibi mater alium addi optaverat, vocatur anomentum.*" See R.D.D. Ruperti,
Abbatis Monasterii S. Heriberti Tuitiensis, *De Trinitate et operibus ejus: Libri XLII*, "Commentariorum
in Genesim, Liber Septimus, Caput XXXII, De nominibus filiorum Jacob," *PL*, 167:478D. Rupert's use
of *anomentum* here may reflect the ανόμος-type "adding" toward Joseph's fortune and virtue, found
in the unexpected details of his life — his birth to an otherwise barren mother, his rise from slavery
in Egypt to a position of power, and his compassion toward his brothers who initially sold him into
slavery.

[103] Mt 1:21 (NAB). Marginal Note: "*Matt. c. 1.*"

[104] For Vincent's imitation of Saint Paul see, *Abelly*, 3:94. "He loved and venerated Saint Paul, the
master and teacher of the gentiles, who had worked harder than anyone else. Since he bore his name,
he also strove to imitate his virtues."

[105] For a discussion of Vincent's humility with regards to the level of his education see, *Abelly*, 3:84,
182. See also Coste, *Life*, 1:14-25, 42. Also, *Robineau*, 30.

[106] The identity of this Jesuit is unclear; but see *Abelly*, 1:251, n. 3, which suggests it was Jean-Baptiste
Saint-Jure, S.J.

[107] Prayer from the preparation of the gifts in the Roman Catholic Eucharist, drawn from Daniel 3:39-
40 (NAB): "But with contrite heart and humble spirit let us be received." See *Abelly*, 3:75-76:

> He pronounced the words of the mass so distinctly, devoutly, and affectionately
> that his heart was obviously in what he did... He recited the Confiteor, the words *in
> spiritu humilitatis et in animo contrito* ...and others with sentiments of humility and
> contrition.

> See Letter 129, "To A Priest Of The Mission," [15 January 1633], *CCD*, 1:184. See also *Abelly*, 2:19:
> Every day at mass we say the words, *in spiritu humilitas* etc. ...A holy person told me
> once that he had learned from the lips of the blessed bishop of Geneva (Francis de
> Sales) that this spirit of humility, which we ask for in each of our masses, consists
> chiefly in a continuous attitude of humbling ourselves, on all occasions, both
> interiorly and exteriorly. "But, gentlemen, who can give us this spirit of humility?
> Our Lord alone, if we ask it of him, and if we remain faithful to his grace, and
> exercise this virtue in ourselves. Please do this, then, and let us remind each other
> of this when we say these words at the altar. I hope in your charity you will do this."

[108] Sg 8:6 (NAB).

[109] Here Bishop du Tour presents his own rather poetic rendition of the Doctor of Avila's comments
on the "blessings left in the soul" following an experience of "rapture of the spirit." See Kieran Kavanaugh, Otilio Rodriguez, trans., "The Interior Castle, VI.5.10," *The Collected Works of Teresa of Avila*,
2nd ed. rev., 3 vols. (Washington, D.C.: Institute of Carmelite Studies, 1987), 2:390:

> Three things, especially, are left in [the soul] to a very sublime degree: knowledge
> of the grandeur of God, because the more we see in this grandeur the greater is
> our understanding; self-knowledge and humility upon seeing that something so low
> in comparison with the Creator of so many grandeurs dared to offend Him (and
> neither does the soul dare to look up at Him); the third, little esteem of earthly
> things save for those that can be used for the service of so great a God.

[110] See *Abelly*, 3:196. Here is the only text in *Abelly* that reflects the spirit of this quote from the
oration:

If then we look into ourselves well, we will see that in all we think, say, or do, either in itself or in its circumstances, we are filled with confusion and contempt. If we do not give way to flattering ourselves, we will see that we are not only more evil than other men, but in some way worse than the devils in hell. If these unhappy spirits had been given the graces and opportunities given to us to make us better, they would have used them a thousand times better than we have.

[111] This quotation attributed by Maupas du Tour to Vincent de Paul is not found in any other source. Nevertheless, its meaning resonates in *Abelly*, as noted immediately above; in Conference 91, "Relations With Outsiders, Murmuring, Detraction (Common Rules, Arts. 30-32)," 30 December 1657, *CCD*, 10:352-352; in Conference 38, "Humility," n.d., *Ibid.*, 11:47-48; and in *Coste*, 3:359.

[112] Is 42:8 (NAB). Marginal Note: "*Isay. 42.8.*"

[113] "Seraphim... the highest order of the angels... [who] surround the throne of Glory and unceasingly intone the trisagion ('holy, holy, holy'). They are the angels of love, of light, and of fire." Gustav Davidson, *A Dictionary of Angels* (New York: Collier-Macmillan, 1967), 267.

[114] Marginal Note: "*II PARTIE Sa Charité.*" For a discussion of Vincent's charity see, *Abelly*, 3:106-162. See also Coste, *Life*, 3:320-325. Also, André Dodin, C.M., "Théologie de la Charité selon Saint Vincent de Paul," *Vincentiana* 20:5-6 (1976): 263-284.

[115] Rom 8:35-39 (NAB). Marginal Note: "*ad Rom. 8.*"

[116] Barnabæ Kearnæi, Archiepiscopo Casselensis in Hybernie, "De Circumcisione Domini," *Heliotropium* (Lyon: A. Pillehotte, 1622), 401.

[117] 2 Cor 11:29 (NAB). See also Conference 100, "To Four Sisters Being Sent To Calais," 4 August 1658, *CCD*, 10:444-445.

[118] See Sancti Eusebii Hieronymi, Stridonensis Presbyteri, *Epistola LXXVII: 'Ad Oceanum: de morte Fabiolæ,' PL*, 22:694. Here Maupas du Tour seems to be paraphrasing Saint Jerome, who said of Fabiola: "*Non mihi si linguæ centum sint, oraque centum, ferrea vox, omnia morborum percurrere nomina possim (ex Æneid. 6) quæ Fabiola in tanta miserorum refrigeria commutavit, ut multi pauperum sani languentibus inviderent.*" (Not with a hundred tongues or throat of bronze could I exhaust the forms of disease [cf. Aeneid, 6] which Fabiola so wonderfully alleviated in the suffering poor that many of the healthy fell to envying the sick.) See also J. Stevenson, ed., *Creeds, Councils, and Controversies* (London: SPCK, 1973), 184. Hereafter, *Creeds*.

[119] For further reading on hospitals, see note 64, *supra*.

[120] Maupas du Tour's version of Vincent's Tunisian Captivity is a very condensed description of the much longer account found in Vincent's correspondence and in *Abelly*. Earlier in the *oraison*, Maupas du Tour mentions the captivity, and the various masters that Vincent had during his time as a slave. The second part of Maupas du Tour's version, found here, generally agrees with both Vincent's and Abelly's accounts, excepting that Maupas du Tour implies Vincent and his master escaped with others of the household to France. Maupas du Tour's account of Vincent's acceptance of, and interpretation of, the providential nature of his captivity is not repeated in *Abelly*, 1:42-47. For Vincent's own account see Letter 1, *CCD*, 1:1-11. See also Coste, *Life*, 1:26-34. Also, *Robineau*, 159-160. For the contemporary controversy over the authenticity of the Tunisian Captivity and its implications for Vincentian studies see, Stafford Poole, C.M., "Saint Vincent de Paul, 1595-1617: The Missing Years 1605-1607," *Vincentiana* 28:4-6 (1984): 424-435. See also José-María Román, C.M., Chapter V, "Novel o Historia? Un Grave Problema Critico," *San Vicente de Paul, I Biografia* (Madrid: Biblioteca de Autores Cristianos, 1982), 42-51.

[121] See previous note 62, *supra*, on galley convicts. See also *Superna Hierusalem*, 52.

[122] Maupas du Tour's account at this point seems to be mistaken. Vincent's concern as chaplain-general of the galleys, for the conditions of the galley convicts at Marseille, was also accompanied by his work with the galley convicts imprisoned at Paris. The Daughters and Ladies of Charity worked with the Paris-based convicts, but not the Marseille convicts. For more details see *Abelly*, 1:148-151. See also Coste, *Life*, 2:315-336.

[123] Jb 17:14 (NAB).

[124] For the effectiveness of Vincent's preaching and his methodology see, *Abelly*, 1:100-01; 2:213;

3:38, 96. See also *Robineau*, 49, 57, 79.

[125] For example, see *Abelly*, 3:118:

> Monsieur Vincent's love of the poor produced two effects in his heart. One was his great sense of compassion for their indigence and misery, for he had a most tender affection for them. For example, when the litany of Jesus was said, and he came to the words *Jesu pater pauperum*, ["Jesus, father of the poor"], he pronounced them in a way that showed the sentiments of his heart. When people would speak to him about some particular misery or necessity of the poor, he would sigh, close his eyes, and hunch his shoulders like a person weighed down with sufferings. His face would reveal the deep suffering by which he shared in the misfortunes of the poor.

[126] This quote appears in Book 3, Chapter 1, line 158, of P. Ovidii Nasonsis, *Epistolarum Ex Ponto*. See Roy J. Deferrari, M. Inviolata Barry, R.P. McGuire, eds., *A Concordance of Ovid* (Washington: The Catholic University of America Press, 1939), 977. See also Peter Green, trans., "Black Sea Letters: Book III," *Ovid: The Poems of Exile* (New York: Penguin Books, 1994), 157.

[127] For Vincent's love of the poor see, *Abelly*, and Coste, *Life*, throughout. See also *Robineau*, 41-43, 124-126, 133, and 135.

[128] See notes 3-5, 21, 38, 60, *supra*, and 163, *infra*, on Anne of Austria. See also *Abelly*, 3:122:

> Although, through a sentiment of Christian humility, Her Majesty requested Monsieur Vincent not to reveal the source of his benefactions, he did not feel obliged to accede to her request. He said to her, "Madame, Your Majesty will please pardon me if I no longer keep secret such a marvelous example of charity. It is good, Madame, that all of Paris and even all of France should know of it. I feel obliged to speak of it wherever I go."

Also, *Robineau*, 111-112, 127.

[129] This was the famous Brother Mathieu Régnard. For more information see *Abelly*, 2:330-331. See also Coste, *Life*, 2:139-140, 371, 375, 384-393.

[130] See, for example, *Abelly*, 2:316-331. See also Coste, *Life*, 2:387-392.

[131] Brother Jean Parre. See Coste, *Life*, 2:431-435. See also *Abelly*, 2:341-344.

[132] See *Abelly*, 3:182:

> He had a habitual attitude of concealing his gifts and activities and all he had undertaken for the good of others. He did this to such an extent that even members of his own Congregation knew only a fraction of the good works he had been involved with, and how many spiritual and corporal works of charity he had performed for all sorts of persons. Many of his confreres were astonished to read in this present work things they had never before known.

[133] For more information see *Ibid.*, 1:208-209; 3:121. See also Coste, *Life*, 2:476.

[134] For more information see *Abelly*, 2:298, 343. See also Coste, *Life*, 2:427.

[135] 2 Cor 6:11 (NAB). Marginal Note: "2. Cor. 6."

[136] 2 Cor 12:14-15 (NAB).

[137] This particular incident took place during the great floods of 1652, in the village of Gennevilliers not far from Paris. For more information see *Abelly*, 3:120, and Coste, *Life*, 2:497.

[138] For more information see *Abelly*, 1:185; 2:317-319. See also Coste, *Life*, 2:369, 379, 384, and 389.

[139] 1 Tm 5:18. Marginal Note: "1. Timot. 5.18." See also 1 Cor 9:13, and Lk 10:7 (NAB).

[140] 2 Cor 12:15 (NAB). Marginal Note: "2. Cor. 12.15."

[141] For Vincent's works in Paris see, *Abelly*, throughout. See also Coste, *Life*, throughout.

[142] At the time, the diocese of Le Puy, in the Haute-Loire.

[143] Ps 112:9. [Vulgate, Ps 111:9.] See also 2 Cor 9:9 (NAB). Marginal Note: "Psal. 111."

[144] 1 Kgs 17:14 (1). [Vulgate, 3 Kgs 17:14.] Marginal Note: "3. Reg. 17."

[145] For Vincent's love and care for the poor see, *Abelly*, 1:185-189, 204-205, 208-212, 224-229;

3:116-123.

[146] 1 Kgs 17:14 (NAB). [Vulgate, 3 Kgs 17:14.] Marginal Note: "*Ibid.*" See note 144, *supra.*

[147] See *Abelly*, 1:37:

> He could say with the ancient patriarch that "mercy had been born with him." He had a particular inclination toward this virtue even from his earliest years. It was noticed that he gave what he could to the poor. Whenever his father sent him to the mill to collect the flour, and he met a poor person along the way and had nothing else to give, he would open the sack and give the poor man handfuls of flour. We are told that his father, a good man, would not object to this.

See also *Superna Hierusalem*, 45:

> Like the innocent Abel, he drew upon himself and his offering the benedictions of the Lord; for he led an innocent life, and of the fruit of his savings and abstinences, he offered to the Lord an acceptable sacrifice of piety; he distributed meal to the poor when he brought it from the mill....

Also, *Robineau*, 123.

[148] See S. Petri Chrysologi, Ravennatis Archiepiscopi, *Sermo III*, "De eisdem, ubi de occursu patris ad filium," *PL*, 52:190C-194A.

[149] Lk 15:22 (NAB).

[150] Jb 31:18 (NAB).

[151] See 2 Cor 8:9 (NAB): "For you know the gracious act of our Lord Jesus Christ, that for your sake he became poor although he was rich, so that by his poverty you might become rich." See also *Abelly*, 1:33: "Having made himself poor for the love of Jesus Christ and having left all to follow him, he had no more worldly goods to give."

[152] This quote is not found exactly as Maupas du Tour cites it, neither in *Abelly* or Coste, *Life*. The closest equivalent seems to be found in *Abelly*, 3:117, "We are priests of the poor. God has chosen us for them. They are our chief duty, all the rest is just secondary." See also *Ibid.*, 2:15; and Conference 164, "Love For The Poor," January 1657, *CCD*, 11:349.

[153] Lk 6:36 (NAB).

[154] This quotation is not found either in *Abelly* or Coste, *Life*; but see *Abelly*, 3:22-23.

[155] This quotation is not found either in *Abelly* or Coste, *Life*; but, again, see *Abelly*, 3:22-23.

[156] Marginal Note: "*Sa confiance en la Providence.*" See *Abelly* and Coste, *Life*, throughout. See also *Robineau*, 29, 32, 94, 118, 125, 131-132.

[157] See *Abelly*, 1:187-188:

> Once the collection of alms was two hundred *livres* short of what was necessary. He called the procurator of the house and taking him aside, asked him quietly what money was available. The response was that just enough remained for the expenses of the community for the next day. "And how much is that," asked Monsieur Vincent. "Fifty *ecus*," was the reply. "Is there nothing else in the house?" asked Monsieur Vincent. "No, Monsieur, we have only fifty *ecus*." "Please bring them to me, Monsieur." With that he gave this to make up, almost, what was lacking to maintain the refugee nobility for a month. He preferred to deprive himself and to be forced to borrow to feed his own household rather than allow these people to suffer want.
>
> One of the nobles present heard the reply of the procurator and so admired the generosity of Monsieur Vincent that he reported it to the others present. The following morning one of them brought a small bag with one thousand *francs* to Saint Lazare as an alms for the community.

There is another similar incident reported elsewhere in *Ibid.*, 3:23:

> It became known that one day the treasurer of the house of Saint Lazare came to tell him that there was not a *sou* left in the house to cover either the ordinary or the

extraordinary expenses arising during the ordination retreats about to begin. Full of confidence in God, he raised his voice: "What good news! God be blessed! Fine, now we will see if we have confidence in God."

[158] Ps 55:23 (NAB). [Vulgate, Ps 54:23.] Marginal Note: "*Ps. 54.23.*"

[159] For more about the retreats for men held at Saint-Lazare see, *Abelly*, 1:141-142; 2:229-248. See also Coste, *Life*, 3:1-19.

[160] For more about the ordination retreats see, *Abelly*, 1:138-140; 2:183-209. See also Coste, *Life*, 1:243, 256-258; 2:150-169. Also, *Robineau*, 31, 114.

[161] At Vincent's insistence all the charitable and apostolic works of Saint-Lazare and the missions were provided free of charge, and supported either by income from endowments, grants, or alms. See *Abelly*, 3:23:

> One of his priest friends spoke to him one day about the large expense these ordination retreats must entail. He thought that the house of Saint Lazare was surely put to great inconvenience and could no longer support such a responsibility. He suggested that perhaps each ordinand should be charged something to stay at Saint Lazare. Monsieur Vincent replied, with a smile, "When we have spent all we have for our Lord and nothing remains, then we will leave the key under the door and go."

For more information see José María Román, C.M., Stafford Poole, C.M., trans., "The Foundations of Saint Vincent de Paul," *Vincentian Heritage* 9:2 (1988): 134-160.

[162] Carolus Halm, ed., "De liberalitatel," *Valerii Maximi: Factorum et dictorum memorabilium, libri novem cum julii paridis et januarii nepotiani epitomis* (Lipsiae: in Ædibus B.G. Teveneri, 1865), 4.8.2:213-214. The actual Latin text reads: "*Subnectam huic Acragantinum Gillian, quem propemodum ipsius liberalitatis praecordia constat habuisse, erat opibus excellens, sed multo etiam animo quam divitiis locupletior semperque in eroganda potius quam in corripienda pecunia occupatus, adeo ut domus eius quasi quaedam munificentiae officina crederetur.*" See also D.R. Shackleton Bailey, ed. and trans., "Of Liberality" in *Valerian Maximus: Memorable doings and sayings* (Cambridge, Mass.: Harvard University Press, 2000), 4.8.2:435, which translates the Latin as: "To him I shall append Gillias of Agrigentum, who is agreed to have almost had the heart of liberality herself. His wealth was preeminent, but he was much richer even in mind than in fortune and always busied in disbursing money rather than in grasping it, so that his house was considered a kind of workshop of munificence." Marginal Note: "*Valer. max. lib. c. 8.*"

[163] Marginal Note: "*Charité desinteressée.*" For further details on the disinterestedness of Vincent's charity see, *Abelly*, 1:109, 180-182, 194; 2:398-399; 3:234. See also Coste, *Life*, 1:166; 3:12, 22, 110, 291, 323, 326. Also, *Robineau*, 32. See, in particular, *Abelly*, 1:194:

> What should be remarked mainly is that the queen was inundated with requests from all sorts of petitioners, eagerly seeking various charges, benefices, or other positions in the Church. What shows Monsieur Vincent's disinterest perfectly is that he never asked, or had others ask for him, anything for himself or for his Congregation, although he was as close to the source of these benefits as one could be. Had he asked, the queen would almost certainly have been happy to confer anything upon him in recognition of his merit.

In his notes, Brother Louis Robineau uniquely relates the story of the 1647 rumor that Anne of Austria intended to have Vincent made a cardinal. According to Robineau, when Vincent heard this rumor he immediately sought an audience with the queen and successfully dissuaded her from going through with her intention. See *Robineau*, 150-151.

[164] 1 Cor 13:5. Marginal Note: "*1. Cor. 13. v. 5.*" See also Eccl 3:9-15; Ps 19: 8-12 [Vulgate, Ps 18:8-12], and Sir 31:1-11 (NAB). [Vulgate, Eccles 31:1-11.]

[165] Exact quotation is not found in *Abelly* or Coste, *Life*; but see *Abelly*, 1:122; 3:23-31, 242-243, 249-253. See also *Robineau*, 32, 36, 65.

[166] Sir 31:8-9 (NAB). [Vulgate, Ecclus 31:8-9.]

[167] In the weakness of his old age, when it became increasingly difficult for him to walk and impossible for him to ride a horse, the Duchesse d'Aiguillon provided him with a carriage and horses. It took the express commands of the queen and the archbishop of Paris to persuade Monsieur Vincent to make use of this means of transportation. He always referred to this carriage as his 'ignominy.' For more details see, *Abelly*, 1:202-203. In particular, *Ibid.*, 3:129:

> One day while returning in a carriage from the country to Paris, Monsieur Vincent saw a poor person along the road. He was all covered with sores and had an otherwise revolting appearance. He had the poor man step into the carriage, and took him to his destination in Paris. He often did similar things, particularly during the winter when he would meet older or handicapped persons. He would have them get in the carriage with him, which through humility he called "my infamy," out of his sense that he was unworthy of this convenience. His attitude was that whatever he had, whether possessions or advantages, ought to be shared with the poor, so great was his love, tenderness, and compassion for them.

See also *Robineau*, 42, 128-129.

[168] Ps 20:8 (NAB). [Vulgate, Ps 19:8.] Marginal Note: "*Psal. 19. v. 8.*" See *Abelly*, 3:110: Another religious of this same order (the Visitation) ...left us this testimony about Monsieur Vincent. "We can truthfully say that this holy man strove to imitate the life of Jesus Christ, who did good to everyone during his sojourn upon earth. Who has not felt the charity of Monsieur Vincent in fulfilling the needs of their lives, whether of body or soul? Can anyone be found who had recourse to him and went away without receiving some help? Is there anyone who turned away from him when he spoke or consoled them? Who had a greater claim on the goods of his community than the person in need?"

[169] Eccl 1:7 (NAB). Marginal Note: "*Eccl. 1, v. 9.*" See also *Abelly*, 1:164.

[170] See Cornelius à Lapide, *The Great Commentary*, trans. by Thomas W. Mossman and W.F. Cobb, 8 vols. (Edinburgh: John Grant, 1908), 8:172. Lapide's commentary on the epistles of Paul was completed in 1614, and would have been available to Maupas du Tour as a current and highly-respected source for Scriptural study. Mossman's English translation of Lapide's statement reads: "Anselm and Theophylact say beautifully: 'Everywhere Paul teaches, but he also suffers greatly. He endures his own sufferings, and at the same time bears the sufferings of others. He bears the infirmities of individuals, and at the same time is anxious about the salvation of all.'" See also Cornelius à Lapide, S.J., "Commentaria in Epist. II ad Corinthios. Cap. XI," *Commentaria in omnes divi Pauli epistolas* (Venetiis: Belleoniana, 1761), 314 B-C. Also Etienne-Michel Faillon, *Vie de M. Olier: fondateur du séminaire de S.-Sulpice*, 2nd ed., 2 vols. (Paris: Poussielgue-Rusand, 1853), 2:10-11.

[171] Lk 24:32 (NAB). Marginal Note: "*Luc 24. 33*"

[172] For a biographical sketch of Charles de Condren see Letter 627, "Saint Louise To Saint Vincent," [1642 or 1643], *CCD*, 2:346, n. 3.

[173] For details on the foundation and operations of these seminaries, see, *Abelly*, 1:164-166; 2:249-258. See also Coste, *Life*, 1:511-529; 2:170-191.

[174] Marginal Note: "*Pardon des iniures.*" On Vincent's pardon of injuries see, *Abelly*, 3:156-162. See also Coste, *Life*, 3:320-322. Also, *Robineau*: 31-32, 35, 87, 112, for Saint Vincent's spiritual basis for forgiving injuries; and 36, 55, 89-91, 93, 96-97, 113, 134-141, for particular acts of forgiveness of injury.

[175] For a biographical sketch of Charlotte-Marguerite de Gondi, the Marquise de Maignelay see, Letter 471, *CCD*, 2:109, n. 1. See also Marc de Bauduen, *La vie admirable de tres-haute, tres-puissante, tres-illustre, et tres vertueuse dame Charlote Marguerite de Gondy, marquise de Magnelais: où les ames fideles trouveront dequoy admirer & des vertus solides à imiter* (A Paris: Chez la veusve Nicolas Buon..., 1666).

[176] Details of this incident are found nowhere else.

[177] For details of this incident see, *Abelly*, 3:157.

[178] See, for example, *Ibid.*, 3:264: "The infirmarian of the house at Saint-Lazare had said that Monsieur Vincent suffered frequent sicknesses.... Even though his legs were inflamed he continued to take his trips on foot, until he had to travel on horseback because of his afflictions."

[179] See *Ibid.*, 1:188:

> Monsieur Vincent always was the first to give. He opened his heart as well as his purse. If anything was lacking he contributed what he had, depriving himself of what was necessary to achieve his goal. On one occasion, to reach a certain sum, three hundred *livres* were needed. He gave it at once, but it was known that he had just been given this money to buy a horse better than the one he had, which was old and feeble and had fallen under him several times. He preferred to run the risk of injury rather than to leave those in need unassisted.

[180] This incident is not specifically related in *Abelly*, but there is an event that seems to be in the same vein at *Ibid.*, 3:157:

> Another incident illustrates both his humility and his charity. Returning once from the city to Saint Lazare, he met in the faubourg Saint Denis a man who was aware of Monsieur Vincent's close association with the queen and her chief ministers. He publicly blamed him for the troubled times, and for the heavy taxes borne by the people. The holy priest himself customarily blamed his own sins as the cause of public difficulties. On this occasion he got off his horse, fell to his knees, and admitted that he was a miserable sinner. He begged pardon of God and of his accuser, the source of the troubles being spoken of. The person in question was so taken aback at the sight of this humble priest abasing himself and so aware of his own boldness, that he came to Saint Lazare the next day to ask pardon of Monsieur Vincent. He received him as an old friend. He was persuaded to stay six or seven days in the house, and to take the occasion to make a spiritual retreat and a good general confession. The story illustrates how charity completed what humility began.

See also *Robineau*, 113.

[181] Marginal Note: "*Gratitude.*" For Vincent's gratitude see, *Abelly*, 3:233-241. See also Coste, *Life*, 3:315-317.

[182] Mt 25:40 (NAB). Marginal Note: "*Matt. 25.40.*"

[183] See *Abelly*, 3:239. See also Letter 1769, "To A Priest Of The Mission," 5 September 1654, *CCD*, 5:180-181; and *Robineau*, 118-119, 141.

[184] See *Abelly*, 3:239-240. See also at Note 514, Letter 1769, *Ibid.*, 5:181. Also, *Robineau*, 131-132.

[185] Marginal Note: "*Charité heroïque.*"

[186] Jn 21:15 (NAB). Marginal Note: "*Joan. 21.15*"

[187] Jn 21:15, 17 (NAB).

[188] Gregorii Theologi, vulgo Nazianseni, Archepiscopi Constantinopolitai, *Orationes*, "Oratio I: In sanctum Pascha et in tarditatem," *PG*, 35:401A. The Latin text reads: "...atque a vero et primo pastore...," *PG*, 35:402A. Marginal Note: "*lib. 1. Ep, 135.*" It must be noted that Bishop du Tour correctly referred to St. Gregory's "Oration 41" when delivering the funeral oration. However, when J.P. Migne published his *Patrologia Græca* in the late nineteenth century, a "reordering" of these works was carried out. *PG*, 36:1259-1260, contains an index of Gregory's orations comparing the old numbering system with the revised one. What had been Oration 41 in 1660 became Oration 1 in the series published by Migne in 1885. What is now identified as Oration 41, "In Pentecosten," does not contain the words quoted here by Maupas du Tour.

[189] Sancti Isidori, Hispaensis Episcopi, *Etymologiarum: Liber VII*, "Caput II: De Filio Dei," *PL*, 82.3-4:266.36. Marginal Note: "*lib. 1. pædag. C. 6.*" Note: More commonly referred to today as Saint Isidore of Seville, this learned bishop is considered one of the Latin Fathers of the Church. The *PL* citation given here reads: "*Pastor, quia custos. Magister, quia ostensor.*"

[190] Clementis Alexandrini, Episcopus. *Pedagogus, Liber tertius*, "Caput XII: Brevis optimæ vitæ similiter periractatio, et quot loca: Hymnus Christo Servatoris a sancto Clemente compositus," *PG*, 8.3:681B. The Latin translation reads: "*Pastor agnorum regalium*," *PG*, 8.3:682B.

[191] 1 Pt 2:25 (NAB). Marginal Note: "*1. Pet. 2. ult.*"

[192] *Ibid.*, 5:4 (NAB).

[193] Heb 13:20 (NAB).

[194] Jn 10:14 (NAB).

[195] S.P.N. Joannis Scholastici, vulgo Climaci, Abbatis Montis Sina, *Liber ad Pastorem*, "Caput V: Pastoris industria in quo spectanda," *PG*, 88:1178B. The Greek text reads: "*Ποιμένα ἀληθινὸν ἀποδείξει ἀγάπη · δι᾽ ἀγάπην γὰρ ὁ ποιμὴν ἐσταυρώθη*," *PG*, 88:1177B. Marginal Note: "*Tract. de officio pastoris in Ps. 37.*"

[196] S.P.N. Basili, Casareæ Cappadociæ Archepiscopi, *Homilia XXIII*, "In Sanctum Martyrem Mamantem," *PG*, 31:598A. The Greek text reads: "*Ἀρχεῖ σοι εἰδέναι, ὅτι ποιμὴν καλός • ὅτι ἔθηκε τὴν ψυχὴν αὐτοῦ ὑπὲρ τῶν προβάτων. Οὗτος ὅρος τῆς τοῦ Θεοῦ ἐπιγνώσεως*," *PG*, 31:597A.

[197] For a full text of this prayer "*Concede mihi, misericors Deus*," with English translation, see: **http://www.preces-latinae.org/thesaurus/Varia/Concede.html** (accessed 23 January 2012).

[198] 2 Cor 11:28 (NAB). Marginal Note: "*Cor. 11. v. 28.*"

[199] Sancti Aurelii Augustini, Hipponensis Episcopi, *De Doctrina Christiana*, "Liber Quartus, Caput VII," *PL*, 34:94.

[200] Maupas du Tour may be summarizing the words of the great Latin Father here. See Sancti Ambrosi, Mediolanensis Episcopi, *In Epistolam B. Pauli ad Corinthios Secundam*, "Caput XI," *PL*, 17.2:346C-D, where it is said of St. Paul: "*Sollicitudo hæc, quam dicit quotidianam, de traditionis usu descendit, ut omnibus diebus commissum sibi populum instruat... Dies enim ad opera datus est, nox ad requiem: sed quia instabat necessitas, ut omnibus succurret, etiam noctu docebat. Se enim affligere non dubitabat, ne Dei gratia esset in otio.*" (Tradition holds that he taught those committed to his care daily... [and] though the day is for working and the night for resting, their needs were so great that he taught even at night, for he knew that God's grace was not to be found in idleness.)

[201] See 2 Tm 4:10-12 (NAB).

[202] See notes: 68, 71-72, 129-131, 133-134, *supra*. See also *Robineau*, 87, 92, 110, 116-117, 123-124, 136. Also, *Superna Hierusalem*, 56-57.

[203] See note 73, *supra*. See also *Robineau*, 116.

[204] Tertulliani, Presbyteri Carthaginiensis, *Libri Apologetici*, "Apologeticus Adversus Gentes Pro Christianis, Caput 50: At vero, dum cruciatibus sese objiciunt, etc.," *PL*, 1.1:603A. The Latin text reads: "*Plures efficimur, quoties metimar a vobis: semen est sanguis Christianorum.*" Marginal Note: "*Tertull.*" See also *Abelly*, 2:134, 159. See also Letter 1057, "To Denis Gautier, Superior, In Richelieu," [July 1648], *CCD*, 3:351.

[205] Toussaint Bourdaise, who died in Madagascar on 25 June 1657. See *Abelly*, 2:156-157:

> You see then, Monsieur, the rich and beautiful opportunities for extending the kingdom of Jesus Christ in this large island. At least six hundred of the inhabitants have already received the light of the Gospel and the number of those who await baptism is much greater. If we can judge from the favorable dispositions and the lack of resistance of these first converts how the others of the island may react, we can have great hopes for the remainder of the people of the island. We are speaking of the 400,000 inhabitants, plus the unnumbered multitude of those future generations who will owe their faith to this generation of converts. However, though I am a poor, small useless servant, if something should happen to me, alas, what would become of this poor Church? What would become of these people who live in ignorance, without the sacraments, and lacking all direction? God, who makes me aware of this pressing necessity, inspires me in spirit to throw myself at your feet to say on behalf of so many souls, with all humility and all possible respect, *Mitte*

quos missurus es ["Send those whom you are going to send"]. Send us missionaries, for those who have died on our shores were not destined to serve in Madagascar. They were called to pass this way on their journey to heaven. No place on earth that needs your Congregation more than here.
See also Coste, *Life*, 2:100-101.

[206] Gn 14:21 (NAB). Marginal Note: "*Genes. 14, v. 21.*"

[207] For Vincent's zeal see *Abelly*, 3:97-105. See also Coste, *Life*, 3:304. Abelly comments in 3:180:
> It is true that after his death it was said of him, as indeed it was said during his life, that his true character was not well known. He was admittedly a humble man. Yet the common opinion never regarded his humility as the main disposition which attracted the graces with which he was inundated, and which were the foundation and root of all the great works he did. Those who judged him most favorably felt that his zeal was the main source of his works, and his prudence happily guided them to a successful conclusion. While these two virtues were indeed highly developed in him and contributed much to his success, we must recognize that his profound humility drew down the plenitude of lights and graces which caused his works to prosper. To speak of this in a better way, we could say that his zeal led him to humble himself at every turn, and his prudence consisted in simply following the maxims and examples of the Son of God and the inspirations of the Holy Spirit.

[208] For Vincent's principle of yielding to other communities see, for example, *Abelly*, 2:18, 29. See also *Robineau*, 112.

[209] See *Abelly*, 2:85.

[210] See *Ibid.*, 3:98:
> Even as old and decrepit as I am, I should also adopt this attitude, even being ready to go to the Indies to gain souls for God knowing that I would probably die on the way. Do not think God asks us for the strength of a healthy body. No, he asks only for our good will, and a true and sincere readiness to seize every opportunity to serve him, even at the risk of our lives. We should cultivate in our hearts a desire to sacrifice ourselves for him, even to suffer martyrdom.

See also *Ibid.*, 2:137-138:
> What more can I say Monsieur, except that I pray that our Lord will give you some share in his charity, and his patience. There is nothing I desire more upon this earth, if it were permitted, than I might be your companion on this mission....

[211] See Sancti Gregorii Magni, Romani Pontificis, *XL Homiliarum in Evangelia, Liber Primus*, "Homilia III, Habita ad populum in basilica Sanctæ Felicitatis martyris, in die natalis ejus: Lectio S. Evangelii sec. Matth. XII, 46-50," *PL*, 76:1086A-1089A.

[212] Roman Catholic Church, "Festa Novembris 11, S. Martini Episcopi, Confessoris," *Antiphonale sacrosanctæ Romanæ ecclesiæ pro diurnis horis SS. D. N. Pii X, Pontificis Maximi jussu restitutum et editum* (Rome: Typis Polyglottis Vaticanis, 1912), 766-767.

[213] Marginal Note: "*Sa patience.*" For Vincent's patience see *Abelly*, 3:280ff. See also Coste, *Life*, 3:332-333.

[214] On Vincent's mortification see, *Abelly*, 3:254-267. See also Coste, *Life*, 3:360-364.

[215] Both Maupas du Tour and Abelly portray Vincent as being eighty-four or eighty-five-years-old at his death, which would place his birth-date at 1575 or 1576. Abelly specifically states, "On the Tuesday after Easter, in the year 1576, Vincent de Paul came into this world...." The Congregation of the Mission recognized this date, as testified to by the memorial plaque affixed to Vincent's tomb at Saint-Lazare which read, "*ætatis vero suæ circiter octogesimo quarto.*" All of Vincent's early biographers deduced Vincent's age at any given point in his life to this birth-date. Vincent himself, while never specifically stating his year of birth, made several explicit statements concerning his age that challenge the 1576 date. Modern scholarship indicates this dating was a deliberate falsification on

the part of the community, and that his biographers perhaps meant to hide the fact that Vincent had been ordained at the age of nineteen (a violation of the Tridentine decrees). For a discussion of this issue see, Douglas Slawson, "The Phantom Five Years," *Vincentian Heritage* 2 (1981): 81-93.

[216] For more on the physical illnesses of Saint Vincent see, for example, *Abelly*, 1:250ff.

[217] *Ibid.*, 1:254.

[218] Ps 39:4 (NAB). [Vulgate, Ps 38:4.] Marginal Note: "*Ps. 38.4.*"

[219] For Vincent and prayer see, *Abelly*, 3:59-71. See also Coste, *Life*, 3:335. Also, *Robineau*, 54.

[220] See *Abelly*, 3:191, for example.

[221] Mt 11:8 (NAB). Marginal Note: "*Matt. 11. 8.*"

[222] S.P.N. Gregorii, Episcopi Nysseni, *De Instituto Christiano*, "De Proposito Secundum Deum," *PG*, 46:297D. The Latin translation reads: "*Etenim decet in præfectura constitutos, majorem quidem quam alii laborem suspicere...,*" *PG*, 46:298D-299A. Marginal Note: "*Tract. de scopo Christiani.*"

[223] Sancti Leonis Magni, Romani Pontificis, *Epistola XV: Ad Turribium Asturicensem Episcopum*, "Caput XVI: De Dictinii scriptis," *PL*, 54:690A. Marginal Note: "*Ep. 93. c. 6.*"

[224] See *Abelly*, 3:313. "In a word, he considered nothing beneath his dignity or unworthy of his attention." See also *Robineau*, 41-42.

[225] Marginal Note: "*Penitence pour autruy.*"

[226] This is an allusion to the occasion of Saint Vincent supposedly taking on the temptation of the theologian described by Coste as "a famous doctor of theology, remarkable for his learning and piety, a skillful controversialist and a redoubtable antagonist of Protestants." This episode has been one of the key events cited by all biographers of Vincent in their reconstruction of the discernment of his vocation to serve the poor. In light of contemporary studies, however, the veracity of this event has now come under challenge. For traditional accounts of this episode see, *Abelly*, 3:113-115; Conference 20, "A Temptation Against Faith," n.d., *CCD*, 11:26-27; and Coste, *Life*, 1:48-49. For a complete bibliographical account of the details of the traditional interpretation, and the contemporary challenge to its relevance and accuracy, see Stafford Poole, C.M., and Douglas Slawson, "A New Look at an Old Temptation: Saint Vincent's Temptation Against Faith and His Resolution to Serve the Poor" (unpublished article).

[227] See *Abelly*, 3:266: "Later he told a friend in confidence that he did this penance because his sins were the cause of the evil that had arisen. Therefore it was only right that he should be the one to do the penance for it."

[228] Ps 69:5 (NAB). [Vulgate, Ps 68:5.] Marginal Note: "*Psal. 68. v. 5.*"

[229] See Rom 9:3 (NAB).

[230] Jn 10:11 (NAB).

[231] Marginal Note: "*Support du prochain.*"

[232] Although this specific incident is not found in *Abelly*, it is clearly reminiscent of various accounts found in this work. The first section calls to mind several stories of people who approached Saint Vincent for favors as a member of the Council of Conscience. The second part of this story is similar to incidents found in *Abelly* concerning Saint Vincent's mildness and charity in dealing with others. For example see *Abelly*, 3:174, for this short narrative by a confrere troubled with scrupulosity:

> Monsieur Vincent was always a great support for me, and treated me with great kindness during my depression. I interrupted him continually, even when he was preparing to celebrate mass or to recite the divine office. When I had heard his response, and left, and then came back again to speak with him several times in succession and at length, I never heard from him a single harsh word. On the contrary, he would always speak to me gently, and never scolded me, something he would have been entirely justified in doing, seeing the constant demands I made upon him. Even after he told me what I must do, I would allow new doubts to arise. He took the trouble to write out in his own hand what he had said to help me remember it, and to support this effort he would then have me read it aloud in his

presence. Whatever hour I went to see him, even late in the evening, or even when he was occupied with others in matters of business, he would always receive me with the same kindness. He would listen to me, and reply with such gentleness and charity that I can hardly express it.

[233] For Vincent's response to calumnies see, *Ibid.*, 3:156-162, 190-191. See also *Robineau*, 36, 86-87. Marginal Note: "*Souffrir les calomnies.*"

[234] Ps 38:14. [Vulgate: Ps 37:14-15.] Marginal Note: "*Psal. 37. v. 14.*" See also Is 53:7 (NAB). [Vulgate, Is 53:7, reads: "*obmutescet et non aperiet os suum.*" (He was silent and opened not his mouth.)]

[235] Antiochi Monachi Lauræ Sabæ Abbatis, *Pandectes Scripturæ Divinitur Inspiratæ: Epistolæ,* "Homilia CXI: De his qui præsunt," *PG,* 89:1773C. The Latin translation reads: "*Debet igitur pastor totus esse mens et oculus...*," *PG,* 89:1774C.

[236] Ps 121:4 (NAB). [Vulgate: Ps 120:4.] Marginal Note: "*Psal. 120 v. 4.*"

[237] Jer 1:11 (NAB). Marginal Note: "*Ierem. 1. p. 11.*"

[238] Gn 31:40 (NAB). Marginal Note: "*Genes. 31. 40.*"

[239] For example, see *Abelly,* 3:265, 316.

[240] Marginal Note: "*Sa force & constance.*"

[241] An apothegm traditionally attributed to the Emperor Vespasian. See C. Suetonii Tranquilli, *The Lives of the Twelve First Roman Emperors,* John Clarke, trans. (London: Printed for A. Bettesworth and C. Hitch at the Red-Lion in Pater-Noster-Row, 1732), 338.

[242] See Sancti Ambrosii, Mediolanensis Episcopi, *Expositio in psalmum CXVIII,* "Sermo Decimus Quintas: ᴅ," *PL,* 15:1494A. The Latin text reads: "*Habes apostolicum cibum manduca illum, et non deficies. Illum ante manduca, ut postea venias ad cibum Christi, ad cibum corporis Dominici, ad epulas sacramenti, ad illud poculum quo fidelium inebriatur affectus.*" For an English translation see, Louis-Marie Chauvet, *Symbol and Sacrament: A Sacramental Reinterpretation of Christian Existence,* Patrick Madigan, S.J., and Madeleine Beaumont, trans. (Collegeville, MN: Liturgical Press, 1995), 214: "[Similarly, St. Ambrose apropos Scripture:] 'Eat this food first, to be able to come later to the food of Christ, to the food of the Body of the Lord, to the sacramental feast, to the cup where the love of the faithful becomes inebriated.'"

[243] For a biographical sketch of Philippe-Emmanuel de Gondi see Letter 6, *CCD,* 1:18, n. 1. See also *Robineau,* 47-69.

[244] For details of the first mission given at Folleville in January 1617, and the other early missions on the Gondi lands, see *Abelly,* 1:56-62. See also Coste, *Life,* 1:68-70.

[245] For a detailed discussion on the role of general confessions in the ministry of Vincent de Paul see, for example, Alexandrette Bugelli, *Vincent de Paul: une pastoral du pardon et de la réconciliation: la confession générale* (Paris: Éditines Universitaires Fribourg Suisse, 1997).

[246] Gal 4:19 (NAB).

[247] For Vincent's comments on the principles and practices of effective preaching see, for example, *Abelly,* 2:19-20, 257; 3:68, 86, 219-221. See also Coste, *Life,* 2:197-225; and *Robineau,* 49, 57, 79, 114.

[248] H.J. Schroeder, O.P., ed., "Concilii Tridenti, Sessio Vigesima tertia de Reformatione, Canones et Decreta, Caput XVIII: Forma erigendi seminarium clericorum, præstertim tenuiorum; in cujus erectione plurima observanda; de educatione promovendorum in cathedralibus et majoribus ecclesiis," in *Canons and Decrees of the Council of Trent* (St. Louis: Herder and Herder, 1941), 447. The full Latin text reads: "*...si opus fuerit, expellendo, omniaque impedimenta auferentes, quæcumquæ ad conservandum et augendum tam pium et sanctos institutum pertinere videbuntur diligenter curabunt.*"

[249] For Vincent's respect for the clergy see notes 50-56, and 79, *supra.* See also *Robineau,* 49, 53, and 55. See also, for example, *Abelly,* 3:109:

He was also united to the pastors and other clergy. He honored and served them as dictated by circumstances, both as a general rule and also in each particular case. He was on good terms with the orders and communities of religious and even of seculars....

[250] For Vincent's views about the Congregation of the Mission as the "little Company" see, *Robineau*, 33. See also, for example, *Abelly*, 1:113:

> He led them to think of themselves always as the least of all those who worked in the Church and to judge all others as superior to themselves. We know of no better way to convey his sentiments than to quote what he said once when a new priest recently received into the Congregation had referred to it as "this holy Congregation." This humble servant of God stopped him and said: Monsieur, when you speak of our Company, we ought never use the terms "this holy Company" or "this holy Congregation," or any such terms. Rather, we ought to say "this poor Company," "this little Company," or some such expression. We should imitate the Son of God, who called the company of his apostles and disciples "little flock," or "little company."

[251] For Vincent's respect for religious and religious orders of men and women see, for example, *Abelly*, 1:193; 2:385, 391; 3:101, 145-147. See also Coste, *Life*, 2:237-254. Also, *Robineau*, 49, 53, 112.

[252] For Vincent's attitude toward the Society of Jesus see, for example, *Abelly*, 3:102:

> Likewise, he often spoke favorably of the religious of the holy Society of Jesus, praising God for the great things they had done in all parts of the world in spreading the Gospel and for the establishment of the reign of Jesus Christ his Son.

See also *Robineau*, 113, 140.

[253] Saint Vincent's relationship to the Oratory of Jesus dated from its foundation by Pierre de Bérulle in 1611. It is believed that Vincent lived for a time with the newly-formed community in Paris, though never with any intention to join. Bérulle and the Oratory in Lyon played a role in Vincent's appointment as pastor of Châtillon-les-Dombes. Bérulle and the Oratorians, however, would later oppose the approval of the Congregation of the Mission. After the death of his wife, Philippe-Emmanuel de Gondi entered the Oratory and was ordained. Vincent was thus well acquainted with the community and its activities in Paris and elsewhere during his lifetime. See, for example, *Abelly*, 1:52, 98; 3:158.

[254] See Bergin, *Rochefoucauld*. For more on Vincent's relationship with the cardinal see, *Abelly*, 1:247; 2:373, 385; 3:265. See also Coste, *Life*, 1:166, 168, 172, 525; 2:237-243; 3:104, 233, 300.

[255] For more details on Vincent's relations with Bérulle see, *Abelly*, 1:48-58. See also Coste, *Life*, 1:43-94.

[256] For an extensive treatment of Saint Vincent's opposition to Jansenism, and his participation in the controversies over these theological opinions, see *Abelly*, 1:221-223; 2:346-371; 3:16-18. See also Coste, *Life*, 3:113-181. Also, *Robineau*, 61-64, 108. For a brief discussion of Jansenism see, *Dictionnaire*, 157-159.

[257] See *Abelly*, 3:15-16.

[258] Sancti Leonis Magni, Romani Pontificis, "De jure metropolitarum sub vicario Thessalonicensi degentium conservando," in *Epistola XIV: ad Anastasium Thessalonicensem episcopum*, PL, 54:672A. The full Latin text reads: "*Igitur secundum sanctorum Patrum canones Spiritu Dei conditos, et totius mundi reverentia consecratos, metropolitanos singularum provinciarum episcopos, quibus ex delegatione nostra fraternitas tuæ cura prætenditur, jus traditæ sibi antiquitus dignitates intemeratum habere decernimus; ita ut a regulis præstitutis, nulla aut negligentia, aut præsumptione discedant.*"

[259] Jean Hardouin, S.J., ed., "Concilium Attiniacense, in quo Ludovicus pium Imperator publicam pœnitentiam sua sponte suscepit, in Attiniaco palatio celebratum, anno Christi DCCCXXII," in *Acta Conciliorum et Epistolæ Decretales, ac Constitutiones Summorum Pontificum*, 11 vols. (Paris: Ex Typographia Regia, 1714-1715), 4:248. The actual text in *Acta Conciliorum* reads: "*...sacros canones, qui firmati sunt Spiritu Dei....*"

[260] See J.E. Lynch, "Canon Law, History of," in *NCE 2nd*, 3:37-58.

[261] Sancti Aurelii Augustini, Hipponensis Episcopi, "In Psalmum LXXXVIII, Enerratio, Sermo II (a), De Secunda Parte Psalmi," in *Enerrationes in Psalmos LXXX-CL*, PL, 37:1141. The relevant Latin text reads:

"Tenete ergo, charissimi, tenete omnes unanimiter Deum patrem, et matrem ecclesiam."

[262] S. Thascii Cæcilii Cypriani, Episcopi Carthaginensis et Martyris, *Liber de Unitate Ecclesiæ, PL,* 4:519A. The Latin text reads: *"Habere jam non potest Deum patrem, qui Ecclesiam non habet matrem."*

[263] Mt 28:20 (NAB).

[264] For Vincent's respect for the pope see *Abelly,* 1:107, 222; 2:355. See also *Robineau,* 43, 54, 63, 108.

[265] Because of his strong and vocal opposition to the Jansenist movement, Saint Vincent was an object of their attacks. Here, Maupas du Tour is reacting to a Jansenist's dismissal of Vincent as an *"ignorant dévot."* For more information see *Abelly,* 3:185-186:

> A person given to Jansenism once spoke to him in an effort to persuade him to come over to that party. When he finished speaking, but with little to show for his efforts, he became angry. He reproached Monsieur Vincent, saying that he was a true ignoramus, and he was astonished that his Congregation would tolerate him as superior general. Monsieur Vincent replied that he himself was astonished at the same thing, because, he said, "I am even more ignorant than you know."

[266] The Sorbonne was considered to have one of the premiere theological schools, and its faculty and their opinions on theology were considered to have a certain semi-official status.

[267] For Vincent's submission to the authority of the Holy See, see *Abelly,* 2:126; 3:108, 207; and for his deference to those who spoke on behalf of the pope see, Letter 740, "Cardinal Antonio Barberini, Prefect Of Propaganda, To Saint Vincent," Rome, 25 February 1645, *CCD,* 2:556-557. See also *Robineau,* 50, 54.

[268] P.T. Camelot, "Ephesus, Council of," in *NCE 2nd,* 5:274:

> When the delegates of the pope arrived, they intervened with full authority, and Philip the priest relates that all admitted that "the holy and blessed apostle Peter, prince and leader of apostles, column of the faith, foundation of the Catholic Church, had received from Our Lord Jesus Christ, the Savior and Redeemer of manking, the keys of the kingdom, and the power to bind or forgive sins. It is he who up to now and always lives and gives judgment through his successors."

See also *Creeds,* 281.

[269] See Sancti Eusebii Hieronymi, Stridonensis Presbyteri, *Epistola XV,* "Ad Damasum Papam," *PL,* 22:355-358. For a summary of the contents of this letter in English see: **http://www.ccel. org/ccel/schaff/npnf206.v.XV.html.**

[270] Sanctii Aurelii Augustini, Hipponensis Episcopi, *Sermones de Scripturis,* "Sermo CXXXI, De Verbis Evangelii Joannis: Caput 10, Concilia contra Pelagianos," *PL,* 38:734. The full Latin text reads: *"Causa finita est: utinam aliquando finiatur error!"*

[271] Sanctii Aurelii Augustini, Hipponensis Episcopi, *Contra Epistolam Manichæi, Quam vocant fundamenti,* "Liber Unus, Caput V: Contra titulum Epistolæ Manichæi," *PL,* 42:176. Marginal Note: *"Tom. 6. Contra epist. Manichæi cap. 5."*

[272] See "English Poems, Life of Pico, The Last Things," in *The Yale Edition of the Complete Works of St. Thomas More,* Anthony S.G. Edwards, Katherine Gardiner Rodgers, and Clarence H. Miller, eds., 15 vols. (New Haven: Yale University Press, 1997), 1:365, line 4.

[273] See Jn 19:26-27 (NAB).

[274] For Vincent's particular devotion to Mary see *Abelly,* 3:92-94. See also Coste, *Life,* 1:33, 56. For examples of the Greek Fathers' regard for Mary see:

> • Origenis, *Originis in Lucam Homiliæ: Interprete S. Hieronymo,* "In Lucam Homilia VII: De eo quod scriptum est: 'exsurgens autem Maria cum festionatione venit in montana,' usque ad eum locum ubi ait: 'erit consummatio eorum quæ dicta sunt,'" *PG,* 13:1817-1819. In this homily Origen stated, for example: *"Oportebat quoque Mariam cum Dei prole dignissima, post alloquium Dei, ad montana conscendere, et in sublimioribus commorari."* (It is said that Mary, carrying the issue of God, after

speaking with God, ascended the mountain, and remained there for a long time.) These are interesting uses of symbolic language normally associated with Moses, his encounter with יהוה on Mount Horeb, and the receipt of his commission to free the children of Israel. See *PG*, 13:1817B.

- S.M.D. Leontii Byzantini, *Accedit Evagrii Scholastici Historia Ecclesiastica*, "Quæstiones: Adversus eos qui unam dicunt naturam compositam D. N. J. C.: Contra Monophysitas," *PG*, 86.2:1783D, 1784D. The original Greek text reads: "... ποῦ ἦν ποτε ἡ τελεία ὑπόστασις ἀνθρωπίνη προυπάρξασα Χριστοῦ; Ε τα ἐν τῇ μήτρα τῆς ἁγίας Παρθένου ἐγκαθειρχθεῖσα · κατ᾽ ἐκεῖνο γὰρ τὸ ἅγιον χωρίον ἡ ἕνωσις τῶν Χριστοῦ φύσεων ἀπ᾽ ἀρχῆς ἐγένετο...," *PG*, 86.2:1784D. The Latin translation is: "...ubi erat tunc perfecta subsistentia humana Christo præexsistens? Deinde in utero sanctæ Virginis inclusa; illo enim in sancto cubiculo adunatio Christi naturarum ab initio facta est...," *PG*, 86.2:1783D.

- Beati Joannis Eucratæ, *Pratum Spirituale*, "Caput XXVI: Vita fratris Theophanis, ejusque mirabilis visio, et de communcatione cum hæreticis," *PG*, 87.3:2871. The Greek text reads: "...εἰ μὴ τὸ ὀρθῶς φρονεῖν καὶ πιστεύειν, κατὰ ἀλήθειαν Θεοτόκον τὴν ἁγίαν Παρθένον Μαρίαν ὑπάρχειν," *PG*, 87.3:2872C. The Latin text reads: "...nisi recte sentiamus et credamus (ut revera est) sanctam Mariam Dei genitricem esse," *PG*, 87.3:2871B-C.

- S.P.N. Joannis Damasceni, Monachi et Presbyteri Hierosolymitani, *Homilia VIII*, "Homilia 1: In Dormitionem B. V. Mariæ," *PG*, 96.3:699-722. The homily is replete with praises of Mary and her participation in God's plan of salvation. It ends with the following words (first, the Greek at *PG*, 96.3:721A-B; then, the Latin at *PG*, 96.3:722A-B): "Σὺ δὲ ἐποπτεύοις ἡμᾶς, ἀγαθὴ δέσποινα, ἀγαθοῦ δεσπότου λοχεύτρια, ἄγοις τε καὶ φέροις τὰ καθ᾽ ἡμᾶς ὅπου βούλοιο, καὶ τὰς ὁρμὰς τῶν αἰσχίστων ἡμῶν παθῶν στήσειας, καὶ πρὸς τὸν τοῦ θείου θελήματος ἀχείμαστον λιμένα καθοδηγοῦσα, καὶ τῆς μελλούσης μακαριότητος καταξιώσειας, τῆς γλυκείας τε καὶ αὐτοπροσώπου ἐλλάμψεως, τοῦ ἐκ σοῦ σαρκωθέντος Θεοῦ Λόγου. Μεθ᾽ οὗ τῷ Πατρὶ δόξα, τιμή, κράτος, μεγαλοσύνη τε καὶ μεγαλοπρέπεια, σὺν τῷ παναγίῳ καὶ ἀγαθῷ, καὶ ζωοποιῷ αὐτοῦ Πνεύματι, νῦν καὶ ἀεὶ, καὶ εἰς τοὺς αἰῶνας τῶν αἰώνων. Ἀμήν."; "Tu itaque, bona Domina, boni Domini parens, nos velim inspicias, resque nostras arbitrio tuo regas ac modereris; fœdissimarum nostrarum affectionum impetum comprimas, ut, compositis fluctibus, nos ad tranquillum divinæ voluntatis portum dirigas, ac futura beatitudine dones; illa, inquam, dulci Dei Verbi incarnate per ejus conspectum illuminatione; cum quo Patri gloria, honor, imperium, majestas et magnificentia, cum sanctissimo, bonoque et vivifico ejus Spiritu, nunc et semper, et in sæcula sæculorum. Amen."

- S.P.N. Joanni Damasceni, Monachi, *Hymni Sex: Hymnus in Sanctum Basilium*, "Ode X: Ne lugeas super me, O Mater," *PG*, 96.3:1377-1378. Several hymns for use in the Eastern Church's liturgies are attributed to St. John. *PG*, 96.3:1363-1408 contains hymns in honor of Saints Basil the Great, John Chrysostom, Nicholas of Myra, Peter the Apostle, George, and Blaise. Rather than ending with a doxology, each "ode" in these hymns ends with a verse to the Mother of God (Θεοτοκίον/Deiparæ). Typical of these bows to Mary as παναγία Παρθένε (most holy Virgin) are the Greek ending and its Latin translation of Ode X in the hymn in honor of St. Basil: "Σὲ, παναγία Παρθένε, ἀκαταίσχυντον πρέσβιν καὶ μεσιτείαν εὐμενῆ προβάλλομαι πιστῶς τῷ ἐκ σοῦ τεχθέντι • καὶ ἱκετεύω σε, τῶν πολλῶν μου πταισμάτων τὰ πλήθη τὰ πολλὰ μητρικαῖς σου πρεσβείαις ἄρδην ἐξάλειψον." *PG*, 96.3:1377B; "Te, sanctissima Virgo, honorandam legatam optimamque mediatricem præmitto libenter ad Filium de te genitum, teque supplico, plurimos lapsus meos et peccata materna intercessione tua omnio dele." *PG*, 96.3:1378B.

²⁷⁵ For a biographical sketch of Francis de Sales see Letter 29, "To Saint Louise," [Between 1626 and May 1629], *CCD*, 1:55, n. 4. For more on the relationship between Francis de Sales and Vincent de Paul see, Dodin, *François de Sales*. See *Abelly*, 1:90-92; 2:266-267; 3:165-167. See also Coste, *Life*, 1:114, 132-143. Also, *Robineau*, 30.

²⁷⁶ Francis de Sales was canonized in 1665.

²⁷⁷ See *Abelly*, 1:90; 2:266; 3:208.

²⁷⁸ Saint Francis' successor in the see of Geneva was his younger brother Jean-François de Sales, consecrated as his coadjutor and bishop of Chalcedon on 21 January 1621. At Francis' death on 28 December 1622, he automatically succeeded to the see of Geneva. Jean-François de Sales died in 1635.

²⁷⁹ Maupas du Tour's great emphasis on Vincent's relationship with Francis de Sales, Jeanne de Chantal, and the Visitation is explained by his own close relationship with, and devotion to, them. He was the author of the first biographies of both figures, and preached the funeral oration for Jeanne de Chantal in Paris.

²⁸⁰ For a biographical sketch of Jeanne-Françoise de Chantal see *Abelly*, 1:90. See also du Tour, *Vie de Frémiot*. For more details of the relationship between Vincent de Paul and Jeanne de Chantal see, *Abelly*, 1:90-92; 2:266-285; and Coste, *Life*, 1:132-143; 3:194-216. See also Document 34, *CCD*, 13a: 137-139.

²⁸¹ Ps 137:6 (NAB). [Vulgate Ps 136:6.]

²⁸² See S. Thascii Cæcilii Cypriani, Episcopi Carthaginensis et Martyris, Operum Pars II: Opuscula, *Liber de Habitu Virginum*, *PL*, 4:461B-462B. Here Saint Cyprian encourages wealthy virgins to use their resources in charitable works.

²⁸³ See 1 Chr 22:5-17 (NAB).

²⁸⁴ Lk: 2:14 (NAB). Marginal Note: "*Luc. 2.14.*"

²⁸⁵ On 16 August 1652, Vincent de Paul wrote to Innocent X and described the desperate situation in France caused by the rebellions of the Fronde. See Letter 1539, "To Pope Innocent X," Paris, 16 August 1652, *CCD*, 4:445-447.

²⁸⁶ Sg 1:6 (NAB). Marginal Note: "*Cant. 1.5.*" See also *Robineau*, 92, 107, 110, 124.

²⁸⁷ See Lk 10:25-36 (NAB).

²⁸⁸ For the impact of war see *Abelly*, 1:185-189, 204-220; 2:317-345. See also Coste, *Life*, 2:398-402.

²⁸⁹ For more details see *Abelly*, 1:291, 294, 301; 2:273, 407. See also Coste, *Life*, 2:279.

²⁹⁰ See Coste, *Life*, 3:388-392. See also *Robineau*, 95, and 108.

²⁹¹ See *Abelly*, 1:220: "No, no, we must not stop now, we must beseech God for universal peace." The war between France and Spain began in 1635 and lasted for twenty-four years. The Peace of the Pyrenees, the treaty which finally ended the long war, was signed on 7 November 1659. See also Coste, *Life*, 2:398.

²⁹² The praise referenced here is unclear. See note 11, *supra*.

²⁹³ Sancti Ambrosii Mediolanenis Episcopi, *De Virginibus ad Marcellinam sororem suam*, *PL*, 16:200C. The full Latin text reads, "*Satis prolixa laudatio est, quæ non quæritur, sed tenetur.*"

²⁹⁴ One of the traditional titles accorded to the King of Spain was, "the most Catholic King," whereas that of the King of France was, "the most Christian King."

²⁹⁵ See Francois Cottelet, *La Nouvelle Relation Contenant L'Entreveue et Serments des Roys, pour L'Entiere Execution de la Paix. Ensemble Toutes les Particularitez & Ceremonies qui se sont faites au Mariage du Roy, & de l'Enfante d'Espagne. Avec tout ce qui s'est passé de plus remarquable entre ces deux puissant Monarques jusqu'à leur depart* (Paris: Jean-Baptiste Loyson, 1660).

²⁹⁶ For Mazarin's role in the war between France and Spain, as well as in the peace negotiations and treaty, see Paul Guth, *Mazarin* (Paris: Flammarion, 1972), 728-739. For Mazarin's development as a diplomat and his involvement in furthering his vision of the cause of France on the European scene,

see Geoffrey Treasure, *Mazarin: the Crisis of Absolutism in France* (London: Routledge, 1995).

[297] From the closing prayers of the "Litany of the Saints." See the full litany with both a Latin and English translation at: **http://www.preces-latinae.org/thesaurus/Sancti/LitSanctorum.html** (accessed 8 August 2012). See also 1 Tm 1:17.

[298] Louis XIV married the Spanish Infanta in the city of Saint Jean-de-Luz on 6 June 1660.

[299] The hard work of negotiating the lengthy treaty was indeed the work of Mazarin as Louis XIV's representative, while Don Luis Mendez de Haro acted as the representative of Philip IV of Spain. They served as the plenipotentiaries of their respective monarchs. See *Traitté de Paix entre les couronnes de France et D'Espagne...du 31, May 1660* (A Paris: De L'Imprimerie Royale, 1659).

[300] Part of the terms of the Peace of the Pyrenees was the marriage of the Spanish Infanta, Maria Theresa, to her first cousin, Louis XIV.

[301] For more on the horrors of war and its aftermath in France during Vincent's life, see: *Abelly*, 2:317, 331-336; Coste, *Life*, 1:400; 2:366-377, 398-402, 412-419, 425-430, 475-478; and *Robineau*, 124-125. Also, letters to Saint Vincent from members of the Company, and from town officials in the devastated areas, paint a vivid picture of conditions in the war-ravaged areas of France during this time. See, for example: Letter 887, "To Jean Dehorgny, Superior, In Rome," Paris, 8 November 1646, *CCD*, 3:111; Letter 1266, "A Priest Of The Mission To Saint Vincent," [La Fère, 26 September 1650], *Ibid.*, 4:94; Letter 1274, "Some Priests Of The Mission To Saint Vincent," [1650], *Ibid.*, 4:104; Letter 1282, "A Priest Of The Mission To Saint Vincent," [1650], *Ibid.*, 4:112; Letter 1309, "A Priest Of The Mission To Saint Vincent," [1650 or January 1651], *Ibid.*, 4:142; Letter 1316, "Edme Deschamps To Saint Vincent," [December 1650 or January 1651], *Ibid.*, 4:150-151; Letter 1317, "Some Priests Of The Mission To Saint Vincent," [1650 or January 1651], *Ibid.*, 4:151-152; Letter 1359, "The Town Magistrates Of Rethel To Saint Vincent," Rethel, 8 May 1651, *Ibid.*, 4:199-201; Letter 1363, "The Town Magistrates Of Rethel To Saint Vincent," Rethel, 22 May 1651, *Ibid.*, 4:204-205; Letter 1371, "A Priest Of The Mission To Saint Vincent," [1651], *Ibid.*, 4:218; Letter 1381, "The Town Magistrates Of Rethel To Saint Vincent," Rethel, 17 July 1651, *Ibid.*, 4:230-231; Letter 1387, "Monsieur Simonnet, President and Lieutenant General Of Rethel, To Saint Vincent," [Between 1650 and 1655], *Ibid.*, 4:236; Letter 1408, "A Priest Of The Mission To Saint Vincent," [Saint-Quentin, 1651], *Ibid.*, 4:260; and Letter 1652, "The Town Magistrates Of Rethel To Saint Vincent," Rethel, 8 September 1653, *Ibid.*, 5:12.

[302] For a discussion of the importance of "fidelity" in Vincent's society see, Sean Smith, "Fidelity to Founder Under the Bourbon Regime: The Congregation of the Mission, 1660-1736" (unpublished doctoral dissertation, National University of Ireland, 2012), 7-8.

[303] See *Abelly*, 3:73: "To God alone be the glory, and may those who work with you give him this thanks. If their small efforts have any success and produce any good (*A Domino factum est istud*) God has done this, and to him alone should be the glory."

Ibid., 3:293: "In the first place, if we consider the end he proposed either for himself or others, it was always to act for the greater glory of God, and to accomplish his most holy will. This was the sole end this good servant of God proposed to himself in all his plans and enterprises."

The original text of
Henri de Maupas' Oraison Funèbre is
presented here. It mirrors
the published text as closely as possible.
No attempt has been made to correct printing
errors or to update the seventeeth-century
French. The Greek content has been
added since much of the text in the original
publication was corrupted by a
lack of Greek printing fonts. The style of the
printed document is also presented as
closely as possible to the original.

ORAISON

FVNEBRE,

A LA MEMOIRE

DE FEV MESSIRE

VINCENT DE PAVL,

INSTITVTEVR,

FONDATEVR,

ET SVPERIEVR GENERAL

DES PRESTRES DE LA MISSION.

Prononcée le 23. Novembre 1660. dans

L'Eglife de S. Germain l'Auxerrois;

Par Monfeigneur l'Illuftrißime & Reverendißime Evefque
& feul Seigneur du Puy, & Comte de Vellay,
HENRY DE MAVPAS DV TOVR.

A PARIS,

Chez GASPAR METVRAS, ruë Saint Iacques, à la Trinité.
IACQVES LANGLOIS, Imp. ord. du Roy, au Mont Sainte-
Geneviève; & en fa boutique dans la grand' Salle du Palais,
à la Reyne de Paix.

ET

EMM. LANGLOIS, ruë S. Iacques, à la Reyne du Clergé.

M. DC. LXI.

AVEC PRIVILEGE DV ROY.

❀❀❀❀❀❀❀❀❀❀❀❀❀❀❀❀❀❀❀❀❀❀❀❀❀❀❀❀❀❀❀❀❀❀❀

Extrait du Privilege du Roy.

P AR Grace & Privilege du Roy, il eſt permis à Meſſire HENRY DE MAVPAS DV TOVR, Eveſque & ſeul Seigneur du Puy, Comte de Vellay, Conſeiller ordinaire du Roy en ſes Conſeils d'Eſtat & Privé, & premier Aumônier de la Reyne Mere, de faire imprimer vn Livre qu'il a compoſé, intitulé, *Oraiſon Funebre à la memoire de feu Mre*, VINCENT DE PAVL *Inſtituteur, Fondateur & Superieur General des Preſtres de la Miβion*: Avec inhibitions & deffenſes à toutes perſonnes de quelque qualité & condition qu'ils soient, d'imprimer ou faire imprimer ledit Livre ſans le conſentement dudit Seigneur: ſur les peines portées par les Lettres de Privilege, données à Paris le 4. Ianvier 1661.

Par le Roy en ſon Conseil, OLIER.

Et ledit Seigneur Eveſque du Puy a cedé le Privilege cy-deſſus à Gaſpar Meturas, Iacques & Emmanuël Langlois, pour en jouyr conjointement, ſuivant l'acte paſſé entr'eux le sixiéme jour de Ianvier 1661.

A SON
EMINENCE.

Monseignevr,

Vn ancien diſoit que la plus ſouveraine autorité des grands de la terre, pouvoit jetter de la crainte pour vn temps, dans quelques eſprits timides; mais que dans le ſiecle ſuivant, leur puiſſance ne pourroit plus eſteindre la liberté des langues, ny des plumes, qui troubleroient leurs cendres avec impunité, pour étaler dans le public la cenſure de leur vie, & les reproches de leur fortune.

Et moy je dis, Monſeigneur, *que les eſprits plus raiſonables auront quelque ſujet de croire que le Ciel vous a élevé dans ce haut étage de credit & de gloire, afin de forcer la jalouſie des grands, la paßion des peuples, & l'inconſtance des ſiecles, à fixer vn reſpect ſolide & conſtant pour honorer vôtre nom; puis qu'ayant menagé la Paix par la prudence & par la force de vos genereux conſeils, vous avez fait en meſme temps que l'envie l'a cedé au merite de voſtre conduite; & que les juges les plus ſeveres, vous regarderont deſormais comme le plus illuſtre arbitre de la felicité publique; qui avez ſacrifié vos propres interests, & qui n'avez peû eſtre vaincu que par vous-meſme, pour faire ceſſer la guerre, afin d'établir le repos des Nations, & le bon-heur de l'Vnivers.*

On ſçait, Monſeigneur, *que Voſtre Eminence entrant dans la Miniſtere a trouvé la guerre allumée, & que parmy le bruit des armes & les grandes agitations de l'Etat, vous avez ſi heureuſement élevé noſtre grand Monarque, que vous avez tiré ſa Couronne autant que ſa perſonne, de la minorité; & avez marqué les progrez de ſon aage, par ceux de ſes victoires. On ſçait que le feu Roy* Lovis le Ivste, *de tres-glorieuſe memoire, & ſon grand Miniſtre, le grand*

Cardinal de Richelieu; *ont tellement estimé vostre puissant genie, & les rares talens de V.E. qu'ils vous ont jugé digne de vous rendre depositaire de tous les plus pretieux interests de nostre Monarchie. On a veu croître le plus beau de nos lys, entre vos mains, dans la blancheur d'vne innocence si pure, que sa Religion a suivy nos vœux & surpassé nos esperances. Vous avez,* **Monseigneur,** *menagé ses Lauriers, entre le bruit de ses conquestes, & les Oliviers de la Paix: vous en aviez donné de glorieux presages, dans cette fameuse journée de Cazal, lors qu'en exposant vostre vie, vous empeschâtes deux puissantes armées de donner la bataille: Et l'on peut dire que V.E. ne s'est point écartée de cette genereuse conduïte, quand elle a espargné le sang de ceux qui vouloient estre prodigues de sa gloire.*

Vous avez fait quelque chose de plus, **Monseigneur,** *quand vous avez honoré de vos faveurs, ceux mesme qu'vne vertu moins heroïque que la vostre, n'auroit peû regarder que comme les objets d'vne juste colere. Et pour porter le dernier effort d'vn parfait courage, jusques au souverain periode de la magnanimité; vous avez pris à tâche de payer les injures avec des caresses; en sorte que les ennemis que vous avez peû vaincre par la force, ont esté contraints de rendre les armes, aux sentimens de la gratitude, qu'ils devoient à vos bien-faits.*

Mais apres tout, **Monseigneur.** *V.E. a fait connoître, qu'en procurant la Paix à toute l'Europe, vous pouviez encor'faire d'vn seul coup quelque chose de plus grand, en vous rendant le bienfaicteur vniversel des peuples, & des plus belles Couronnes du monde. Voila,* **Monseigneur,** *ce que la voix publique admire dans la conduite de V.E. Et moy, qui par les loix de ma profession, dois regarder celles de l'Evangile, pour bein mesurer mes respects, & qui condamne la loüange si elle n'est conform eà l'esprit de l'Eglise, je veux donner ma veneration jusqu'à des actions de V.E. qui semblent bien plus basses & bien plus cachées. Ie considere V.E. dans le Conseil du Roy, qui observe les pratiques de vertu de feu Monsieur Vincent, Superieur General de la Mißion; & qui les fait remarquer aux autres: Qui témoigne après la mort de ce grand homme, qu'elle veut proteger les suiets de sa Congregation; qu'elle estime les emplois de ces bons Prestres; & qu'elle a crû que les prieres de ce grand Serviteur de Dieu, n'avoient point esté inutiles pour la Paix, & pour le Mariage du Roy.*

Ie me souviens encor, **Monseigneur,** *qu'vn iour que j'avois l'honneur d'estre deputé des Evesques, pour parler à V.E. d'vne affaire tres-importante à la Religion, vous me dites de si bonne grace, que vous donneriez vostre sang de bon cœur pour le service de l'Eglise. Apres cela,* **Monseigneur,** *cette Oraison Funebre*

ſe preſente d'elle-meſme à V.E. dans laquelle peut-eſtre que j'auray mieux
expliqué mes pensées: elles ſont innocentes, n'eſtant point mercenaires; ſi ce n'eſt
que ie pretens la protection que V.E. doit à mon Dioceze & qu'elle m'a promis,
& à quatorze de nos grands Prelats, leſquels en corps de Deputation, la Cour
eſtant à Fontainebleau, luy ont recommandé mes droicts, comme inſeparables
des obligations de noſtre commun Caractere. Il eſt vray, Monſeigneur, *que V.E.*
m'a fait la grace de m'offrir autresfois quelques autres Benefices, & que je luy
ay la meſme obligation que ſi je les avois accepté; & depuis ce temps-là, j'ay
achevé de perdre mes neveux dans les armées, pour le ſervice du Roy, en ſorte
qu'il ne m'en reſte plus; ſi bien que ma famille en eſt preſque eſteinte: mais
auſſi, Monſeigneur, *mon ſort qui eſt l'effet d'vne particuliere providence de*
Dieu, m'ayant reduit à ce point, que j'ay moins d'intereſts que jamais; je tireray
cet avantage de mes diſgraces, que le public donnera plus de creance à mes
diſcours, quand je parleray des reſpects que l'on doit à vos grandes actions, &
que ie paroîtray plus fidel & plus libre, en vous aſſeurant de la paßion que i'ay
d'eſtre toute ma vie,

MONSEIGNEVR,

De V.E.

Les tres-humble & tres-obeïſſant
Serviteur, Henry, E. du Puy.

ORAISON FVNEBRE

A LA MEMOIRE

DE FEV MESSIRE

VINCENT DE PAVL,

INSTITVTEVR,

FONDATEVR,
ET SVPERIEVR GENERAL

DES PRESTRES DE LA MISSION.

Prononcée le 23. Novembre 1660. dans l'Eglife de S. Germain l'Auxerrois, par Monfeigneur l'Illuftriffime & Reuerendiffime Evefque & feul Seigneur du Puy, & Comte de Vellay, HENRY DE MAVPAS DV TOVR.

Cujus laus eft in Euangelio per omnes Ecclefias. C'eft celuy de qui la loüange eft eftablie dans l'Euangile par toutes les Eglifes.   S. Paul 2. Cor. c.8.

L A loüange que nous rendons à la memoire des Iuftes, eft vn hommage innocent, & vn tribut bien legitime; puif-qu'il eft vray que la loüange des Iuftes fait partie de la gloire que nous devons à Dieu. Les ames venales & mercenaires, qui fans pudeúr & fans repentance ont proftitué la confcience aux faillies de la volupté, ou bien aux interefts de la fortune & de l'ambition, ne meritent qu'vn mépris eternel: parce qu'ils on tari la fource de la loüange dans fon principe, en faifant outrage à l'efprit de la grace, qui en eft le fondement folide & la premiere femence. Comme au contraire, les ames genereufes, qui ont renoncé à ce trafic pervers, qui fait commerce de l'eternité pour le temps, *qui cælestibus terrena mercantur*, dit faint Bernard, & qui n'ont recherché que la gloire de la grace pour parler aux termes de l'Efcriture, elles ont merité la veritable loüange; parce que leur morale & leur politique n'ont point reconnu d'autres loix que celles de l'Evangile, ny d'autre appuy que celuy de la grace. Et dautant que la grace, au langage du premier des Apoftres, rend les ames qui font fidelles à fes attraits, participantes de l'effence Divine, *Divinæ confortes naturæ*, dit faint Pierre; de là vient que ces ames choifies participent aux loüanges de Dieu, & que leur gloire fait partie de celle que nous devons à Dieu. *Tunc laus erit vnicuique à Deo. (I. Cor. 4.)*

C'eft icy, Meffieurs, où fans differer davantage, d'abord je dois expofer à vos yeux l'image vivante du grand Vincent de Pavl, & vous dire hardiment avec vne liberté d'efprit toute entiere, que la loüange eft deuë au recit de fes rares vertus; puis qu'on peut dire de fa tres-fainte vie & de fa tres-heureufe mort, que la grace en a fait le plan, & l'Evangile en a fait la couronne.

Cujus laus eft in Evangelio per omnes Ecclefias.

La loüange qui ne doit eftre qu'vn illuftre falaire des belles actions, fe corrompt neantmoins trop fouvent, & dans la bouche de celuy qui la prononce, & dans l'oreille de celuy que l'écoute.

La foibleffe ou l'intereft, la crainte ou l'efperance de celuy qui parle; la jaloufie ou l'envie de celuy qui prefte l'attention, font bien fouvent que la loüange qui doit eftre écoutée fur la terre comme la voix du Ciel, degenere neantmoins en des fons irreguliers; fi bien que l'armonie qui doit refulter du concert de toutes les vertus, n'eft plus qu'vn faux ton, que l'organe de l'impofture, & l'Echo de l'enuie.

Icy, Meffieurs, il n'en eft pas de mefme: Si je donne des loüanges à le memoire du grand Vincent de Pavl, ie n'en puis affez dire pour arriuer à l'eftime que l'impreffion de fes vertus a fait naître dans vos efprits; & fi peu que j'en dife, j'en diray trop, fi je confulte les fentimens de la profonde humilité de ce grand homme, & du parfait mépris qu'il a fait de foy-mefme durant tout le cours de fa vie.

Son humilité.

Vn Ancien ne pût cacher fa vanité, quand il avoüa que de tous les fons de la mufique, il n'en connoiffoit point qui luy fut plus agreable que celuy qui chantoit fes loüanges: Vincent de Pavl, Meffieurs, n'auoit pas des penfées fi profanes; on peut dire tout au contraire de fa modeftie, que celuy qui difoit quelque chofe à fon avantage, mettoit fon ame à la torture, & faifoit fouffrir le plus cruel de tous les fupplices à fon humilité. *Qui me laudat, me flagellat.* L'horreur qu'il avoit de fes propres loüanges, eft quelque chofe fans doute difficile à comprendre, & je puis dire, à la face des SS. Autels, en repaffant dans ma memoire ce que j'aẏ veu dans fa converfation durant le cours de tant d'années que je l'ay pratiqué, qu'il me femble que c'eft avoir trouvé vne explication litterale & admirable des facrez devoirs de l'humilité du Chriftianifme, que d'avoir étudié le gefte, la parole, le logement, la nourriture, l'habit & tout le refte de l'equipage du grand VINCENT DE PAVL, qui fe nommoit vn gueux, que j'eftimois vn Saint, & que vous avez fi fouvent admiré, Meffieurs, comme vn exemplaire achevé d'vne parfaite humilité.

Cujus laus eft in Evangelio per omnes Ecclefias.

On donne des loüanges à des perfonnes dont le fouvenir eft execrable, & dont la voix publique commence de châtier la memoire auffi-toft apres leur mort, par le reproche des crimes, dont ils ont flétri leur vie; cependant que dans vne autre vie d'vne plus longue durée, leur ame reprouvée en fouffre les fupplices: *Laudantur vbi non funt, cruciantur vbi funt. On loüe ces criminels fur la terre, où ils ne font plus, & ils brûlent où ils font.* Icy tout au contraire; nos loüanges font foibles pour des vertus heroïques, que le Ciel & la voix publique ont couronné de Gloire.

On donne des loüanges aux enfans du fiècle, à ces grands de la terre, plus grands quelquefois par l'enormité de leurs vices, que par l'éclat de leur fortune & de leur dignité: On cherche des pretextes apparens d'vne vertu imaginaire pour déguifer le débauches ou les concuffions d'vne vie toturiere & fouvent fcandaleufe: On flate les paffions les plus honteufes, on couvre fous les voiles de l'impofture & de la flatterie des veritez fâcheufes dignes de la haine des peuples: On veut des Harangues Funebres pour des fourberies infideles, que la plus grand indulgence des Loix ne fçauroit punir qu'avec feverité: On fait violence aux regles du blafon; on fauffe les fourreures, les metaux, les émaux, les ourles, les lambels, & les brifures: On force les loix de la fcience heroïque; on fait des lignes obliques dans les genealogies; on emprunte des quartiers eftrangers de plus illuftres familles; on fait couler le fangs des Roys à tort & fans caufe dans des veines obfcures, dans des races qui ont merité plus d'vne fois les châtimens des premiers tribunaux de la Iuftice, & les difgraces de nos plus grands Monarques & de nos Souverains, pour s'eftre voulu élever de la pouffiere au dépens des larmes des pupils, & par vne profufion cruelle du fang des miferables: On fouïlle dans les myfteres fabuleux de la mitologie, pour donner quelque luftre à des noms fauuages, qui n'en peuvent avoir du cofté de la vertu dont ils ont efté les ennemis hereditaires & les perfecuteurs: on fait vn mélange confus de l'hiftoire avec la fable, pour compofer les ornemens frauduleux, les fauffes parures, ou pour mieux dire, pour forger les mafques d'vne nobleffe farouche, qui fe trouve en mefme temps engagée dans l'obligation d'vne double reftitution, & de la loüange dont ils font indignes, & de la fubftance des vefves dont ils font engraiffez. Soûpirons, Meffieurs, pour ces creatures infortunées, & difons en gemiffant avec le Prophete Ifaye 5. 18. *Væ qui trahitis iniquitatem in funiculis vanitatis. Malheur à ceux qui s'attirent l'iniquité par les liens de la vanité.* Mais quoy! l'orgueil & l'avarice font deux confeillers infideles & fanguinaires, qui leur infpirent en mefme temps & le mépris de l'humilité, & le carnage des pauvres. Cependant que tout au contraire, Vincent de Pavl fait gloire de fa baffeffe, & de fe rendre gueux pour enrichir les pauvres.

Venez, efprits fuperbes, qui n'ayant rien de loüable en vous, faites trop de vanité d'vne gloire étrangere; apprenez d'vn Poëte Latin, puis que vous cherchez dans la fable des menfonges de voftre nobleffe, *Et genus & proauos, & quæ non fecimus ipfi, Vix ea noftra voco.*

Ou pour mieux dire, apprenez de la doctrine du grand S. Ambroife, & de la morale du grand Vincent de Pavl; *Probati viri genus, virtutis profapia eft. La vraye nobleffe eft celle qui tire fa genealogie de la pratique des plus excellentes vertus.* (*lib. de Noë & Arca. c. 4*) Vincent de Pavl eft d'vne baffe naiffance; mais d'vne vertu eminente: & ce qui eft admirable dans la pratique de fon humilité, c'eft qu'il cache de tout fon pouvoir l'eminence de fa vertu, & il produit aux yeux de tout le monde l'obfcurité de fa naiffance.

Nous honorons les cendres & le memoire d'vne bergere, d'vne Geneviéve qui gardoit les troupeaux aux portes de Nanterre: nous honorons le fer de la charruë d'vn Ifidore, d'vn laboureur d'Efpagne: nous avons veu ces jours paffez des folemnitez extraordinaires pour honnorer vne partie des offemens d'vn Iean de Dieu, qui paroiffoit aux yeux des hommes comme vn objet de mépris; mais je ne fçay pas fi ces grandes ames ont plus recherché le mépris que Vincent de Pavl, qui recherchoit avec tant de foin de paffer dans le monde pour le dernier des hommes.

Moïfe ce grand Legiflateur du peuple de Dieu, ofte fa chaufure & marche fur la montagne, à pieds nuds; il fait paroître cette partie la plus baffe & qui touche la terre; & en mefme temps il fe couvre d'vn voile, & cache fa face toute brillante par l'éclat des lumieres qui fortent de fon vifage.

Voila l'image, Meſſieurs, de la rare humilité de Vincent de Pavl: il a la face toute rayonnante & toute inveſtie de lumiere comme vn autre Moïſe, & c'eſt le ſeul qui ne voit goute dans le beau iour de ſes eminentes vertus. *Ignorabat quod cornuta eſſet facies ſua ex conſortio ſermonis Domini*, dit le Texte ſacré, *(Exod. 34.) radijs coruſcans*, dit le docte Liranus, Moïſe oſte ſes ſouliers, il montre ſes pieds à nud pour approcher la montagne, & il couvre d'vn voile les rayons de ſa face. Vincent met à découvert l'obſcurité de ſa naiſſance, il fait voir, pour ainſi dire, la craſſe de ſes pieds, il veut que tout le monde ſçache qu'il eſt fils d'vn laboureur, qu'il a gardé les troupeaux comme vn autre Moïſe; mais quand il eſt queſtion de le conſiderer comme vn Legiſlateur choiſi de la main de Dieu pour la conduit de ſon peuple; ah! c'eſt pour lors qu'il couvre ſa face, qu'il ſe cache de honte, & veut eſtre inconnu: & neantmoins, Meſſieurs, il faut vous le dire avec liberté, & ſans aucune chaleur de diſcours, c'eſt Vincent de Pavl que la main de Dieu a choiſi pour porter à ſon peuple les tables de la Loy, c'eſt luy qui par ſon zele admirable, & par celuy de ſes dignes enfans, a ſanctifié des millions d'ames dans les Miſſions; Qui a procuré les ſecours ſpirituels & temporels à des provinces entieres, ruïnées par les malheurs de la guerre; Qui a retiré des millions de creatures des portes de la mort: Qui a ſauvé du dernier naufrage des ames infortunées, leſquelles par vne funeſte alliance & preſque neceſſaire, avoient joint à vne profonde ignorance de nos ſacrez myſteres, & des veritez Chrétiennes neceſſaires au ſalut, vne proſtitution honteuſe au crime & au libertinage, & qui ſembloient en vn mot ne devoir jamais connoître Dieu, que par la rigueur de ſes vangeances, & dans l'eternité des ſupplices. Oüy, Meſſieurs, il faut vous le dire; c'eſt luy-méme, c'eſt ce Vincent de Pavl qui a preſque changé la face de l'Egliſe par les Conferences, par les inſtructions, par tant de Seminaires, dont il a procuré les établiſſemens; C'eſt luy qui a rétably la gloire du Clergé dans ſa premiere ſplendeur, par les exercices des Ordinands, par les Retraites ſpirituelles, par l'ouverture de ſon cœur & de ſa maiſon, lors qu'il a tendu les bras à tous venans, pour embraſſer amoureuſement tous ceux qui vouloient profiter dans cette ſainte école de la veritable diſcipline Eccleſiaſtique: C'eſt luy qui a retiré du déreglement tant de Miniſtres des Autels, qui ſans conſulter les regles d'vne vocation legitime, s'eſtoient engagez temerairement dans les fonctions redoutables de ces ſacrez Miniſteres, par des motifs profanes d'vn intereſt ſordide: c'eſt luy qui a formé de ſi grands ſujets, pour remplir pluſieurs de nos Dioceſes de Vicaires Generaux, d'Officiaux, de Vicegerans, de Promoteurs, & qui meſme a fourny de ſi grands Prelats à la France: C'eſt luy qui a ſeruy d'inſtrument & d'organe à tous les plus grands deffeins, & aux plus importantes affaires, & pour la gloire de Dieu, & pour l'avantage de la Religion, & pour le bon-heur de l'Eftat. Et neantmoins apres tant de couronnes de gloire que l'on doit pofer fur la tefte de ce grand homme, le voir tout caché fous les voiles de fon humilité, tout obfcurci fous les plus fombres nuits des plus profonds abifmes, tout plongé dans la veuë de fon neant; tout ardant d'vn defir extréme d'eftre traité comme l'objet du dernier mépris. C'est cette humilité confommée, Meffieurs, qui merite la loüange des hommes & l'eftime des Anges.

Cuius laus eft in Evangelio per omnes Ecclefias.

Vous ne pouvez fouffrir, Meffieurs, ces petits efprits infolens, qui font tellement bouffis de vanité par les progrés de leur fortune, qu'il femble qu'on doit écouter toutes leurs paroles comme des oracles; que la plus foible de leurs actions doit avoir des panegyriques; & que chacune de leurs démarches les doit élever fur la tefte des hommes: Mais quel remede plus falutaire aux faillies de leur ambition, que de prendre & d'expofer à leurs yeux vn peu de poufliere dont ils font extraits; ou de celle de leur fepulchre, ou la caducité des chofes mortelles fera bien-toft la diffolution de leurs corps, & les reduira dans la terre de leur premiere origine: Il ne faut qu'vn peu de poufliere, difoit la Poëte latin, pour éteindre la chaleur des combats des mouches à miel, & pour r'amener ces legions volantes dans leur quartier d'hyver, lors qu'enyvrées par le fuc des fleurs elles s'écartent de la ruche; ou bien lors qu'eftant charmées par les douceurs du Printemps, elles prennent l'effor dans ces agreables journées, qui compofent les plus belles faifons;

Hi motus animorum atque hæc certamina tanta,
Pulveris exigui iactu, commota quiefcunt.

Voila les reftes chetifs de la vanité des humains. Mais voicy les beaux reftes de l'humilité du grand VINCENT DE PAVL: dites-luy fi fa modeftie le peut fouffrir, que toutes les fleurs des plus beaux parterres n'ont pas tant de varietez, ny tant de beautez que celles de fes vertus; Que la plus vertueufe, auffi bien que la plus grande Reyne du monde eft dans l'admiration de fes rares talens de grace & de fainteté: Que le plus grands hommes & dans l'Eglife & dans la Cour, & dans les Confeils de nos Roys admirent fa vertu. Que le Louvre & le Palais font d'accord qu'il a fait des biens infinis & dans Paris, & dans tout le Royaume, & dans toute l'Eglife de Dieu: Que tout le monde eft échauffé par les faintes ardeurs de fa charité; rien de tout cela ne peut ébranler la conftance de fon humilité. Dites-luy fi vous voulez qu'il faut paffer les Mers, & les limites du Chriftianifme, pour fuivre les faillies de fon zele; Qu'il faut creufer les prifons &

les plus noirs cachots; Qu'il faut fouiller dans tous les hofpitaux; Qu'il faut jetter les fondemens du grand Hofpital General; Qu'il faut fonder toutes les playes des malades; Qu'il faut tâcher d'effuyer les larmes de tous les affligez; Qu'il faut couvrir la nudité de tous les indigens; Qu'il faut que tous les jours, cinq mille, fix mille, & fept mille perfonnes languiffantes & bien davantage, felon le calcul fidel qu'vne perfonne digne de foy en a fait affez exactement, foient affiftez par les Confrairies de la Charité dont il est l'Inftituteur, par les Sœurs & par les Dames de la Charité, dont il eft auffi l'Inftituteur, & dans le Royaume, & dans le Savoye, dans le Piedmont, fi vous voulez, & dans l'Italie, & dans la Pologne & autres lieux auffi éloignez, & tout cela par les mouvemens de fon amour & de fa charité: Dites luy qu'il faut defcendre dans les galeres: Qu'il faut eftre à la cadene pour apprendre la compaffion que l'on doit avoir de ces pauvres forçats; Qu'il faut eftre à la chaîne pour brifer leurs fers; Qu'il faut eftre efclaue pour ménager la liberté des captifs; Qu'il faut effuyer la cruauté d'vn Comite, & fléchir fous fon empire; Qu'il faut eftre valet d'vn Empiric, d'vn Turc, d'vn Renegat, pour ménager la falut d'vne ame. Dites luy qu'il faut aller dans Tunis & dans Alger au milieu de la Barbarie pour fuivre les tranfports de fon zele; Qu'il faut paffer dans les Ifles de Madagafcar; Qu'il faut que les Miffions du Canada, du Iapon, de la Chine, de la Cochin-chine, de Laos, du Tunquin, ou les Peres de la Compagnie de IESVS ont travaillé fi faintement & fi vtilement, reffentent encor en partie les effets de fes foins charitables, & les impreffions de fon zele: Dites luy qu'il faut qu'il expofe vn bon nombre des principaux fujets de fa Congregation, à la fureur ou à la perfidie des Idolatres; à la pefte, au fervice des malades, infectez de la contagion, à mille autres dangers de la mort: Dites-luy, qu'il faut étendre les conquêtes de l'Evangile; & planter les trophées de la Foy, dans des pays perdus, dans des contrées prefque inconnuës, où le Paganifme a fait tant de ravages. Et puis adjoûtez encor vne fois, que rien ne fçauroit ébranler la conftance de fon humilité. Apres cela, Meffieurs, permettez-moy de vous dire deux chofes.

La premiere, Que tout cecy n'eft qu'vn foible échantillon, & vne legere montre, d'vn fonds de vertus qu'on ne peut épuifer. Que le courage de VINCENT DE PAVL eft à l'épreuve de toutes les craintes, & au deffus de toutes les efperances; Que tout ce que la flaterie de la Cour a de plus careffant, tout ce que la complaifance des grands de la terre a de plus charmant, & tout ce que la paffion la plus emportée des Puiffans du fiecle a de plus violent. Tout cela mis enfemble, eft incapable de donner la moindre fecouffe au cœur genereux de VINCENT DE PAVL. Tout cela ne fçauroit ébranler tant foit peu la conftance de fon humilité.

En vn mot; tout ce que les refpects humains ont de plus doux, de plus agreable, & de plus innocent, pour les promeffes d'vne profperité certaine, de laquelle on pretend mefme relever les avantages par les interefts de la gloire de Dieu: & tout ce que les mefmes refpects humains ont de plus terrible pour établir les menaces d'vne ruïne entiere des biens, de l'honneur de la fortune & de la vie, & mefme avec vn dommage évident de fa Congregation, & des interefts de la gloire de Dieu. Tout cela mis enfemble, n'eft pas capable de donner le moindre atteinte à la conftance de cette grande Ame plus ferme qu'vn rocher, au milieu des vagues de la mer: parce que, *Fundatus erat fupra firmam petram. Il a fondé fa confiance fur la fermeté de la pierre. (Luc 6. 48.) Petra autem erat Chriftus (I. Cor. 10.)* C'eft vn rocher qui fe jouë de la colere des vents, & du mépris des flots: de qui nous pouvons dire ce que faint Chryfoftome difoit des Apoftres, *Pulfata fluctibus rupe, firmius conftiterunt.* C'eft vn homme qui ne veut aucun autre foûtien pour fa perfonne, pour les fiens, pour fa conduite, & pour celle de tous ces grands deffeins que la Providence de Dieu luy avoit confiée, finon les pures maximes de l'Evangile, incapable de gauchir ny de biaifer tant foit peu, non pas pour vne Couronne, ny pour vn Empire.

Tout le monde fçait le profond refpect qu'il avoit pour les Evefques, dans vn temps où les Mitres facrées ont efté traitées trop fouvent avec bien du mépris. Vn jour parlant à vn Evéque, il luy dit ces paroles; *Monfeigneur, jamais les maximes de l'Evangile ne pofent à faux.*

Apres cela, Meffieurs, jugez fi nous n'avons pas fujet de dire; *Cujus laus eft in Evangelio,* quand nous parlons d'vn homme incomparable, tout vuide des maximes du fiecle, & tout remply de celles de l'Evangile?

Vn jour qu'vn des Grands du Royaume demandoit vn Benefice à la Cour pour quelqu'vn des fiens, & fçachant que Monfieur Vincent eftant dans le Confeil, avoit fait refiftance à fa pretention, il luy fit ce reproche: *Hé quoy! Monfieur* Vincent, *c'eft donc vous que me refiftez?* Voicy la réponfe que Monfieur Vincent luy fift avec vne parfaite douceur, & vne fermeté nompareille. *Monfeigneur, je fçay le refpect que ie vous dois; mais par la grace de Dieu, vous n'avez aucun pouvoir fur ma confcience.* C'est avoir trouvé le jufte temperament, entre la douceur de l'humilité & la fermeté d'vne conftance, qui ne fléchit jamais fous les refpects humains: car fi l'humilité n'eft accompagnée de la force, elle n'a rien que l'apparence de la vertu, & n'en a plus l'effet.

J'ay appris de bonne part, qu'on s'eft eftonné de l'heureux fuccez de plus grandes affaires qu'il manioit bien fouvent par des voyes, toutes contraires aux conduits ordinaires de la prudence humaine; c'eſt parce qu'il travailloit avec étude à ſe dépouïller de l'eſprit humain, à ne rechercher que les mouvemens de l'eſprit de Dieu; & Dieu qui s'approche de ceux qui le cherchent, le rempliſſoit des lumieres de ſa ſageſſe, & luy donnoit des évenemens favorables, dans les plus fâcheuſes conjonctures des affaires les plus difficiles, où la prudence des eſprits les plus éclairez ſembloit évanoüie. *Qui confidunt in Domino ſicut mons Sion, non commovebitur in æternum qui habitat in Ieruſalem.* Pſ. 124. Tout au contraire, la politique des Sages eſt confonduë, lors qu'ils s'écartent dans des intrigues, ennemies de la ſincerité du Chriſtianiſme, *Declinantes in obligationes,* σραγγαλίας dit le Grec, *adducet Dominus cum operantibus iniquitatem. La Iuſtice de Dieu les punira avec les ouvriers de l'iniquité, & toſt ou tard détruira leurs artifices & leurs déguiſemens.*

La ſeconde choſe que j'avois à vous remarquer, Meſſieurs, c'eſt que VINCENT DE PAVL eſt tout ſeul aveugle dans le grand jour de ſes heroïques vertus, & que tant plus vous élevez ſa gloire juſques dedans le Ciel, tant plus il ſe rabaiſſe dans la pouſſiere de ſon neant, & ne voit que la terre.

N'avez-vous jamais admiré, Meſſieurs, la modeſtie du Patriarche Ioſeph & de ſes freres? Il eſt deſtiné pour eſtre élevé ſur le thrône des Pharaons, & il ordonne à ſes freres de dire qu'ils gardoient les troupeaux: c'eſtoit vn employ que les Egyptiens conſideroient non ſeulement avec mépris, mais encore avec execration, témoin ces paroles de la Geneſe, *Deteſtantur Ægyptij omnes paſtores ovium.* (*c. 46. 34.*) Et que ne dites-vous que vous eſtes les Néveux d'Abraham? que vous eſtes décendu du ſang des Heros? Que vous eſtes de ces races illuſtres, qui ont eſté ſi ſouvent honorées des bendictions de Dieu, qui avez receu les promeſſes de l'heritage, comme les enfans du Tres-Haut? Tout au contraire vous cherchez le mépris: *Quod ſcilicet hominibus non ſolum non placere, ſed etiam diſplicere quæſierunt,* dit Rupert. (*lib. 9. In Geneſim. c. 18*).

De meſme, parlez à VINCENT DE PAVL de toutes ces merveilles que vous avez admiré, & au lieu de vous témoigner de la complaiſance pour l'eſtime que vous faites de ſa vertu, il ſe plongera devant vos yeux, dans la terre, & dans le fumier des troupeaux qu'il gardoit autres fois à la campagne pluſtoſt par pratique d'humilité, que par la neceſſité de ſa fortune. Ah! grand homme, que tant de peuples peuvent nommer Abrech, comme vn autre Ioſeph; qui avez plus fait que de ſoulager la famine de l'Egypte, qui avez garanty de l'extremité de la faim, la Lorraine, la Champagne, la Picardie, les frontieres du Luxembourg; tant de pauvres refugiez des Iſles de la grande Bretagne, de l'Eſcoſſe & de l'Irlande; tant de perſonnes dans la neceſſité qui ont ſouffert l'exil, & la perte de leurs biens pour la Foy; eſt-ce ainſi qu'apres tant de ſaintes actions, au lieu de la loüange, vous cherchez le mépris?

Autrefois en entrant dans Paris, il cacha ſon ſurnom; par la crainte qu'il eut, que ce nom de PAVL, ne le fit prendre pour quelque perſonne noble: & ſe perſuada qu'eſtant ſimplement nommé Monſieur VINCENT, comme qui diroit, Monſieur Pierre ou Monſieur Iean, il paſſeroit pour vn homme inconnu. Quel plus innocent artifice de ſon humilité? Nous voyons bien que Cæſar, Xenophon, Caton, Sylla, Brutus, ont couché leurs belles actions par écrit; mais de cacher ſon nom parce qu'il eſt trop beau, c'eſt l'effet d'vne modeſtie dont les exemples ſont rares. Nous voyons bien par la diſpoſition du Droit en la Novelle 13. que l'Empereur Iuſtinien voulut, que le Prefet du Guet, que les Grecs appelloient d'vn nom trop obſcur & trop ſombre νυκτεπαρκòς changeât de nom, & que par ſon ordre il fut depuis nommé le Preteur du peuple. Mais vous, VINCENT DE PAVL, pour quoy changer de nom, ou pourquoy cacher dans le ſilence, la moitié de voſtre nom? vous pouviez ſans doute porter ces deux noms differens, l'vn de tenebres, & l'autre de lumieres; l'vn ſombre, & l'autre éclatant; l'vn du jour, & l'autre de la nuit, puiſque vous veillez ſur les deſordres de la nuit pour empeſcher les œuvres de tenebres; & que vous eſtiez en meſme temps dans la pratique des œuvres de lumiere, puis que vous eſtiez plus vtile au public, que le Préteur du peuple, par les charitables ſecours que vous avez procuré à tant de peuples affligez, & dans les bourgades de la campagne, & dans les plus grandes villes du Royaume; *ut non ſit qui ſe abcondat à calore ejus.* (*Pſal. 18.*)

Ne vous imaginez pas, Meſſieurs, que ce ſoit vne trop foible penſée, de chercher l'origine des grandes actions, dans la ſignification des noms illuſtres de ceux qui les ont faites: Socrate chez Platon, veut que les peres prennent vn ſoin particulier de donner de beaux noms à leurs enfans, afin de les engager par là, à la pratique des vertus: afin de les rendre plus conſiderables dans l'eſtime des peuples; & afin que par des noms agreables, ils puiſſent avoir vn accez plus libre chez les Princes, deſquels ils eſperent la faveur & les graces: Et ne ſemble-t'il pas que le Poëte avoit donné dans l'étude des Loix, quand il a dit, *conueniunt rebus nomina ſæpè ſuis*, puiſque la Iuriſprudence nous enſeigne parlant des noms propres que *debent eſſe convenientia rebus.* (§ *3. inſtit. de donatio.*) Et ſaint Thomas le maiſtre de l'Eſcole ſacrée, n'enſeigne-t'il pas 3. queſt. 37, art. 2. que les noms ſont impoſez par la conſideration des proprietez de la choſe nommée. Ie laiſſe quantité d'exemples de cette verité qui ſe rencontrent dans l'Eſcriture: Abram & Abraham, pere des Nations & pere des Croyans: Ioſeph, qui nous marque dans fon nom, les progrez de fa fortune, & ceux de fa vertu: Le Sauveur de nos ames a mefme voulu prendre le nom de IESVS, qui fignifie Sauveur: *Ipfe enim falvum faciet populum fuum à peccatis eorum* (*Matt. c. 1.*), pour témoigner le deffein qu'il avoir de racheter le monde. Et pourquoy ne dirons-nous pas que par vne finguliere providence du Ciel, VINCENT DE PAVL, a porté ces deux beaux noms de Vincent & de Paul, pour nous marquer d'vne part fes genereux combats, & fes illuftres victoires dans le nom de VINCENT: & d'autre part pour nous faire connoiftre dans le nom de PAVL, qu'il devoit eftre vn parfait imitateur du zele du grand S. Paul. Et neantmoins, Meffieurs, perfeverant dans vne conftante pratique d'humilité, dont il ne s'écarte jamais, il veut eftre inconnu, ou bien n'eftre connu que pour vn homme de neant.

Quand il parloit de fes eftudes, il difoit qu'il n'eftoit qu'vn chetif Quatriéme, bien qu'il fut Bachelier en Theologie; & ledifoit fi fouvent, que mefme la plufpart de ceux de fa Congregation ont efté trompez en ce point, & ont crû qu'il n'avoit pas paffé ces premieres claffes de la Grammaire. C'eft la feule exception que la candeur de cette ame plus blanche que la neige, plus pure que les lys, pouvoit fouffrir dans les loix inviolables de fa fincerité; mais quoy! il faut que dans l'innocente querelle de plus belles vertus, l'humilité l'emporte; bien que fous fes voiles ordinaires, elle tienne fecretes fes plus belles victoires. Vn grand Religieux Iefuite (comme les ferviteurs de Dieu fe recherchent, & fe lient d'amitié) vn jour dans l'extremité d'vne grande maladie, dont on n'attendoit que la mort, l'eftant allé vifiter, luy demanda, quel eft Monfieur le penfée qui occupe maintenant voftre efprit? Ce faint humble ferviteur de Dieu répondit fur le champ; *In fpiritu humilitatis, & en animo contrito fufcipiamur à te Domine.* Vous euffiez dit que cette grande ame, si dégagée de la corruption du peché, ne meritoit que des fupplices.

En effet, Meffieurs, il faut qu'vne ame aneantie, qui ne cherche dans tous les momens de fa vie, que la gloire de Dieu, fe creufe le dernier des abyfmes, pour établir le fond de fon humilité. Qul eft, Meffieurs, ce dernier abyfme au deffous de la terre? C'eft l'enfer, le trifte & l'eternel fejour des ennemis de Dieu; *Dura ficut infernus æmulatio. (Cant. 8. 6.)*

Ce faint homme, tout remply de l'efprit de Dieu, qui pour ainfi dire, met en mefme temps dans la creature l'efprit du neant; témoin les expreffions admirables de la grande fainte Terese: O grand Tout! parlant de la grandeur infinie de l'effence de Dieu: O grand neant! parlant de la petiteffe infinie de la creature oppofée à la grandeur de Dieu. Ce grand homme, dif-je pour témoigner l'eftime qu'il faifoit de foy-mesme, il s'eftimoit, Messieurs, oferois-je le dire, il s'eftimoit pire qu'vn diable: il exhortoit Meffieurs de fa Congregation, à fe regarder comme des creatures plus méprifables que les damnez, & à fe mettre au deffous des diables; parce que, difoit-il, ils n'ont peché q'vne fois, & nous, helas! combien d'offenfes & combien de pechez? Les diables n'ont pas eu les exemples du Fils de Dieu pour s'humilier, comme nous les avons: ils n'ont pas eu le temps de faire penitence, ce que Dieu nous donne; de combien de momens pouvons-nous profiter, pour effuyer nos fautes? Et fi les demons avoient encore la liberté & la grace que nous avons d'honorer & de fervir l'adorable Majefté de nôtre Dieu; O qu'ils s'en acquitteroient bien d'vne autre maniere que nous ne faifons pas! De quoy pouvons nous nous glorifier? Quoy! de nostre naiffance? Helas! ils font d'vne plus noble extraction que nous? Quoy! de noftre science? hé! le moindre des diables en a plus que tous les hommes enfemble: toutes les Bibliotheques & toutes les Vniverfities du monde, n'ont rien de comparable aux lumieres de ces efprits perdus: Quoy donc! fera-ce du cofté de nos bonnes œuvres, que nous voudrons tirer fujet de vanité? O mon Dieu! qui eft-ce qui en peut faire aucune par foy-mesme? Vous feul, ô mon Dieu, eftes l'Autheur de tout bien; & fi l'homme s'en veut attribuer l'honneur, il le dérobe, Meffieurs, il le dérobe à Dieu, & fert comme de valet au diable, ennemy de fon Createur, pour dérober la gloire qui n'appartient qu'à luy. *Gloriam meam alteri non dabo. (Ifay. 42.8.)*

Meffieurs, ce n'eft plus moy qui parle c'eft l'efprit de Vincent de Pavl qui anime vos bons cœurs, & qui part en mefme temps du plus haut des Cieux par les mouvemens de fa charité; & du plus creux des abyfmes par les pratiques de fon humilité. C'eft quelque chofe de bien étonnant, Meffieurs, qu'vne humilité fi prodigieufe; mais de partager en mefme temps fon cœur entre les brafiers de l'enfer par l'étude de fon humilité, & les brafiers innocens dont les Serpahins brûlent dans le Ciel, par les ardeurs de fon zele & de fa charité, c'eft le genie miraculeux de la grace abondante, & de la fidelité du courage invincible du grand Vincent de Pavl, qui fait aujourd'huy l'étonnement de vos efprits; & que fera à l'advenir l'admiration de tous les fiècles dans l'Eglife de Dieu. Et c'eft icy où il faut abreger, en attendant que l'Histoire de fa Vie en dife davantage, & qu'il faut paffer du recit de quelques pratiques de fon humilité, à celuy de quelques effets de fon amour & de fa charité: & ce fera la feconde & la derniere Partie du difcours.

II. PARTIE.

Sa Charité

Il faut donc dire avec liberté, oüy Meſſieurs, Vincent de Pavl nous donne lieu de vous dire, que le zele du grand ſaint Paul, ſemble avoir eſté l'objet de l'imitation de Vincent de Pavl. C'eſt ce digne Superieur General de la Miſſion, qui a eſté le veritable imitateur du grand Apoſtre, & qui a peû dire avec luy; *Quis nos ſeparabit à charitate Chriſti? Certus ſum enim quia neque mors, neque vita, &c. (ad Rom. 8.) O animam furentem inſania,* dit ſaint Iean Chryſoſtome, *ſed quæ ſobrietatem pariat!* Vincent de Pavl, ie vous en dis de meſme: Ne doit-il pas dire avec l'Apoſtre, *Quis infirmatur, & ego non infirmor?* Fut-il jamais vne ſeule occaſion de ſecourir les affligez, qu'il ne l'ait embraſſée tendrement? Mais que dis-ie, qu'il n'ait couru au devant avec vne chaleur extréme? On peut dire du luy, ſans exagerer la matiere, ce que ſaint Hieroſme diſoit de Fabiole; *Morbos in tanta miſerorum oblectamenta commutavit, vt multi ſani languentibus inviderent.* Ie ne vous parle point de trois ou quatre hoſpitaux qu'il a fait établir dans Paris; ny de ceux qu'il a étably dans les Provinces; ce diſcours ſeroit infiny.

Ie le regarde ſeulement dans les galeres en deux manieres; premierement, lors tque faiſant voyage ſur mer, il fut pris par des Pirates, & mis à la chaîne avec pluſieurs autres perſonnes qui eſtoient avec luy dans ce meſme vaiſſeau: on les mene à Tunis, & on joint ce jenue eſclave avec d'autres, leſquels pour eſtre compagnons de ſa peine, ne l'eſtoient pas de ſa vertu: parmy tant de captifs, ils ſe trouverent quelques perſonnes aſſez libres, pour admirer la modeſtie, la douceur, la patience, & mille autres qualitez tres-aimables, en la perſonne de Vincent de Pavl: Si les vns accuſent le ſort d'vn traitement ſi rigoureux qu'eſt celuy qu'ils endurent, Vincent de Pavl ne reconnoît point d'autre deſtinée que la conduite de la divine Providence, à laquelle il ſe ſoumet avec amour: Les vns ſe plaignent & ſoupirent parmy tant de ſouffrances; & luy tout au contraire y trouve ſes delices, puiſque c'eſt vn Dieu qui l'ordonne. On en voit qui par des cris & des ſanglots témoignent l'amertume de la douleur qui leur ſaiſit le cœur, cependant que Vincent de Pavl chante les Cantiques de Sion, au milieu de cette Babylone. La femme de ſon Patron preſte l'oreille, lors qu'il chante les Pſeaumes de David; ſon cœur en eſt touché; elle s'adreſſe à son mary, & au lieu de luy porter la contagion du peché, comme fit noſtre premiere Mere au premier des humains & au premier des coupables, elle luy porta des paroles de vie bien plus heureuſement, en ſorte qu'au lieu de flater ſon crime, elle luy reproche la honte de ſon apoſtaſie, & en meſme temps luy met devant les yeux l'exemple de la conſtance & de la pieté de cét amiable captif. C'en eſt fait, voicy l'ouvrage des prieres & de la charité de Vincent de Pavl; il ménagea ſi bien l'affaire avec ſon Patron, & quelques autres de ſa ſuite, qu'il les rendit capables d'aborder Avignon, où ils renoncerent à l'Alcoran, & se rangerent dans le ſein de l'Eglise: Voila, l'vne des premieres conqueſtes de Vincent de Pavl, voila des preludes de ces gands butins qu'il devoit faire vn jour dans les Miſſions. dans leſquelles il a depuis retiré tant d'ames du naufrage & de l'eſclavage, pour les gagner à Dieu.

Secondement, je le considere qui regarde les ſouffrances des forçats dans les Galeres de Marseille, & qui ne peut enviſager leurs miſeres, ny beaucòup moins en faire le recit à ces Dames charitables qui les ont ſecouru, qu'il net fut tout baigné de ſes larmes: Il les expoſoit à vos yeux, Mes-dames, tous couverts de vermine & tous mangez des vers: & pour lors il ſemble qu'il pouvoit dire avec Iob, *Putredini dixi, Pater meus*, & *Soror mea vermibus:* Il ſembloit vouloir careſſer ces pauvres qui n'eſtoient qu'vne maſſe de pourriture & les vers euſſent eſté ſes freres & ſes ſœurs. Le voyez-vous ce cœur debonnaire, dans le milieu de ſes exhortations toutes ferventes; au milieu de ſes entretiens ſpirituels, & de ſes conferences toutes embrazées du feu de ſa charité, qui eſt constraint de s'interrompre ſoy-meſme? Eſtoit-ce la violence de ſon amour, ou la tendreſſe de ſa compassion, qui ſembloit luy vouloir impoſer le silence, & qui le rendoit plus eloquent, lors qu'il eſtoit muet? O divine miſericorde du chaſte cœur de Iesus Christ mon Sauveur, qui avez allumé tant de flammes celuy de Vincent de Pavl, expliquez-nous ces myſteres. La parole tarit dans ſa bouche preſſé qu'il eſt de douleur & d'amour, sur le ſpectacle de la miſere de ce cher prochain, qui luy eſt bien plus cher que la vie; & en meſme temps on voit naitre vne source de larmes qui coule de ſes yeux: *Interdum lachrymæ pondera vocis habent.*

Ses yeux s'expliquent eloquemment au defaut de ſa voix; & en meſme temps, Mes-Dames, vous demeurez d'accord qu'vn ſeul de ſes ſoûpirs vaut dix piſtoles aux pauvres: vous ouvrez vos bourſes avec largeſſe; ſes larmes ſont naiſtre les voſtres; vous joignez les ſentimens de vos bon cœurs à la compaſſion du ſien: & puis, que devez-vous attendre, Meſſieurs, d'vn mélange ſi innocent & ſi divin, de tant de feux, & de tant de larmes?

Ie laiſſe à part ce que noſtre grande Reyne, Mere de noſtre grand Roy, a fait en ces occasions, la part qu'elle a au merite de ſes grandes aumoſnes; Sa modeſtie en ce rencontre m'impoſe le ſilence. Mais je dois dire, qu'vne ſeule personne de la Maiſon de Monſieur Vincent a fait cinquante-trois voyages dans la Lorraine, & y a porté prés de quinze cens mille livres, ſans jamais eſtre volé: qu'il a paſſé au milieu des gens de guerre, ſans rien perdre, tout ſeul chargé de vingt mille francs à chaque voyage; & fouvent portant de plus grandes fommes, n'ayant point d'autre efcorte que les prieres & la charité de celuy qui l'envoye.

Ie ne vous dis point la quantité d'estoffes & d'habits qu'il a fait paſſer dans la Lorraine, pour fecourir tant d'honneſtes filles, pour reveſtir tant de bonnes Religieufes, lefquelles après avoir fouffert vne pauvreté extréme, fe trouvoient enfin parées de la robe nuptiale, puis qu'elles portoient la livrée de la charité, qui est l'époufe des ames faintes, & la Reyne de toutes les vertus, Faut-il vous cacher, Meſſieurs, qu'vn des fujets de ce grand Miſſionnaire, a porté plus de huict mille paires d'habits dans vne autre province? Qu'vn autre a fait paſſer par fes mefmes foins dans vne autre frontiere, plus de cinq cent millivres pour en faire part à tous les miferables? Non, non, Meſſieurs, il n'eſt plus temps de tenir des hiſtoires fecretes; au contraire vous le devez fçavoir, Que Monſieur Vincent a fourny des hommes & de l'argent pour nettoyer les fumiers, les cloaques, les voiries des chevaux morts qui caufoient vne infection mortelle dans la ville d'Eſtampes; Qu'il en a fait des mefme après la bataille de Retel, en procuranr la fepulture à douze ou quinze cent corps morts, qui faifoient vne puanteur infupportable, & commençoient à caufer vne mortalité generale, qui eut achevé la ruïne entiere de ces triſtes contrées.

Mais, Meſſieurs, la charité de ce digne Inſtituteur & Premier General de la Miſſion, a bien d'autres characters d'vne charité confommée, comme eſtoit celle du grand saint Paul, dont il porte le nom. Il ne feroit jamais fatisfait de fon zele, s'il ne fe dépoüilloit foy-mefme, pour eſtre prodigue envers les affligez: S'il ne pouvoit dire avec faint Paul, lors qu'il écrivoit à ceux de Corinthe: *Os noſtrum patet at vos, ô Corinthij, cor nostrum dilatatum, & (2 Cor. 6.)* ou bien avec le mefme Apoſtre au chapitre 12. *Nec enim decent filij parentibus thefaurizare, fed parentes filijs: Ego autem libentiſſime impendam & fuperimpendar.*

Vous avez fçeu, Meſſieurs, que ces grands débordemens des rivieres, qui fembloient faire vn deluge aux portes de Paris, & dans la ville & dans la campagne, avoient reduit des villages entiers à la faim; mais vous n'avez pas fçeu qu'on vous a caché jufqu'à prefent avec tant de foin. Oüy, Meſſieurs, il faut vous le dire: Monſieur Vincent fit ouvrir les greniers de fa Maifon de faint Lazare, où il n'avoir de bled qu'autant qu'il eſtoit neceſſaire pour la fubfiſtance de fa famille aſſez nombreufe; il fit faire des pains en quantité, dont il fit remplir des charetes, que l'on déchargeoit en fuite dans des bateaux, & puis avec vne échelle, on portoit le pain dans les feneſtres des étages d'enhaut, ou ces pauvres refugiez, preſſez en mefme temps des eaües & de la faim, attendoient le dernier naufrage dans leurs propres maifons: Il expofa la vie de fes bons domeftiques, qui plufieurs fois fe trouverent en danger d'eftre noyez, en voulant fauver les autres.

Ie ne vous ay pas dit que dans la ville de Toul ces bons Miſſionaires, animez de l'efprit de leur General, fouffrirent beaucoup dans la neceſſité publique, & neantmoins ils ne voulurent jamais prendre part aux aumofnes qu'eux mémes & leurs freres diftribuoient aux autres. Ne devoient-ils pas, Meſſieurs, y prendre tout au moins vne double part? *Dignus eſt operarius mercede fua: L'ouvrier n'eſt-il pas digne de recompenfe? (1 Timot. 5. 18.)* Celuy qui fert à l'Autel ne doit-il pas pretendre fa fubfiftance du miniftere de l'Autel?

Oüy, Messieurs, fans doute cette conduite eft innocente, ces loix font legitimes: mais les mouvemens violens de l'ardente charité de Vincent de Pavl, ont bien d'autres maximes: *Ego autem libentiſſime impendam & fuperimpendar (2. Cor. 12. 15.)* difoit l'incomparable S. Paul; & vous dit encore aujourd'huy l'incomparable Vincent de Pavl: Vous avez fçeu les mouvemens de Paris; & moy qui eftois dans mon Dioceze, ie n'ay pas fçeu pour lors, & ne l'ay fçeu que depuis peu de jours, que Monfieur Vincent donna ordre que l'on diftribuaft le bled de S. Lazare, avec tant de profufion, qu'en ce rencontre il parût pluftoft vn prodigue, qu'vn pere de famille. Et quoy! Vincent de Pavl voftre Famille eft fi nombreufe, vous l'avez endebtée par tant de precedentes aumônes, ajuftez voftre prudence à voftre charité, voyez ce que vos greniers peuvent fournir; il n'importe, Meſſieurs, fa charité eft mieux fournie que tous ces magazins. Il fit fi bien, que durant l'efpace de trois mois, on nourriſſoit tous les jours, avec quatre vingts dix grands pains de braſſée, deux mille pauvres, & quelquefois jufqu'à trois milles & trois mille cinq cens par jour, à la porte de saint Lazare. *Difperfit, dedit pauperibus iuftitia ejus manet en fæculum fæculi. (Pfal. III.)* Et ce qui eft admirable, c'eft que la paix fe fit, lors que le bled manqua.

Adorable Providence de mon Dieu! qui tenez dans vos mains l'abondance & la fterilité; qui partagez voftre conduit entre les châtimens de voftre justice & les faveurs de vos mifericordes; qui conduifez aux portes de la mort, & qui retirez du tombeau; ne femble-t-il pas que vous vouliez renouveller les miracles du grand Propehte Helie, pour honorer la vertu du grand Vincent de Pavl? Vn vefve charitable a nourri le Prophete avec vn peu d'huile & vn peu de farine, & pour recompenfe d'vne liberalité qui parôit fi legere, elle merite qu'Helie luy prononce ces agreables paroles & de la part de Dieu: *Hæc autem dicit Dominus Deus Ifraël: Hydria farinæ non deficiet, nec lecythus olei minuetur, ufque ad diem in qua Dominus daturus eft pluviam fuper faciem terræ.* Ne vous femble-t-il pas, Meſſieurs, qu'on en peut dire de méme charitable Vincent de Pavl? Allez hardiment charitable Pere des pauvres, ouvrez vos greniers, foulagez dans voſtre maison de Saint Lazare deux & trois mille cinq cens affamez, & les nourriſſez tous les jours durant l'eſpace de plusieurs mois; *Hyrdria farinæ non deficiet, nec lecythus olei minuetur,* vos magazins ne ſe vuideroint point, que lors que par le merite de vos prieres, de vos aumônes, & de vos penitences, vous aurez fait ceſſer les troubles de Paris, vous aurez attiré l'abondance ſur cette grande Ville, & la benediction du Ciel ſur toute voſtre famille.

N'eſtoient-ce pas, Meſſieurs, de tres-heureux preſages de ſes profuſions, lors qu'eſtant jeune garçon, allant au moulin pour y porter du bled, qu'il prenoit dans le grenier de ſon pere, il en diſtribuoit la farine aux pauvres, avant que de r'entrer dans la maiſon de ſon pere? O l'aimable prodigue! ſi vn pere, au langage de ſaint Chryſologue, a trouvé dans ſon ſein, vn ſolliciteur domeſtique, pour ménager le pardon d'vn fils qu s'eſt perdu dans la débauche; que dirons-nous d'vn ſaint prodigue, qui ayan vécu ſur la terre prez d'vn ſiecle, comme dans vne terre étrangere, eſt enfin retourné dans le Ciel, comme nous l'eſperons, dans l'aimable ſejour de la celeſte patrie, pour y eſtre honnoré des careſſes du grand Pere de famille? *Citò proferte ſtolam primam.* Sans doute qu'il pouvoit dire avec Iob, dés ſa premiere jeuneſſe, *Ab infantia crevit mecum miſericordia.* Vous euſiez dit, examinant les mouvemens de ſa conduite, & les ſentimens de ſon cœur, que Dieu ne l'avoit crée que pour eſtre pauvre, & pour ſervir les pauvres; Nous ſommes aux pauvres, diſoit-il, les pauvres ſont à nous: vn chaſſeur ſuit ſon gibier par tout; en quelque lieu du monde que nous ſçachions des miſerables, il faut les ſecourir, deut-il nous en coûter la vie.

Voila, Meſſieurs, l'image d'vn cœur charitable au ſouverain degré de la parfaite charité du prochain; vn imitateur du cœur de Dieu, pour anſi dire, qui embraſſe tout & ne refuſe rien; *Eſtote miſericordes, ſicut & pater veſter cæliſtis miſericors eſt.* Dites-luy qu'il metttra ſes freres à l'aumône, s'il n'eſtablit quelque regle d'œconomie, & ſ'il ne considere les domeſtiques de ſa famille par preference aux étrangeres: Non, non, Meſſieurs, ces menaces ſont inutiles pour arreſter la cours de ſes profuſions: Ce qui pourroit donner de la crainte à vn moindre courage; c'eſt ce qui fait l'objet de ſes eſperances, & la matiere de ſes delices. *Ayons ſoin,* diſoit-il, *des affaires de Dieu, & Dieu ſans doute, aura bien ſoin des noſtres. Qu'importe,* diſoit-il, *que nous ſoyons des gueux, pourveu que nous ſoyons aſſez heureux pour ſoulager les pauvres?*

Sa confiance en la Providence.

Vn soir, on luy vient dire, qu'il n'y avoit pas dequoy fournir le refectoire pour le dîner du lendemain; *Ah, mon frere,* répondit-il, *l'heureuse nouvelle! puis qu'elle nous donne sujet d'établir noftre confiance uniquement en Dieu. Iacta cogitatum tuum in Domino, & ipse te enutriet. (Ps. 54. 25.)* Sa confiance ne fut point vaine, le foir mefme on luy apporta vne fomme notable en aumône. Reprefentez-vous vn homme qui a vne grande Communauté fur les bras, qui donne d'extraordinaire gratuitement la nourriture fpirituelle & temporelle, à vingt & trente perfonnes par jour lefquelles durant les cours de l'année, tantoft les vns, tantoft les autres rempliffent fa maifon, pour y faire les Exercices fpirituels, les Retraites, & les Confeffions generales: I'ay veu environ cent ou fix vingt jeunes hommes dix jours durant, lors qu'en eftant prié par feu Monfieur VINCENT, je faifois les Entretiens fpirituels à ceux qui fe preparoient pour recevoir les Ordres; & au bout de dix jours, après que toutes ces perfonnes avoient efté entretenuës aux frais & aux dépens de la Maifon de faint Lazare fans aucune foundation, pour ce charitable employ, Monfieur VINCENT & ces bons Meffieurs de faint Lazare remercioient Meffieurs les Ordinands comme f'ils en euffent receu des thresors: vous euffiez dit que de toutes parts on venoit fondre dans le cœur de ce charitable Pere, pour en tirer du fecours: On pouvoit dire de luy à plus jufte titre, ce que Valere le grand difoit de Gillias; *que fa maifon fembloit eftre la boutique de la munificence: il fembloit n'eftre pas vn mortel; mais le fein bening & bien faifant de la mefme fortune. (Valer. Max. lib. c.8.)*

Charité defintereffée.

Quelle charité plus defintereffée? *Non quærit fua funt:* Iamais ne faire vn pas, ny dire vne parole pour acquerir du bien. Iamais n'avoir la penfée de procurer le moindre benefice à pas vn des feins, ayant neanmoins des occafions fi favorables dans les mains. *Ie n'irois pas jufqu'au ruiffeau* (difoit-il vn jour) *en eftant à quatre pas, pour procurer du bien pour nous:* Endebter fa maifon jusques dans l'excez, pour ne jamais refufer de pratiquer vne bonne œuvre, fi toft qu'il voyoit la moindre ouverture, pour en ménager l'occafion. *Qui poft aurum abijt nec fperavit in pecuniæ thefauris; Quis eft hic & laudabimus eum?* Ah combien d'hiftoires agreables aurois-je à vous dire, fi j'en avois le temps, des charitable fecours qu'il a donné à des creatures toutes perduës d'vlceres & de pourriture qu'il mettoit dans ce petit caroce (qu'il appelloit fon infamie, par vn étrange terme de fon humilité) pour les conduire au port du falut? *Hi in curribus & hi in equis, nos autem in nomine Dei noftri invocabimus. (Pfal. 19. v. 8,)*

Vne charité confommé qui n'a point de limites; fon cœur eſt comme vne vaſte mer: *Omnia flumina intrant in mare, & mare non redundat (Eccl. 1, v. 9.)* Tout y entre, & tout y eſt receu; tout y eſt noyé dans les deluge de ſes bien-faits: En tout temps, en tous lieux: Toute ſorte de perſonnes: Le Barbare & le Scyte, le Iuif & l'infidel; le juſte & le pecheur.

I'ay bien connu des Serviteurs de Dieu; mais jamais je n'ay rien veu de pareil à ces deux grands Serviteurs de Dieu, feu Monſieur l'Abbé Ollier, & feu Monſieur VINCENT, que l'eminence de leurs vertus avoit parfaitement vnis, par les liens ſacrez d'vne ſainte & parfaite amitié: C'eſt qu'eſtant ſurchargez d'affaires, & toutes affaires importantes à la gloire de Dieu, ſi toſt que l'on demandoit leurs ſecours, vous euſſiez dit que toutes les affaires ceſſoient, & qu'ils n'avoient plus rien à faire, ſinon de conſoler voſtre cœur affligé. Avez-vous quelque peine extraordinaire ou d'eſprit ou de corps? addreſſez-vous à Monſieur VINCENT ou à M. l'Abbé Ollier; & je diray de l'vn & de l'autre ce que ſaint Anſelme & Theophylacte diſoient de ſaint Paul: *Patitur ſuas & ſimul aliorum infirmitates tolerat & ſolatur: tolerat infirmitates ſingulorum, & ſimul de communi ſalute & de toto orbe ſolicitus est.* Il ſouffre ſes peines, & en meſme temps il a ſoin de ſoulager celles de toute le monde.

Combien de fois a t-on dit en ſortant de leur converſation; *Nonne cor noſtrum ardens erat in nobis dum loqueretur in via? (Luc 24.33)* Combien de fois a-t-on dit, en adorant l'infinie bonté de noſtre Dieu? O que le cœur de Dieu eſt bon! ô que le cœur de Dieu eſt amiable; puis qu'il a formé de ſi bons courages, puis qu'il a logé de ſi bons cœurs dans la poictrine des hommes! L'vn eſtoit le fils ſpirituel, & l'autre eſtoit le pere.

Monſieur VINCENT avoit eſté comme le premier Directeur de Monſieur l'Abbé Ollier; & Monſieur l'Abbé Ollier l'appelloit ſon pere. Apres cette premiere conduite, le Pere de Condran, General des Peres de l'Oratoire fut auſſi Directeur de ce jeune Abbé: il falloit ſans doute deux grands maiſtres de la vie ſpirituelle, pour former ce grand ſujet. & le rendre capable des plus hautes maximes de la perfection; puiſque la Providence de Dieu s'en vouloit ſervir pour établir ce beau Seminaire de ſaint Sulpice, & pour le rendre luy-meſme tel qu'il a paru depuis dans la ſuite du temps, vn Pere & vn Maiſtre de tant de vertueux Eccleſiaſtiques, qui maintenant à l'heure que je parle, travaillent dedans nos Diocezes avec abondance de graces & de benedictions; & l'on peut dire que Monſieur VINCENT a eſté en quelque façon le premier, qui a jetté les precieuſes ſemences de ces riches moiſſons: ſans parler des Seminaires des Bons-Enfans, proche la porte Saint Victor, de Saint Charles proche de S. Lazare, pour les jeunes gens, du Seminaires d'Anneſſy en Savoye, pour l'examen des Ordinands, & de tant d'autres établiſſemens; les vns plus petits, les autres plus grands; les vns pour la jeuneſſe, les autres pour les perſonnes plus avancées dans l'aage. Et tout cela par les mouvemens de ſon zele & de ſa charité.

Pardon des iniures.

Charité qui n'avoit point de bornes: Comme il eſtoit prodigue de ſes benfaits; il eſtoit inſatiable à ſouffrir les injures, & à rendre le bien pour le mal. Vn jour, en preſence de feu Madame la Marquiſe de Maignelet, de tres-ſainte memoire, il exhortoit vne jeune Damoiſelle à changer de vie: Cette creature emportée ne voulant point fléchir ſous ſes ſaintes remonſtrances, au lieu de rendre graces à la charité de ſon bienfaiteur, elle luy jetta vn ſiege à la teſte: Monſieur VINCENT recut cet outrage avec vn agreable ſouris, en continuant son diſcours ſans changer de viſage ny de langage.

Vne autrefois, vne perſonne de qualité, qui crut qu'il avoit reſiſté à la pretention qu'il avoit d'avoir vn benefice, luy chanta des injures atroces, qu'il receut avec vne douceur extréme. La Reyne Mere en fut avertie, & voulut faire ſortir de la Cour, celuy qu en avoit ſi mal vsé. Monſieur VINCENT se met à genoux devant Sa Majeſté pour obtenir ſa grace. Vn jour, qu'à cause de la grande incommodité de ſes jambes, il eſtoit monté ſur ce méchant cheval qui avoit vingt-quatre ans; vn homme qui avoit beu, le voyant paſſer dans la rüe, luy dit toutes les injures que la chaleur du vin, & la fureur d'vn eſprit égaré luy peurent fournir: Monſieur VINCENT met pied à terre, ſe donne le tort à ſoy-meſme en preſence de cét homme emporté, & luy demande pardon avec tant de civilité, que cét homme le lendemain au matin vient trouver Monſieur VINCENT, reconnoit ſa faute, fait la Retraite dans la Maiſon & aux dépens de Monſieur VINCENT, fait vne bonne Confeſſion, change de vie, & d'vn homme diſſolu, devient vn penitent, vn homme converty.

Gratitude

S'il avoit tant d'amour pour tous ſes enemis? Quelle charité pouvoit-il avoir pour ceux qui luy rendoient quelque office, ou au moindre des ſiens? Il eſtoit tout remply de l'eſprit & des maximes du Fils de Dieu, & pouvoit dire en quelque façon, comme le Sauveur de nos ames, *Quamdiu feciſtis vni ex his fratribus meis minimis, mihi feciſtis. (Matt. 25. 40.)*

Le moindre ombrage de plus leger office qu'il eut recue de vous, vous rendoit maiſtre de ſon cœur, de ſa personne, de tout ce qu'il pouvoit, de tout ce qu'il avoit. On feroit vn juſte volume des hiſtoires ſignalées de ſa generoſité

nompareille, & des reſſentimens immortels qu'il conſervoit pour tous ſes bien-
faicteurs. *Iamais*, diſoit-il, *les perſonnes fondées n'aurant aſſez de gratitude pour
leurs Fondateurs:* Telle eſtoit ſa pensée, ſa parole, ſon écrit, & ſa pratique. Vn
jour il écrivit ces paroles, qui ont eſté extraites d'vne des ſes Lettres: *Dieu nous a
fait la grace ces jours paſſez, d'offrir au Fondateur d'vne de nos Maiſons, le bien
qu'il nous à donné; parce qu'il me ſembloit qu'il en avoit beſoin: Il me ſemble
que s'il l'avoit accepté, que i'en aurois ſenty vne tres ſenſible consolation, & croy
qu'en ce cas ſa divine bonté ſe rendroit elle meſme noſtre fondatrice, & que rien
ne nous manqueroit. Et quand cela n'arriveroit pas, quel bon-heur, Monſieur, de
s'eſtre apauvry, pour accommoder celuy qui nous auroit fait du bien? Dieu nous
a fait la grace d'en vſer vne fois de la ſorte; & j'en ay vne conſolation toutes les
fois que j'y penſe, que ie ne vous ſçaurois exprimer.*

Charité heroïque.

Enfin la Providence de Dieu, qui avoit des grands deſſeins sur la perſonne
de ce grand homme, vouloit de luy vne charité heroïque, pour en faire vn paſteur
des ames. Le Fils de Dieu, voulant confier le ſoin de ſon Egliſe à S. Pierre, luy
demanda, *Simon Ioannis, diligis me plus his? (Ioan. 21.15.)* m'aimez-vous plus
que Thomas, que Nathanaël, que Iacques & Iean, & que les deux autres Diſciples
qui alloient enſemble à la peſche? Vous ſçavez la réponſe que fit le Prince des
Apoſtres; Seigneur, vous ſçavez que ie vous aime: & pour lors le Fils de Dieu luy
dit, après pluſieurs demandes & pluſieurs réponſes; *Pais mes agneaux, & pais
mes oüailles.*

Voila Meſſieurs de ſouverain periode de l'amour, que nous avons pour la
Fils de Dieu; s'eſt d'aimer ſon troupeau, c'eſt d'aimer ſon Eglise. Pourquoy cela,
Meſſieurs? Parce que c'eſt luy qui par excellence, prend la qualité tres-aimable
de Paſteur de nos ames. Saint Gregoire de Nazianze en l'Oraiſon 41. le nomme
τοῦ ἀληθινοῦ καὶ πρώτου ποιμένος. *(Lib. 1. Ep 135.) Le veritable & le premier
Paſteur.* S. Isidore l'appelle ποιμανγίκης ἡγεμων, *le Capitaine de l'art paſtoral,
(Lib. 1. Pædag. C. 6.)* & S. Clement Alexandrin, Ποιμὴν ἀρνῶν βασιλικῶν,
le Paſteur des agneaux du troupeau Royal; S. Pierre l'appelle *Paſtorem &
Epiſcopum animarum, le Paſteur & l'Eveſque des ames. (1 Pet. 1. ult).* Et au Ch.
5. *Principem paſtorum, le Prince des paſteurs;* Et S. Paul aux Hebreux Ch. 13.
v. 20. *Paſtorem magnum ovium. Le Grand Paſteur des brebis.* Et le Fils de Dieu
parlant de ſoy-meſme en ſaint Iean Ch. 10. dit ces paroles. *Ego ſum Paſtor bonus,
Ie ſuis le bon Paſteur.*

Demandez-vous quel eſt le charactere de cette qualité de Paſteur des ames?
la Charité. ſuivant ces paroles de ſaint Iean Climacus, *Verum Paſtorem charitas
demonſtrat: per charitatem enim Paſtor cruxifixus eſt, (Tract. de officio paſtoris*

in Pf. 37). ou bien de faint Basile; *fatis fit fcire Paftorem effe bonum, animam fuam pofuiffe pro ovibus: terminus hic fit divinæ cognitionis.*

C'est icy, Meffieurs, où nous devons dire, que la loüange que nous rendons à la memoire de Monfieur Vincent, eft bien folide & bien legitime, puis qu'il s'intereffe avec tant de zele, dans tous les befoins de l'Eglife de Dieu. *Cujus laus eft in Evangelio per omnes Ecclefias.*

Vous euffiez dit, Meffieurs, que rien ne pouvoit exciter la tristeffe ou la joye de ce grand cœur, que les avantages ou les difgraces de l'Eglife de Dieu, *De nullo gaudeam, vel doleam, nifi de eo quod ducit at te, vel abducit à te,* difoit faint Thomas d'Aquin parlant à Dieu tous les jours dans la ferveur de fes prieres: Difons-en de mefme de Vincent de Pavl, pour ce qui regarde les interefts de l'Eglife de Dieu. *Inftantia mea quotidiana, follicitudo omnium Ecclefiarum,* dit faint Paul; *(Cor. 11. v. 28.)* & tout de mefme Vincent de Pavl. *Incurfus meus quotidianus,* dit faint Augustin parlant du grand Apoftre: *Vrgentes omnium Ecclefiarum curæ,* dit S. Ambroise. S. Paul au milieu de fes chaifnes, au milieu des prifons, envoye fes Difciples pour embraffer le foin de toutes les Eglifes; Crefcent en Galatie, Tite à Crete en Dalmatie, Tychichus à Ephefe, Marc & d'autres en differens endroits: Vincent de Pavl envoye des fujets de fa famille en Lorraine, quelque autres dans la Champagne & dans la Picardie: les vns dans la Barbarie, les autres dans la Pologne: Il envoya par diverfes fois plufieurs de fes Preftres en l'Ifle de Madagascar, dont il en mourut fix: il en fit embarquer trois autres fur vn vaiffeau, qui fit naufrage au port: quelque temps apres, il en fit embarquer quatre autres dans vn autre navire, qui fut pris des Efpagnols. Qui est-ce n'auroit perdu le courage après tant de morts, tant de mauvais fuccez, après tant de naufrages? Mais luy tout au contraire, a vn zele Apostolique, à l'épreuve des contradictions qui pourroient rebuter vn plus foible courage. Il difoit que l'Eglife vniverfelle a efté établie par le Mort du Fils de Dieu, confirmée par celle des Apoftres, des Papes, & des Evéques Martyrs: Qu'elle s'est multipliée & affermie par la perfecution; & que le fang des Martyrs a efté la femence des Chrêtiens. *(Tertull.)* Il eftoit affeuré d'ailleurs que ces peuples eftoient difposez à recevoir les lumieres de l'Evangile, & qu'vn grand nombre des habitans de ces Ifles, avoient déja recue le Baptefme par les travaux d'vn feul de ces Miffionaires, qui Dieu y avoit confervé, & qui feul eftoit refté parmy tant de morts dont nous avons parlé. Pensez-vous, Meffieurs, qu'il puiffe abandoner ce Preftre qui demande fecours? Penferiez-vous qu'il pêut abandonner ce peuple qui tend les bras pour recevoir l'instruction, & qui déja ouvre le cœur & les aureilles pour écouter les paroles de vie? Non, non, Meffieurs, nous n'avons rien à craindre: O qu'il n'a garde d'abandoner les ames:

Da mihi animas, cætera tolle tibi: (Genes. 14. v. 21).

O que fon cœur eft trop vafte & trop genereux, pour ne pas vaincre tous les obftacles, qui s'opposent à fes deffeins Apoftolics. Il envoya au commencement de céte année 1660. cinq de fes enfans, en céte Ifle éloignée.

Sur quoy, Meffieurs, nous remarquons trois chofes. La premiere, qu'en matiere de Miffion, d'employ, ou d'établiffement, foit qu'il fut vtile, foit qu'il fut honorable, il en quittoit la place, la gloire, & tous les avantages, à toute autre perfonne qu'il eut trouvé dans vn mefme deffein. O que de belles hiftoires il faut paffer fous filence en céte occafion?

La fecond, qu'il envoyoit jamais perfonne dans la Barbarie, ny dans d'autres perils, que ceux-là mefme qu'il y envoyoit ne l'en euffent inftamment follicité.

La troifiéme qu'il portoit l'efprit du martyre en toutes ces rencontres; qu'il entroit en efprit par fes vœux & par fes fouhaits, dans tous les travaux de ceux qu'il envoyoit; & eut fouhaité de pouvoir foulager leurs peines, aux dépens de fon sang & de fa vie.

Il me femble que nous luy devons appliquer les paroles d'vn Pere de L'Eglife parlant de fainte Felicité mere de sept marytrs, puifqu'aujourd'huy nous en faifons la feste, laquelle fept fois endura le martyre en la perfonne de fes enfans, auparavant que de l'endurer en la fienne. Dirons-nous pas de luy, ce que la fainte Eglife dit du glorieux faint Martin, *O fanctiffima anima! quam etfi gladius perfecutoris non abftulit, palmam tamen martyrij non amifit.*

Il faudroit icy, Meffieurs, vous dire au moins quelque chofe des grandes qualitez qui compofent celle d'vn vray Pafteur des ames; d'vn tres-digne Superieur General des Preftres de la Miffion. Mais l'on peut dire que le temps eft trop court pour vne fi vafte matiere. On vous a parlé quoy que trop legerement, de l'amour qu'il avoit pour les fiens; mais il faudroit vous entretenir, de la patience, de la vigilance, & de la conftance qu'il avoit dans ces penible emplois.

Sa patience.

Sa patience admirable, & dans les pratiques de la mortification, & dans le fupport du prochain.

Vne austerité de vie, au delà de toutes les mesures ordinaires de plus rigoureufe penitence.

Six vingt coups de difcipline tous les matins & davantage: ne pas manquer vn jeûne d'Eglife à l'âge de plus de quatre vingts ans: ne vouloir jamais la moindre delicateffe en fa nourriture, & mefme en fes maladies; mais au contraire, demander les reftes de la table. I'en fçay des hiftoires admirables, que j'ay veu de mes yeux. Coucher sur vne paillaſſe, & meſme dans les maladies; ne pas perdre l'Oraiſon Mentale dans l'ardeur de la fiévre. Il pouvoit dire en deux manieres bien differentes: *In meditatione mea exardeſcet iginis (Pſ. 38. 4.)* le feu de la fiévre & celuy de ſa devotion. Trois heures de ſuite à genoux tous les matins dans l'Egliſe, nonobſtant les playes & les douleurs de ſes jambes. Paroître dans le Conſeil du Roy plus pauvrement & plus chetifvement veſtu qu'il n'eſtoit pas auparavant, noſtre grand Cardinal y a pris garde, & l'a fait remarquer à d'autres. *Qui in domibus Regum ſunt, mollibus veſtiuntur. (Matt 11. 8.)* Vincent de Pavl voſtre eſprit de penitence & de pauvreté fait icy vne exception qui n'eſt pas ordinaire. Saint Gregoire de Nice a dit bien à propos, qu'vn Superieur étably en authorité au deſſus des autres, doit porter la plus grande charge du fardeau, Δεῖ γὰρ ἐν τῇ ἐπιστασίᾳ] μείζονα μὲν τῶν ἄλλων τοὺς προεστῶτας πονεῖν *(Tract. de ſcopo Chrtſtiani.)* On n'a garde de reprocher à ce digne Superieur General de la Miſſion, ce que diſoit ſaint Leon: *Beſtiæ irruunt, & ovium ſepta non claudunt.* Il prend les clefs à la main, cependant que le Frere Portier prend ſa refection. Et ſi cét employ vous choque en la perſonne d'vn General, il s'en va laver les écuelles dans les bas offices d'vne cuiſine, & vous n'en verrez rien.

Penitence pur autruy.

Mais de faire penitence pour les fautes d'autruy, & meſme pour des perſonnes eſtrangeres: demander à noſtre Seigneur, qui exauça ſa priere, que pour ſoulager vn de ſes penitens, qui eſtoit travaillé d'vne violent tentation, il en fut attaqué luy-meſme durant quelque années. Mais ſçachant le peché d'vn autre, dire à vne perſonne de confiance, il faut qu'il en couſte à mon corps, & en faire vne rude penitence; où trouve-t-on des exemples d'vne vertu ſi rare? où trouve-t-on des Paſteurs animez de ce zele? Sans doute qu'il pouvoit dire à l'exemple du ſouverain Paſteur de nos ames; *Quæ non rapui tunc exolvebam (Pſal. 68. v. 5.)* C'eſt vn homme Apoſtolique, vn imitateur de S. Paul, qui ſemble vouloir eſtre anathéme pour ſes freres. *Bonus paſtor animam ſuam dat pro ovibus ſuis.*

Support du prochain.

Que dirons-nous du ſupport du prochain? vne personne le preſſe de luy quelque chose que Monſieur Vincent luy refuſe par principe de conſcience: qu'arrive-t-il, Meſſieurs? Cét homme importune Monſieur Vincent par de tres-frequentes & tres-inutiles viſites; Monſieur Vincent le reçoit avec vn viſage content, ſans jamais ſe pleindre d'vne importunité ſi extreme, qui ſembloit eſtre inſupportable à tout autre qu'à luy.

Souffrir les calomnies.

Mais fouffrir les noires calomnies fans s'excufer & fans vouloir ouvrir la bouche pour fe justifier, *ficut mutus non habens in ore fuo redargutiones (Pfal. 37. v. 14.)* Beaucoup moin vouloir fouffrir, qu'on fit connoistre qui eftoit le coulpable; ô rigoureufe modeftie! ô neceffité du filence! ie refpecte vos Loix, lefquelles neantmoins en cét endroit me femblent bien cruelles: Paffons outre, Meffieurs, fans nous expliquer davantage.

La vigilance d'vn Pafteur, doit eftre l'ame de fa conduite: S. Antiochus homil. III, dit ces belles paroles: Ὀφείλει οὖν ὁ ποιμὴν ὅλος νοῦς καὶ ὀφθαλμὸς εἶναι. Que le Pafteur doit eftre tout efprit & tout œil. Ah! c'est icy, Meffieurs, où nous pouvons dire de noftre General de la Miffion: *Non dormitabit neque dormiet qui cuftodit Ifraël. (Pfal. 120. v. 4.)* Ou bien avec vn autre Prophete, *Virgam vigilantem ego video. (Ierem. 1. p. 11.)* Oüy fans doute, il pouvoit dire de foy-mefme, ce que Iacob difoit, paiffant les troupeaux de fon beau pere Laban: *Die noctuque œftu vrebar & gelu: fugiebatque fomnus ab oculis meis.* Puis qu'il eft vray, que fe levant tous les jours à quatre heures, & fe couchant tous les jours bien plus tard ques les autres, il déroboit à fon fommeil ces precieux momens qu'il donnot au foin des ames de fon cher troupeau.

Sa force & conftance.

Sa force & fa conftance meriteroit icy vn nouveau difcours. On loüe la vertu, en quelque temps qu'on la trouve. Mais de trouver vne vertu consommé, durant l'efpace prefque d'vn fiecle; durant le cours d'vne vie de quatre vingt cinq ans; fans relâche, fans interruption; avoir encor couché fur la paillaiffe la veille de fa mort. *Oportet ftantem Imperatorem mori.* Quelle ame affez froide, n'aura pas quelque chaleur d'eftime pour vn fi beau fujet?

Il faudroit avant que finir ce Difcours, vous faire voir avec quelle force de courage il nourriffoit les ames de ces trois excellentes nourritures que fainct Ambroise remarque dans l'Eglife de Dieu; Iesus-Christ méme, les Sacrements, & l'Efcriture: Quand il commença les Miffions, le propre jour de la Conuerfion de faint Paul, par vn tref-bon augure; ce fut premierement dans les terres de feu Madame Françoife Marguerite de Silly, époufe de Monfieur le Comte de Joigny, Chevalier des Ordres du Roy, pour lors General des Galeres de France, & à prefent Preftre de l'Oratoire. Cette fainte & vertueufe Dame, qui avoit Monfieur Vincent pour son Confeffeur & pour fon Directeur, & qui luy fit promettre de ne la point abandonner jufqu'à la mort, commença pour lors à fe rendre la premiere Fondatrice de la Miffion, & à procurer des Miffions dans toutes fes terres.

O l'agreable fpectacle! Qui faifoit naiftre la joye des Anges par la Converfion des pecheurs! vous euffiez veu Monfieur Vincent dan la chaire tout animé de zele pour le falut des ames, qui préchoit avec vne fi fainte vehemence de l'efprit de Dieu, qu'il fondoit en larmes, & touchoit tous les cœurs de ceux qui l'efcoutoient: vous euffiez veu vn commun deluge de larmes du Predicateur & de fes Auditeurs: On vient à luy de toutes parts; tout le monde l'aborde; tous les habitans d'vne Parroiffe font la Confeffion generale; les autres villages imitent cét exemple; les peuples ont recours à la Penitence, aux Sacremens, à la Parole de Dieu; on ne parle que de Converfions, on voit par tout des changemens de vie qui furprennent les plus indifferens & qui étonnent le plus opiniaftres; Monfieur Vincent infatigable dans fon travail ne fe rend point qu'il n'ait achevé fon ouvrage qu'il n'ait formé Iesus-Christ dans les cœurs; *Donec formetur Chriftus in vobis.* Et qu'il n'ait porté cette benediction dans l'Eglife de Dieu, d'avoir rendu les Confeffions generals plus frequentes que jamais, dans vn temps où à piene en connoiffoit-on l'vfage: C'est luy-méme qui a retiré les peuples de la profonde ignorance de nos myfteres, qui a donné les methods & les exemples à tant de dignes Ecclefiaftiques, & tant de grands Religieux, de donner les inftructions neceffaires aux Fidelles. C'eft luy qui a fait ce grand œuvre, que le faint Concile de Trente appelle, *Opus tam pium, & tant fanctum, vn œuvre fi pieux & fi faint,* en établiffant des Seminaires, pour former des fujets dans le Clergé, capables de reffentir le poids & la dignité de leur facré ministere.

Qui pourroit vous exprimer les mouvemens de fa Religion pour l'administration des Sacremens; & la maniere fimple, familiere, mais forte & puiffante, pour traiter refpectueufement la Parole de Dieu?

Le refpect merveilleux qu'il avoit pour les Preftres, voulant que les fiens fuffent les derniers de tous: la veneration profonde qu'il avoit pour les Ordres du Clergé, & pour les Cloîtres, & pour la Hierarchie; l'eftime qu'il faifoit de ces faintes Congregations, de ces Corps fi celebres, & de la Compagnie de Iesus, & de l'Oratoire de Iesus: De cecy j'en puis eftre temoin. De la liaifon qu'il avoit avec tous les grands Serviteurs de Dieu qui ont vécu de fon temps; C'eft tout dire en deux mots; que deux grandes lumieres de l'Eglife, Meffeigneurs les Cardinaux de la Rochefoucaut & de Berule, tres-fignalez par l'eminence de leur pieté, comme par celle de leur pourpre facrée, avoient vne tres-haute eftime pour les rares merites de feu Vincent de Pavl: Qui pourroit vous dire le grande parte qu'il avoit à toutes les grandes œuvres de fon fiecle, de la pluf-part defquelles il a jetté les premiers fondemens.

De vous parler de zele qu'il avoit pour maintenir la Pureté de la bonne doctrine, ce n'eft pas icy le temps de m'engager dans vn fi vafte fubjet: on peut dire feulement, qu'en cecy fa conduit femble avoir imité celle des Apoftres: Quelle plus raifonnable cenfure de toutes les nouveautez, que le refpect qu'il avoit pour les facrez Conciles, & pour les faints Canons? que le grand faint Leon appellée excellemment, *Canones fpiritu Dei conditos, & totius orbis reverentia confecratos.* Le Concile d'Attigni les appelle *Firmatos fpiritus Dei Canones.* Les Conciles les nomment, *Divinos Canones.* Petits efprits, qui vous rendez rebelles aux plus faintes Loix; enfans dénaturez, qui méprifez votre Mere la fainte Eglife, apprenez de faint Augustin, que le repete après faint Cypien; *Que celuy-la n'aura jamais Dieu pour Pere, qui n'a point l'Eglife pour Mere.* Apprenez de VINCENT DE PAVL, qui avoit folidement étudié en Theologie, & dans Paris, & dans Tholofe, & dans Rome, que c'eft faire vn injuste querelle à cette chafte Epoufe du Fils de Dieu, qui eft la Mere commune de tous les Chreftiens, de partager fon authorité, puis qu'elle eft également infaillible aujourd'huy comme au temps des Apoftres. *Ego vobifcum fum vfque ad confummationem fæculi.* La parole de noftre Divin Maistre y eft engagée; il en eft l'Efpoux; il l'anime de fon efprit; & l'animera toûjours, dans la fuite de tous les fiecles.

Quel refpect n'avoit-il pas pour l'authorité de noftre faint Pere? Dites-nous, VINCENT DE PAVL, que vous n'eftes qu'vn chetif Quatriéme; cachez-nous vos études; cachez-nous les lumieres de voftre fcience, & celles de voftre efprit, par vn excez d'humilité qui n'a rien de pareil; qu'vn Predicateur, qu'vn Miffionnaire, qu'vn General d'vne Congregation, à qui les talens de la doctrine & de la parole font neceffaires pour foûtenir fes employs, pour foûtenir vne loüable reputation, qui femble neceffaire pour ne pas rendre fes fonctions inutiles, veüille neantmoins paffer pour ignorant? Et moy, Messieurs, je fçay bien qu'en cette matiere, la Sorbonne la plus fçavante & la plus fainte Efcole du monde n'en fçait pas davantage.

Fléchir fous les orders du faint Siege, & reconnoiftre dans vne fincere foumission d'efprit l'authorité toute entiere du Vicaire de IESUS-CHRIST en la perfonne de celuy qui fuccede à S. Pierre: Combien de fouverains Pontifes f'en font autrefois expliquez? Entr'autres, Luc, Marc, Felix, Agathon, Nicolas I. Leon IX. Innocent III. & fur tout le grand faint Leon. Combien de Conciles en on parlé de mefme? Tous les Fideles ont reconnu les Successeurs de S. Pierre & les ont honnorez de ces beaux noms de *Maiftre de la Foy, Chef de l'Eglife, Pafteur vniverfel; Iuge des contreverfes, Docteur de tout l'vnivers.* Philippe Legat de faint Celeftin, dans le Concile d'Ephefe, eft approuvé de tous les Peres de cette fainte & illuftre Affemblée, quand il dit, que S. Pierre regle les matieres de la Foy en la perfonne de fes Succeffeurs, qu'en eux il eft vivant, & il vivra toûjours. Saint Ierome, l'vn des plus grands hommes du monde, fe foûmet aveuglement à la decifion du Pape, pour regler cette controverfe des premieres fiecles fi obfcure & fi difficile, touchant les hypofthafes. Saint Augustin, apres que le Pape a pronouncé fur les erreurs des Pelagiens; qu'il a confirmé deux Conciles d'Affrique, qui n'eftoient point œcumeniques, S. Augustin, dis je, conclud que la caufe eft finie, *caufa finta est.* C'eftoit vne doctrine, Meffieurs, qui charmoit le cœur de Monsieur VINCENT, tant il eftoit foûmis à l'Eglife, à noftre faint Pere, & aux Nonces du Pape; & lors qu'il avoit befoin d'vn confeil plus prompt fur certaines matieres, il confultoit les plus grands hommes de la Sorbonne, & fuivoit leur avis. En vn mot, il fuivoit en tout & part tout les maximes & la doctrine de l'Evangile, mais expliquée par l'efprit de l'Eglife, & non pas par celuy de l'ambition ou de la vanité. Il avoit parfaitement étudié ces paroles de faint Augustin: *Ego vero Evangelio non crederem, nifi me Ecclefiæ commoveret auctoritas. (Tom 6. Contra epift. Manichœi cap. 5.)*

Apres cela, Meffieurs, ne faut-il pas conclure; *Cujus laus eft in Evangelio per omnes Ecclefias.* Toutes les Eglifes prennent interest à honoré la memoire du grand VINCENT DE PAVL parce que l'on peut dire qu'il a honoré toutes les Eglifes, & a rendu fervice à toutes les Eglifes: Tous ces grands perfonnages, Meffieurs les Curez de Paris, fi celebres par leur doctrine & par leur vertu, n'ont-ils pas témoigné le refpect qu'ils avoient pour le memoire de ce grand homme: les vns ayant fait des Services pour luy dans leurs paroiffes; les autres fe difposant à faire quelque chofe de mefme; & tous d'vne commune voix élevant les merites de fa vie, jusques dan le Ciel; *Æqua enïm laus eft, laudari à laudatis & improbari ab improbis,* difoit Pïc de la Mirande. C'eft icy l'vn des endroits ou je n'acheve pas. Mais s'il eft vray, que la voix publique eft vne caution bien fidele du merite des plus grands hommes; qui eft celuy d'vn efprit raisonnable, & non preoccupé, qui peût trouver la moindre tache dans vn fi beau foleil? Meffieurs de faint Germain, dignes fujets de cettte Eglife Royalle, vous faites bien paroître voftre vertu par l'eftime que vous avez pour la fienne, ayant témoigné de fi bonne grace le desir que vous avez, que voftre Eglife fut choisie, parmy tant t'autres qui s'offroient pour le mefme deffein, pour fervir à l'action qui fe fait aujourd'huy.

Mais, Meffieurs, pouvons-nous sortir de la Chaire, & vous cacher vne verité fi confiderable, qu'eft celle je m'en va vous dire? Le Fils de Dieu qui a aimé fon

Eglife & fa Mere avec tant d'ardeur, ayant deux Apoftres quy luy étoient bien chers; S. Pierre & S. Iean; a confié le foin de fon Eglise à S. Pierre; & le foin de la plus fainte perfonne de fon Eglife, à saint Iean; c'eft à dire, fa tres-fainte Mere, que les Grecs ont nommé excellemment, παναγία, toute Sainte. Nous avons eu de nos jours vn Prelat d'vne eminente fainteté, le grand François de Sales, Evéque & Prince de Geneve; nous efperons fa Canonization dans peu de temps, fi Dieu benit nos vœux les plus ardents, & nos petits travaux: Il avoit deux trefors dans les mains qui luy eftoient bien chers; fon Eglife & fa Vifitation: non pas fa Mere, comme le Fils de Dieu; mais fes bonnes & fes faintes filles: Il confulte les Autels; il invoque le Ciel, il ne cherche que Dieu, dans tous fes deffeins; il faut qu'il rencontre deux hommes de grand choix, pour leur confier la conduit de ces deux grands trefors: il met le Dioceze de Geneve dans de tres dignes mains, fans m'expliquer davantage des qualitez de celuy qui va remplir sa place: & pour choifir vn Pere Spirituel à ces dignes filles de la Vifitation; dans Paris, dans la premiere & la plus belle ville du monde, il arrefte fon choix vniquement par preference à tout autre, fur la perfonne de Monfieur VINCENT; c'eft à dire fur vn excellente copie de cet parfait Original, fur vn homme remply de fes maximes, & de l'efprit de la Vifitation: c'eft à dire de l'efprit de toutes les vertus, & de plus heroïques vertus; de l'humilité, de la pureté, du parfait aneantiffement; du parfait mépris de foy-méme; de l'efprit d'Oraifon & de Retraite, de la vie cachée avec IESUS-CHRIST en Dieu; de l'vnion pure, fincere & cordiale avec Dieu, avec le prochain. Ah! ma chere Vifitation, de laquelle ie connois particulierement la Sainteté & les rare vertus, à laquelle j'ay des obligations immortelles, & au Pere de voftre faint Inftitut, & à voftre digne Mere de Chantal, & à tant d'auftres excellens fujets de ce faint Ordre; *Adhæreat lingua mea favcibus meis, fi non meminero tui, fi non propofuero Ierufalem in principio lœtitiæ meæ: Que ma langue f'attache à mon palais, fi ie manqué jamais à publier tes loüanges,* & nommément dans vn fi beau fujet; puis que le choix de VINCENT DE PAVL, qui t'a gouverné fi faintement depuis tant d'années, fait partie de ta gloire & de tes ornemens. Les Vierges, difoit faint Cyprien font vne illuftre portion du troupeau du Seigneur; & celles de la Vifitation ont fait vne notable partie des charitables employs de VINCENT DE PAVL, de ce digne Pafteur des ames.

Efin, la Perfeverance qu'vn Pere fpirituel doit avoir pour les interefts de l'Eglife, nous oblige de dire de noftre Superieur General de la Miffion; *Cujus laus eft in Evangelio per omnes Ecclefias.* Il embraffe les interefts de la fainte Eglife avec tant d'ardeur, qu'apres avoir fouvent confideré en la prefence de

Dieu, que l'esprit de l'Eglise est vn esprit de paix, que le vray Salomon pacifique, entrant dans le monde pour fonder son Eglise, fit cesser toutes les guerres qui avoient si long temps agité l'Empire Romain, & voulut que les Anges chantassent vn Cantique de paix; *Pax hominibus bonæ voluntatis. (Luc. 2. 14.)* Il prend vne constante resolution de s'offrir à nostre Seigneur, comme vne victime publique, pour obtenir la Paix: Il soûpire devant les Autels sur les malheurs que la guerre a causez dans le monde; Il considere qu'il est mal-aisé de prendre les armes, sans faire la guerre aux vertus; Que la guerre donne bien souvent la victoire au peché, & fait en mesme temps la ruïne de la pieté, & les playes de la Religion; Que les exercices du Christianisme sont presque éteints parmy la chaleur des combats; les Sacremens méprisez, les Autels profanez, les Prestres presque interdits des saintes fonctions de leur sacré ministere: *Filij matris meæ pugnaverunt contra me. (Cant. 1.5.)* Qui est-ce qui fera l'office du charitable Samaritain? Qui au moins donnera quelques larmes? Que appliquera l'huile & le vin sur les blessures de la sainte Eglise, plus profondes & plus cruelles, que celles de ce pauvre languissant sur le chemin de Iericho? Le voicy, Messieurs, c'est Vincent de Pavl: Il voit par le succez des Missions, qui se répandent en divers endroits du Royaume, que l'ignorance des peuples, & les pechez des Chrestiens augmentent tous les jours sous la licence des armes: qu'il est grand temps d'écarter le soldat de nos Parroisses, à moins que de declarer vne nouvelle guerre à l'Evangile & aux Autels: Il entreprend de traiter de la Paix avec Dieu: mais voicy de quelle maniere: Il entreprend vne neuvaine vn peu extraordinaire: Il fait communier durant le cours de neuf années, deux ou trois personnes tous les jours, chacun à son tour; vn Prestre dit la Messe, vn Frere communie à cette Messe, qu'on peut nommer la Messe de la Paix; & le Prestre & le Frere jeûnent ce méme jour: On voit vne petite table exprez dedans le Refectoire, qu'on appelle la table des jeûnans: Monsieur Vincent pour estre General d'vne Congregation, surchargé d'affaires, d'audiances, & de depéches, accablé de vieillesse, de douleurs, & d'infirmitez, ne veut point de dispense; il subit la même loy: Il fait son tour comme les autres; avec céte seule difference, que son tour arrive plus souvent qu'aux autres, & qu'il en fait deux fois plus que les autres. Enfin au bout de neuf années, la paix generale est concluë entre les deux Couronnes: On propose à Monsieur Vincent de finir cette pratique, qui ne peut estre qu'à grande charge à vne Communauté tres-occupée d'ailleurs, qui sans doute a bien d'autres employs. *Non, Messieurs & mes Freres,* dit-il, *allons jusques au bout, perseverons jusqu'à la fin, attendons que la Paix soit publiée, ne nous rendons jamais.*

De vous dire; Messieurs, qu'vn homme fi humble & fi aneanti; fi meffiant de foy-mefme; fi reglé dans toutes fes actions; fi prudent, que l'on peut dire que c'eftoit la Sageffe mefme; qui n'entreprenoit rien fans confulter la volonté de Dieu, se foit chargé de cette entreprife fans quelque movement extraordinaire de l'efprit de Dieu: c'eft à quoy je ne m'engage point; je vous laiffe la liberté de vos penfées & de vos jugèmens.

Mais de vous dire, Meffieurs, que la loüange de noftre grand Cardinal fe trouve en ce rencontre folidement établie; vous le voyez avec moy: ny vous, ny moy, ne fçaurions nous en taire. *Prolixa laudatio eft quæ non quæritur, fed tenetur,* dit S. Ambroise; c'eft vne grand loüange en peu de paroles, quand nous en tenons le fujet dans les mains, & qu'il n'eft pas befoin d'vne recherché forcée, ny d'vn fecours étranger, pour en trouver la matiere. Oüy, Meffieurs, la Paix generale, qui fait la gloire de noftre Monarchie, le repos de l'Efpagne, & la confolation de toute l'Europe, eft l'ouvrage des Confeils, & des Veilles, & des Genereux Travaux de noftre incomparable Miniftre; qui aux dépens de fa fanté, a voulu faire ceffer les maladies & les langueurs de tant de miferables: Qui a noüé cette Paix par le nœud facré du plus beau & du plus grand Mariage que l'on pût fouhaiter dans le monde: Qui a joint par la prudence & par la force de fes Confeils; non feulement d'alliance, mais d'aimitié; les deux plus grands Roys de la terre, le Roy Tres-Chreftien fils aîné de l'Eglife, & le Roy Catholique: Qui a fortifié cette amitié par vn ferment fi faintement juré: I'en puis parler, puifque la Providence de Dieu a voulu que j'aye efté l'vn des Evefques qui en ont efté les témoins. Cela fans doute, merite des juftes loüanges; puis que ces grandes actions, compofent les grands originaux de plus beaux ornemens de l'Hiftoire: Mais voicy ce qui doit attire le refpect des Couronnes, & la veneration de toutes les Monarchies; C'eft d'avoir formé ces glorieux deffeins avec des penfées Chrétiennes; car la Politique n'eft rien, non, Meffieurs, la Politique n'eft rien qu'vne abomination devant les yeux de Dieu, quand on s'écarte des facrez devoirs de la Religion. Ce qui fait donc la veritable loüange de ce grand Prince de l'Eglife, c'eft d'avoir reconnu, parlant à vn Prelat de fes plus familiers, long temps auparavant que la Paix fut concluë, que la paix devoit eftre l'ouvrage du Ciel, en difant ces paroles, *Quam mundus dare non poteft pacem.* C'eft de m'avoir répondu au mois de Iuin dernier, le jour que noftre jeune Reyne eut la Couronne sur la tefte à S. Iean de Luz, lors que je difois à S.E. que c'eftoit vne illuftre journée pour fa gloire, après tant de fatigues; c'eft dis-je, de m'avoir répondu en ces termes: *Monfieur, ie n'ay rien du tout fait en cecy, c'eft Dieu qui a toute fait.* C'eft en vn mot, d'avoir joint les Conſeils du cabinet, avec la Religion des Autels, & d'avoir ſecondé les vœux de Vincent de Pavl, pour inſpirer les Conſeils de la Paix à noſtre grand Monarque.

Puiſſiez-vous, grand Prince de l'Egliſe, après de ſi glorieuſe demarches, augmenter de plus en plus le zele que vous devez avoir pour embraſſer avec plus d'ardeur que jamais, le plus precieux intereſts de l'Egliſe de Dieu! puiſſiez-vous rendre la Paix feconde en toute force de bonnes œuvres! & puiſſiez-vous maintenant reparer les bréches que le Chriſtianiſme a ſouffert durant les malheurs de la guerre.

Et vous, Vincent de Pavl, qui regnez aujourd'huy dans le Ciel, comme nous le croyons; obtenez à cét incomparable Miniſtre de l'Eſtat, & aux perſonnes ſacrées de leurs Majeſtez, que vous avez si cherement aymez, que vous avez toûjours ſervy avec tant de fidelité; obtenez à tous ces devots Auditeurs, qui ont tant de reſpect pour voſtre memoire; qui ont écouté avec tant de patience, ce foible recit d'vne partie bien legere de vos admirables vertus; obtenez, dis-je, les ſecours de la grace qui leur ſonts necessaires, pour renoncer aux maximes du ſiecle, ſuivant les obligations de noſtre ſaint Baptéme; & pour bien regler leur conduite, & tous les mouvemens de leurs cœrs, par les loix du Fils de Dieu; afin qu'ils ne ſoient point flatez ny ſurpris par la fauſſe eſtime des hommes; mais qu'en vous imitant, leur loüange, pour le temps & pour l'eternité, ſoit établie dans l'Evangile, par toutes les Egliſes.

Et pour moy; puiſqu'étant ſur la terre vous m'avez aimé, & ma perſonne & ma famille; puiſque vous avez tant de fois ſoulagé mes peines, & dans mes beſoins particuliers, & dans les plus grandes necessitez publiques de mes emplois, & de mon Dioceſe; puiſque vous m'avez obligé par tant de ſignalez effets de vôtre charité; faites-moy reſſentir aujourd'huy le credit que vous avez aupres de Dieu; achevez en moy ce que vous avez commencé, obtenez-moy la part que je dois ſouhaiter, aux plus abondantes benedictions du Ciel, que je vous ſouhaite Meſſieurs, du meilleur de mon cœur, autant comme à moy-méme.

Soli Deo honor & Gloria.

FIN.

BIBLIOGRAPHY

ARCHIVAL SOURCES

BIBLIOTHÈQUE NATIONALE DE FRANCE, PARIS

B.N. Ms. fr. Baluze 175, fol. 92: Letter of Maupas du Tour to Cardinal Mazarin, dated 11 June 1658. In *Papiers de MAZARIN et de COLBERT. – Lettres originales adressées à Mazarin (1643-1660); correspondence de Benjamini Priolo (1656 et 1661-1664; notes diverses de Mazarin, datant de son exil à Brühl, en 1651.*

B.N. Ms. fr. Baluze 324, fol. 163: Letter of Maupas du Tour to Cardinal Mazarin, dated 20 January 1661. In *Recueil de pieces, et principalement lettres et billets orig., addresses pour la plupart à MAZARIN. (1651, 1659, 1660 et 1661.).*

B.N. FR 20636 and 20637: *Recueil de pieces concernant Henri de Maupas du Tour, Abbé de Saint-Denis de Reims, évêque du Puy et d'Évreux.*

   . 20636.1: Appointment of Maupas as the commendatory abbot of Saint-Denis at Reims, 14 May 1616.

_____ . 20636.2: Diploma, Pont-à-Mousson, 22 May 1622.

_____ . 20636.3: Licentiate, Pont-à-Mousson, 13 December 1623.

_____ . 20636.28: *Copie d'un lettre de la Reine-Mère escrite au Pape en fauver de M. Évêque du Puy, 31 December 1642.*

_____ . 20636.30: Letter from Maupas du Tour to his sister, a Benedictine nun in Reims, dated 3 October 1643.

_____ . 20637.111: Letter from Cardinal Mazarin to Maupas du Tour, dated June 1656.

B.N. L²⁷ N 11387: Anonymous. *Vie de M. De Lantages: Prêtre de Saint-Sulpice, Premier Supérieur du séminaire de Notre Dame du Puy.* Paris: Adrien le Clere, 1830.

B.N. LN²⁷ 13814: St.-Michel, Monsieur de. *Oraison funèbre prononcée dans l'eglise paroissiale de St. Nicolas d'Evrevux, aux service solennel fait par Messieurs les Ecclesiastiques de la conference d'Évreux, le 8 Oct, 1680, pour Msgr. L'Illustrissime, & Reverendissime évêque d'Évreux, Henry de Maupas du Tour.* À Rouen, chez la veuve de Louis du Mensil, 1681.

L ⁴³ 12 fo 178 (8 Juillet 1648), 233 (13 Jan 1644), and 238 (6 Mai 1645): Jacotin, M. Antoine. *Inventaire-Sommaire des Archives Départementales: Haute-Loire, Archives Ecclesiastique - Série G: Clergé Seculier, antérieur à 1790.*

SECRET VATICAN ARCHIVES, THE VATICAN

Acta Camerararii Sacri Colegi S.R.E. Cardinalum: Henricus (de Cauchon) de Maupas du Tour, Aniciensis (Le Puy en Velay), 22 June 1643. AC 18 f. 159.
Processus Episcoporum Sacræ Congreg. Consistoralis, P. Con. 42ff. 72, 82-83. Sacred Congregation of Rites [Latin: *Congregatio pro Sacri Ritibus et Caeremoniis*, 1588-1969]:

_____ . *Congr. Riti, Processus* 2221-2222: versio processus ordinarii super fama (years 1705-1706), ff. 1856;

_____ . *Congr. Riti, Processus* 2223: versio processus super virtutibus (years 1710-11), f. 1062;

_____ . *Congr. Riti, Processus* 2224: versio processus super virtutibus (years 1712-1713), ff. 1085;

_____ . *Congr. Riti, Processus* 2225: versio processus super miris post beatificationem (years 1731-1733), ff. 1582;

_____ . *Congr. Riti, Processus* 2226-2227: processus ordinarius super fama (1705-1706), ff. 1749;

_____ . *Congr. Riti, Processus* 2228: processus apostolicus Parisien. super fama in gen. (1709-1710), ff. 87+48;

_____ . *Congr. Riti, Processus* 2229: processus ordinarius super non-cultu cum versione (1705-1706), ff. 178+39;

_____ . *Congr. Riti, Processus* 2230: processus apostolicus super virtutibus (1711-1712), ff. 632;

_____ . *Congr. Riti, Processus* 2231: processus apostolicus super virtutibus ne pereant...(1710-1711), ff. 358;

_____ . *Congr. Riti, Processus* 2232: processus apostolicus Parisien. super miris post beatificationem (1731-1733), ff. 1030.

PRINTED SOURCES

JOURNAL ARTICLES

Blanc, Paul le. *Annuaire de la Haute-Loire*. Le Puy: Marchessou Fils Ed. (1879): 12-17.

Blet, Pierre, S.J. "Saint Vincent and the Episcopate of France." *Vincentian Heritage* 10, no. 2 (1989): 102-135.

Bossuet, Jacques Bénigne. "On the Eminent Dignity of the Poor in the Church." Translated and annotated by Edward R. Udovic, C.M. *Vincentian Heritage* 13, no. 1 (1992): 37-58.

Dicharry, Warren, C.M. "Saint Vincent and Sacred Scripture." *Vincentian Heritage* 10, no. 2 (1989): 136-148.

Dodin, André, C.M. "M. Vincent de Paul et la Bible." Under the direction of Jean-Robert Armogathe. *Le Grand Siècle et la Bible*. Vol. 6 in *La Collection Bible de Tous les Temps*. 8 vols. (Paris: Éditions Beauchesne, 1989), 6:627-642.

_____ . "Théologie de la Charité selon Saint Vincent de Paul." *Vincentiana* 20, nos. 5-6 (1976): 263-284.

Forrestal, Alison. "Venues for Clerical Formation in Catholic Reformation Paris: Vincent de Paul and the Tuesday Conferences and Company." *Proceedings of the Western Society for French History* 38 (2010): 44-60.

Grès-Gayer, Jacques M. "The *Unigenitus* of Clement XI: A Fresh Look at the Issues." *Theological Studies* 49, no. 2 (1988): 273-281.

Guerra, Guiseppe, C.M. "I miracoli di S. Vincenzo de' Paoli: Dalla storia della sue beatificazione (1729) e della sue canonizzazione (1737)." *Carità e Missione: Rivista de Studi e Formazione Vincenziana* 13, no. 1 (2013): 55-64.

Kolk, Caroline zum. "The Household of the Queen of France in the Sixteenth Century." *The Court Historian* 14, no. 1 (June 2009): 3-22.

Merrick, Jeffrey. "The Cardinal and the Queen: Sexual and Political Disorders in the Mazarinades." *French Historical Studies* 18, no. 3 (Spring 1994): 667-699.

Mezzadri, Luigi, C.M. "Humility in St. Vincent's Apostolic Dynamism." *Vincentian Heritage* 1 (1980): 3-30.

Padberg, Collette and Daniel Hannefin, D.C. "Saint Vincent's First Foundation: The Ladies of Charity." *Vincentian Heritage* 3 (1982): 105-130.

Poole, Stafford, C.M. "Saint Vincent de Paul, 1595-1617: The Missing Years 1605-1607." *Vincentiana* 28, nos. 4-6 (1984): 424-435.

——— . "Brother Bertrand Ducournau." *Vincentian Heritage* 6, no. 2 (1985): 247-255.

Quantin, Jean-Louis. "A Godly Fronde? Jansenism and the Mid-Seventeenth-Century Crisis of the French Monarchy." *French History* 25, no. 4 (2011): 477.

Renouard, Jean-Pierre, C.M. "Châtillon: Les Charités." *Vincentiana* 31, nos. 4-6 (1987): 629-649.

Rocher, Ch. "Un Évêque et un Conspirateur en Velay." *Annuaire de la Haute-Loire*. Edited by M.D. Marcessou. Le Puy, 1877.

Román, José María, C.M. Stafford Poole, C.M., trans. "The Foundations of Saint Vincent de Paul." *Vincentian Heritage* 9, no. 2 (1988): 134-160.

Slawson, Douglas. "The Phantom Five Years." *Vincentian Heritage* 2 (1981): 81-93.

Smith, James E., C.M. "The Vincentian Mission, 1625-1660." *Vincentian Heritage* 4, no. 2 (1983): 40-60.

Smith, Jay M. "'Our Sovereign's Gaze': Kings, Nobles, and State Formation in Seventeenth-Century France." *French Historical Studies* 18, no. 2 (Fall 1993): 396-415.

Udovic, Edward R., C.M. "Caritas Christi Urget Nos": The Urgent Challenges of Charity in Seventeenth Century France." *Vincentian Heritage* 12, no. 2 (1991): 85-104.

Winsen, Gerard van, C.M. "Saint Vincent and Foreign Missions." Jacqueline Kilar, D.C., trans. *Vincentian Heritage* 3 (1982): 3-42.

BOOKS

Abelly, Louis. *La vie du vénérable serviteur de Dieu Vincent de Paul, instituteur et première superior général de la Congrégation de la Mission.* Paris: Florentin Lambert, 1664 & 1667.

___ . *Life of the Venerable Servant of God: Vincent de Paul.* Edited by John E. Rybolt, C.M. Translated by William Quinn, F.S.C. 3 vols. New York: New City Press, 1987. Originally published as *Vie de S. Vincent de Paul: fondateur de la Congrégation des prêtres de la Mission et de la compagnie des Filles de la Charité.* Paris: F. Lambert, 1664.

Acta Apostolica, Bullæ, Brevia et Rescripta in gratiam Congregationis Missionis. Parisiis: Typis Excudebat Georges Chamerot, 1876.

Alexandre, Philippe and Béatrix de L'Aulnoit. *Pour mon fils, pour mon roi: la reine Anne, mère de Louis XIV.* Paris: R. Laffont, 2009.

Allier, Raoul. *La compagnie du Très Saint-Sacrement de l'autel: La "cabale des dévots" 1627-1666.* Paris: A. Colin, 1902.

Arnaud, J.A.M. *Histoire du Velay, jusqu'a la fin du regne de Louis XV.* 2 vols. Le Puy: J.B. La Combe, 1816.

Barcos, Martin de. *Defense de feu M. Vincent de Paul, Instituteur et Premier Superior General de la Congregation de la Mission contres les faux discours du livre de sa vie publieé par M. Abelly, Ancien Evesque de Rodez, et contre les impostures de quelques autres ecrits sur ce sujet.* Paris, 1668.

Bauduen, Marc de. *La vie admirable de tres-haute, tres-puissante, tres-illustre, et tres vertueuse dame Charlote Marguerite de Gondy, marquise de Magnelais: où les ames fideles trouveront dequoy admirer & des vertus solides à imiter.* A Paris: Chez la veusve Nicolas Buon..., 1666.

Baussonnet, G. *Reste des Vers de la Composition de feu tres-genereux Seigneur, Messire Charles de Maupas, Chevalier, Baron du Tour: Seigneur dudit Maupas, du Cosson, Montaneux, & Sainct Imoges: Conseiller du Roy en ses Conseils d'Estat and Privé, Plus un Elogue pour le mesme Seigneur.* Reims: Chez François Bernard, 1638.

Bell, David. *Lawyers and Citizens: The Making of a Political Elite in Old Regime France.* New York: Oxford University Press, 1994.

Bergin, Joseph. *Cardinal de La Rochefoucauld: Leadership and Reform in the French Church.* New Haven: Yale University Press, 1987.

___ . *The Making of the French Episcopate, 1589-1661.* New Haven: Yale University Press, 1996.

Bois, Albert. *Les sœurs de Saint-Joseph: Les Filles du petit dessein: de 1648 à 1949.* Lyon: Ed. du Sud-Est, 1950.

Bonnenfant, Chanoine. *Histoire Générale du diocèse d'Évreux.* 2 vols. Paris: Auguste Picard, 1933.

Bossuet, Jacques-Bénigne. *Oraisons Funèbres de Bossuet.* Paris: Librairie de Firmin Didot Frères, 1847.

___ . *Témoignage sur la vie et les vertus éminentes de Monsieur Vincent de Paul (1702).* Edited by Armand Gasté. Paris: Alphonse Picard, 1892.

Broutin, Paul. *La Réforme Pastorale en France au XVIIe siècle: recherché sur la tradition pastorale après le concile de Trente*. 2 vols. Tournai, Belgium: Desclée & Co., 1956.

Bugelli, Alexandrette. *Vincent de Paul: une pastoral du pardon et de la réconciliation: la confession générale*. Paris: Éditiones Universitaires Fribourg Suisse, 1997.

Burns, Marie-Patricia, V.S.M. *Françoise-Madeleine de Chaugy, dans l'ombre et la lumière de la canonisation de François de Sales*. Annecy: Académie Salésienne, 2002.

Chalendard, Marie. *La Promotion de la Femme à l'Apostolat 1540-1650*. Paris: Éditions Alsatia, 1950.

Chaumiel, Abbé. *Vie de Mgr. Henri de Maupas, évêque de Puy et Fondateur de la Congrégation des Dames Religieuses de Saint-Joseph*. St. Flour: Chez l'auteur, au convent de Saint-Joseph, 1837.

Chauvet, Louis-Marie. *Symbol and Sacrament: A Sacramental Reinterpretation of Christian Existence*. Translated by Patrick Madigan, S.J., and Madeleine Beaumont. Collegeville, MN: Liturgical Press, 1995. Originally published as *Symbole et Sacrement: Un Relecture de l'Existence Chrétienne*. Paris: Les Éditions du Cerf, 1987.

Christophe, Paul. *Les pauvres et la pauvreté, II éme partie, du XVIe siècle à nos jours*. Bibliothèque d'histoire du Christianisme, no. 7. Paris: Desclée, 1987.

Circulars of the Superiors-General and the Superioresses to the Daughters of Charity: and notices upon the deceased Sisters of the Community. Emmitsburg, Md.: St. Joseph's, 1870.

Collet, Pierre, C.M. *La Vie de St. Vincent de Paul: Instituteur de la Congrégation de la Mission, et des Filles de la Charité*. 2 vols. Nancy: A. Lescure, imprimeur ordinaire du Roy, 1748.

———. *La vie de M. Henri-Marie Boudon, grand archidiacre d'Évreux*. 2 vols. Paris: Jean-Thomas Herissant, 1753.

Conchon, Anne, Bruno Maes, et al. *Dictionnaire de l'Ancien Régime*. Paris: A. Colin, 2004.

Corbinelli, Jean de. *Histoire genealogique de la maison de Gondi*. 2 vols. Paris: Jean-Baptiste Coignard, 1705.

Coste, Pierre, C.M. *The Life & Works of St. Vincent de Paul*. 3 vols. New York: New City Press, 1987.

Cottelet, Francois. *La Nouvelle Relation Contenant L'Entreveue et Serments des Roys, pour L'Entiere Execution de la Paix. Ensemble Toutes les Particularitez & Ceremonies qui se sont faites au Mariage du Roy, & de l'Enfante d'Espagne. Avec tout ce qui s'est passé de plus remarquable entre ces deux puissant Monarques jusqu'à leur depart*. Paris: Jean-Baptiste Loyson, 1660.

Cunningham, Lawrence S. *A Brief History of the Saints*. Malden, MA: Blackwell, 2005.

Davidson, Gustav. *A Dictionary of Angels*. New York: Collier-Macmillan, 1967.

Deferrai, Roy J., M. Inviolata Barry, and R.P. McGuire, eds. *A Concordance of Ovid*. Washington: The Catholic University of America Press, 1939.

Dodin, André, C.M. *François de Sales, Vincent de Paul: les deux amis*. Paris: O.E.I.L., 1984.

Dougherty, Dolorita M., C.S.J., Helen A. Hurley, C.S.J., Emily Joseph Daly, C.S.J., St. Claire Coyne, C.S.J., et al. *Sisters of St. Joseph of Carondelet*. St. Louis: B. Herder Book Co., 1966.

Faillon, Etienne-Michel. *Vie de M. Olier: fondateur du séminaire de S.-Sulpice*. 2ⁿᵈ ed. 2 vols. Paris: Poussielgue-Rusand, 1853.

Farmer, S.A. "Conclusions on the doctrine of Plato." In *Syncretism in the West: Pico's 900 Theses (1486): The evolution of traditional religious and philosophical systems*. Tempe, Arizona: Medieval & Renaissance Texts & Studies, 1998.

Forrestal, Alison. "Vincent de Paul: The Making of a Catholic *Dévot*." In *Politics and Religion in Early Bourbon France*. Edited by Alison Forrestal and Eric Nelson. Basingstoke, U.K.: Palgrave Macmillan, 2009.

Galibert, Nivoelisoa. *À l'angle de la grande maison: les lazaristes de Madagascar: correspondance avec Vincent de Paul 1648-1661*. Paris: PUPS, 2007.

General Curia of the Congregation of the Mission, 1989. *Constitutions and Statutes of the Congregation of the Mission*. [Eng. Trans.] Philadelphia, 1984.

Grell, Chantal, ed. *Anne d'Autriche: Infante d'Espagne et reine de France*. Versailles: Centre de recherché du château de Versailles, 2009.

Guth, Paul. *Mazarin*. Paris: Flammarion, 1972.

Hérambourg, Pierre. *Le Révérend Jean Eudes apôtre des SS. Cœurs de Jésus et de Marie,...ses vertus*. Paris: P. Lethielleux, 1869.

Hôpital Général de Paris. *L'Hospital General de Paris*. A Paris: chez François Muguet, 1676.

Kavanaugh, Kieran and Otilio Rodriguez, trans. "The Interior Castle, VI.5.10." In *The Collected Works of Teresa of Avila*. 2nd ed. rev. 3 vols. Washington D.C.: Institute of Carmelite Studies, 1987.

Kearnæi, Barnabæ. "De Circumcisione Domini." In *Heliotropium*. Lyon: A. Pillehotte, 1622.

Kettering, Sharon. *Patrons, Brokers, and Clients in Seventeenth-Century France*. New York: Oxford University Press, 1986.

Kroen, Sheryl. *Politics and Theater: the Crisis of Legitimacy in Restoration France, 1815-1830*. Berkeley: University of California Press, 2000.

Lalore, Charles. *L'opinion de M. de Boulogne, évêque de Troyes: touchant la captivité volontaire de Saint Vincent de Paul sur les galères de Marseille*. Troyes: Dufour-Bouquot, 1875.

Lapide, Cornelius à, S.J. "Commentaria in Epist. II ad Corinthios. Cap. XI." In *Commentaria in omnes divi Pauli epistolas*.Venetiis: Belleoniana, 1761.

___ . *The Great Commentary*. Translated by Thomas W. Mossman and W. F. Cobb. 8 vols. Edinburgh: John Grant, 1908.

Lecouturier, Ernestine. *Françoise-Madeleine de Chaugy et la Tradition Salesienne au XVIᵉ siècle*. 2 vols. Paris: Bloud et Gay, 1933.

Lough, John. *An Introduction to Seventeenth-Century France*. New York: Longmans, Green and Co, 1954.

Loyac, Jean de. *Le Triomphe de la Charité en la vie du Bienheureux Jean de Dieu. Institution et Progez de son Ordre Religieux. Avec les Ceremonies de sa Béatification, & de la Translation solmnelle de sa Relique, enuoyee a La Reyne Mère par le Roy d'Espagne*. Paris: Antoine Chrestien, 1659.

Marie, Catherine-Laurence. *De la cause de Dieu à la cause de la Nation: Le Jansénisme au XVIIIe siècle*. Paris: Editions Gallimard, 1998.

Mathieu, Marguerite Robert. *Monsieur Vincent chez les de Gondy: les missionnaires et les Filles de la Charité à Montmirail*. Paris: Brodard-Taupin, 1966.

Maupas du Tour, Henri de. *La vie de la vénérable mère Ieanne Françoise Frémiot: fondatrice, première mère & relígieuse de l'Ordre de la Visitation de Saincte-Marie*. Paris: Simeon Piget, 1647.

McMahon, Norbert, O.S.J.D. *The Story of the Hospitallers of Saint John of God*. Philadelphia: Newman Press, 1959.

Merrick, Jeffrey W. *The Desacralization of the French Monarchy in the Eighteenth Century*. Baton Rouge: Louisiana State University, 1990.

Mezzadri, Luigi, C.M. *Fra Giansenisti e Antigiansenisti. Vincent de Paul e la Congregazione della Missione (1624-1737)*. Firenze: "La Nuova Italia" Editrice, 1977.

——, Francesca Onnis. *The Vincentians: A General History of the Congregation of the Mission*. Translated by Robert Cummings. Edited by Joseph E. Dunne, Felicia Roşu, and John E. Rybolt, C.M. 6 vols. [Vols. 4-6 forthcoming.] Hyde Park, New York: New City Press, 2009-2013.

Mongeron, Louis-Basile Carré de. *La Verité des miracles operés par l'intercession de M. de Pâris: demontrée contre M. l'Archevêque de Sens. Ouvrage dedié au roy*. Utretcht: chez les Libraires de la Compagnie, 1737.

Montigny, Antoine, S.J. *Vie du Père Jean Eudes, missionaire apostolique, instituteur de la Congrégation de Jésus et Marie et de l'Ordre de Notre-Dame de Charité*. Paris: Adrien Le Clere, 1827.

More, Thomas. "English Poems, Life of Pico, The Last Things." In *The Yale Edition of the Complete Works of St. Thomas More*. Edited by Anthony S.G. Edwards, Katherine Gardiner Rodgers, and Clarence H. Miller. 15 vols. New Haven: Yale University Press, 1997.

Mousnier, Roland. *The Institutions of France under the Absolute Monarchy 1598-1798*. Chicago: University of Chicago Press, 1979.

Ovid. "Black Sea Letters: Book III." In *Ovid: The Poems of Exile*. Translated by Peter Green. New York: Penguin Books, 1994.

Patrologiæ Cursus Completus, Series Græca. Edited by J.P. Migne. 161 vols. Paris: Bibliothecæ Cleri Universæ, 1857-1891.

Patrologiæ Cursus Completus, Series Latina. Edited by J.P. Migne. 221 vols. Paris: Garnier Frères, 1844-1890.

Poole, Marie, D.C., Jacqueline Kilar, D.C., et al., eds. and trans. *Vincent de Paul: Correspondence, Conferences, Documents. Newly Translated, Edited, and Annotated from the 1924 Edition of Pierre Coste, C.M.* Vols. 1-14. Hyde Park, New York: New City Press, 1985-2014.

Poole, Stafford, C.M. and Douglas Slawson. "A New Look at an Old Temptation: Saint Vincent's Temptation Against Faith and His Resolution to Serve the Poor." Unpublished article.

Prince Michael of Greece. *Louis XIV: The Other Side of the Sun.* Translated by Alan Sheridan. New York: Harper & Row, 1983.

Pujo, Bernard. *Vincent de Paul: The Trailblazer.* Notre Dame: University of Notre Dame Press, 2003.

Recueil des Principales Circulaires des Supérieurs Généraux de la Congrégation de la Mission. 3 vols. Paris: Georges Chamerot, 1877-80.

Return to the Fountainhead. Tercentenary Addresses published by the Sisters of St. Joseph of Carondelet. St. Louis, Missouri, 1952.

Richardt, Aimé. *Le Jansénisme de Jansénius à la mort de Louis XIV.* Paris: François-Xavier de Guibert, 2002.

Ristretto Cronologico della Vita, Virtù, e Miracoli del B. Vincenzo de Paoli Fondatore Della Congregazione della Missione, e delle Serve de' Poveri, dette le Figlie della Carità. Alla Santità de Nostro Signore Papa Benedetteo XIII. Roma: Antonio de'Rossi, 1729.

Robineau, Louis. "Notebooks of Brother Louis Robineau: Notes concerning the actions and words of the late Monsieur Vincent de Paul our Most Honored Father and Founder." Unpublished English translation by John E. Rybolt, C.M. Originally published as *André Dodin, C.M., présente Louis Robineau. Monsieur Vincent: Raconté par son secrétaire; Remarques sur les actes et paroles de feu Monsieur Vincent de Paul, notre Trés Honoré Père et Fondateur.* Edited by André Dodin, C.M. Paris: O.E.I.L., 1991.

Roman Catholic Church. "Concilium Attiniacense, in quo Ludovicus pium Imperator publicam pœnitentiam sua sponte suscepit, in Attiniaco palatio celebratum, anno Christi DCCCXXII." In *Acta Conciliorum et Epistolæ Decretales, ac Constitutiones Summorum Pontificum.* Edited by Jean Hardouin, S.J. 11 vols. Paris: Ex Typographia Regia, 1714-1715.

_____ . "Festa Novemberis 11, S. Martini Episcopi, Confessoris." In *Antiphonale sacrosanctæ Romanæ ecclesiæ pro diurnis horis SS. D. N. Pii X, Pontificis Maximi jussu restitutum et editum.* Rome: Typis Polyglottis Vaticanis, 1912.

_____ . "Concilii Tridenti, Sessio Vigesima tertia de Reformatione, Canones et Decreta, Caput XVIII: Forma erigendi seminarium clericorum, præstertim tenuiorum; in cujus erectione plurima observanda; de educatione promovendorum in cathedralibus et majoribus ecclesiis." In *Canons and Decrees of the Council of Trent.* Edited by H.J. Schroeder, O.P. St. Louis: Herder and Herder, 1941.

Román, José-María, C.M. "Novel o Historia? Un Grave Problema Critico." In *San Vicente de Paul, I Biografía.* Madrid: Biblioteca de Autores Cristianos, 1982.

Sachet, Alphonse. *Le cœur de Saint Vincent de Paul à Lyon*. Lyon: G. Patissier, 1929.

Sacra Rituum Congregatione Ēmo, & Rm̄o Dn̄o Card. Lercario pro Ēmo, & Rm̄o D. Card. Polignac Ponte Parisien. Canonizationis B. Vincentii A' Paulo, Fundatoris Congregationis Missionis, & Societatis Puellarum de Charitate. Positio super Dubio An, & de quibus Miraculis constet post indultam eidem Beato venerationem in casu etc. Romae: Typis Reverendæ Cameræ Apostolicæ, 1735.

Saint-Albin, Charles de. *Mandement et Instruction Pastorale de Monseigneur l'Archevêque, Duc de Cambray, Portant Condamnation de trois Ecrits, dont le premiere a pour titre: Vie de M. de Pâris, Diacre, à Bruxelles, chez Foppens, à l'Enseigne du Saint Esprit, 1731. Le second: Vie de M. de Pâris, Diacre du Diocése de Paris, en France, 1731. Et le troisiéme: Vie de M. de Pâris, Diacre, 1731.* Paris: Marc Bordelet, 1732.

Saint-Simon, Louis de Rouvroy, duc de. *Mémoires complets et authentique de duc de Saint-Simon.* 20 vols. Paris: Librairie Hachette et Cⁱᵉ, 1874.

Sandars, Thomas Collett, ed. and trans. "Liber II, Tit. VII, De Donationibus." In *The Institutes of Justinian: With English Introduction, Translation, and Notes.* London, 1883.

Scheoll, Rudolfus. "De Prætoribus Plebis." In *Corpus juris civilis, Novellæ, XIII De Prætoribus Populi.* Berolini: Weidmannos, 1912.

Smith, Sean. "Fidelity to Founder Under the Bourbon Regime: The Congregation of the Mission, 1660-1736." Ph.D. diss. National University of Ireland, 2012.

Stevenson, J., ed. *Creeds, Councils, and Controversies.* London: SPCK, 1973.

Strayer, Brian E. *Suffering Saints. Jansenists and Convulsionnaires in France, 1640-1799.* Brighton: Sussex Academic Press, 2008.

Suetonius Tranquillus, G. *The Lives of the Twelve First Roman Emperors.* Translated by John Clarke. London: Printed for A. Bettesworth and C. Hitch at the Red-Lion in Pater-Noster-Row, 1732.

Tallon, Alain. *La Compagnie du Saint-Sacrement, 1629-1667: spritualité et société.* Paris: Cerf, 1990.

Tapié, Victor L. *France in the age of Louis XIII and Richelieu.* Translated by D. McN. Lockie. Cambridge: Cambridge University Press, 1984.

Thiébaud, Jean-Marie. *Dictionnaire de l'Ancien Régime du Royaume de France.* Besançon: CÊTRE, 2009.

Tinniswood, Adam. *Pirates of Barbary: Corsairs, Conquests and Captivity in the Seventeenth-Century Mediterranean.* London: Riverhead Books, 2010.

Traitté de Paix, entre les Couronnes de France et d'Espagne • avec Le Contract de Mariage du Roy Tres-Chrestien et de la Serenissime Infante, Fille aisnée du Roy Catholique. Le 7. Novembre, 1659 • avec l'explication de l'Article XLII. Du susdit Traitté, concernant le Roussillon : du 31, May 1660. Paris: l'Imprimerie Royale, 1660.

Treasure, Geoffrey. *Mazarin: the Crisis of Absolutism in France.* London: Routledge, 1995.

Tronçon, Jean. *L'entrée trimphante de leurs majestez Louis XIV roy de France et de Nauarre, et Marie Therese d'Austriche son espouse: dans la ville de Paris capital de leurs royaumes, au retour de la signature de la paix generale et de leur hereux marriage.* Paris: chez Pierre Le petit...Thomas Ioly...et Louis Vilaine...1662.

Vacant, Alfred, Eugène Mangenot, Elile Amann, Bernard Loth, Albert Michel. *Dictionnaire de Théologie Catholique.* 15 vols. Paris: Letouzey et Ané, 1903-50.

Vacher, Marguerite. *Nuns Without Cloister: Sisters of St. Joseph in the Seventeenth and Eighteenth Centuries.* Translated by Patricia Byrne, et al. Lanham, Md.: University Press of America, 2010.

Valerius Maximus. "De liberalitatel." In *Valerii Maximi: Factorum et dictorum memorabilium, libri novem cum julii paridis et januarii nepotiani epitomis.* Edited by Carolus Halm. Lipsiae: in Ædibus B.G. Teveneri, 1865.

_____ . "Of Liberality." In *Valerian Maximus: Memorable doings and sayings.* Edited and translated by D.R. Shakleton Bailey. Cambridge, Mass.: Harvard University Press, 2000.

Venusinus, Richardus. "De Paulino et Polla." In *Commedie latine del XII e XIII secolo.* Genova: Istituto di Filologia Classica e Medievale, 1986.

Virgil. *The Works of P. Virgilius Maro.* Edited and translated by Levi Hart and V.R. Osborn. New York: David McKay Co., 1952.

Xenophon. "Hiero." *Scripta Minora.* Edited by E. Capps, T.E. Page, W.H.D. Rouse. Translated by E.C. Marchant. London: William Heinemann, 1925.

NEWSPAPERS

Nouvelles Ecclésiastiques 12 (1739).

BIBLES

The Interlinear Hebrew-Aramaic Old Testament. Edited and translated by Jay P. Green, Sr. 3 vols. Peabody, MA: Hendrickson Publishers, 1993.

The New American Bible: Translated from the original languages with critical use of all the ancient sources. Saint Joseph Edition. New York: Catholic Book Publishing Co., n.d.

INDEX

eager to know the life story of Vincent de Paul, 39;

    in attendance at Vincent's funeral, 13;

    sought the canonization of Vincent de Paul, 35

Charity, Ladies of,

    founded by Vincent de Paul, 99

    in attendance at Vincent's funeral, 13

    service to galley slaves, 107

Chrysologus, (Peter), Saint, 113

Clement of Alexandria, (saint), 118

Clement XI, (pope), 64

Clement XII, (pope), 35, 69, 70

Clergy of France, General Assembly of the, 23, 62, 69

Codoing, Bernard, C.M., 18

Coligny, Comte de, 60

Collet, Pierre, C.M., 14, 60

Comet, M. de, 40

Condren, Charles de, Cong. Orat., 116

Conference of Ecclesiastics. *See* Tuesday Conference of Ecclesiastics

Confession, General. *See* General Confession

Congregation of the Mission. *See* Lazarists

Conscience, Council of, 100

convulsionnaires, 65, 69

Cosson, (Château du), 14

Coste, Pierre, C.M., 67, 73, 75

Couty, Jean, C.M., 35, 63-64, 69, 74

Cyprian (of Carthage), Saint, 125-126, 128

Daughters of Charity. *See* Charity, Daughters of

d'Autriche, Marie-Therese, (queen), 49, 132

Dehorgny, Jean, C.M., 40-41

Delahaye, Antoine Philopald, 66

de non cultu. See canonization process

devil's advocate. *See* canonization process

dévots, 18

diâcre de Pâris. *See* Pâris, François de

dubia. See canonization process

Ducournau, Bertrand, C.M., 39, 41

Elijah, (Old Testament prophet), 112

Ephesus, Council of, 126

Etampes, France, 110

Eudes, Jean, Saint, 25

Fabiola, Saint, 106-107

Felicity, Saint, 121

Felix I, (pope), 126

as preacher, 38, 124;

as reformer of clergy in France, 38, 96, 116, 124;

as spiritual director, 108, 116, 124;

as first Superior General of the Congregation of the Mission, 110, 121, 129, 130-131;

as theologian, 47, 126;

as Tridentine reformer in France, 36-37, 46-47, 124;

his beatification, 67-68;

his canonization, 35, 70-72;

his canonization process, 61-71;

his christology, 129;

his death and burial, 13-14, 60;

his education, (formal), 126; (downplayed), 39, 103;

his foundations: Confraternities of Charity, 99; Congregation of the Mission, 17; Daughters of Charity, 99; Ladies of Charity, 99; seminaries, 96, 116; "Tuesday" Conference of Ecclesiastics, 14, 96;

his hidden (early) life, 39, 41;

his humble beginnings, 41, 102;

his life of virtue: in

   care for abandoned children, 49;

   charity, 98, 106-113, 114-117, 118-121;

   confidence in Divine Providence, 38, 44-46, 99-100, 107, 112-114;

   constancy, 123-124;

   forgiving, 116-117, 122;

   generosity, 111-113, 117;

   gratitude, 117-118;

   humility, 37-39, 44-46, 92-105, 131;

   long-suffering, 117;

   meekness, 116;

   modesty, 95;

   mortification, 121-122;

   patience, 107, 121-122;

   penitence for others, 122;

   peacemaking, 47, 49, 112, 129;

   self-imposed poverty, 44, 46, 94;

   zeal, 47, 96, 98-99, 122, 124;

   zeal for (charity), 98, 105-115, 119; (foreign missions), 99, 120-121; (prisoners), 96, 99; (refugees), 102; (the hungry), 102; (the poor), 38, 46, 107-108, 111-113, 115-118, 130-131; (the sick), 99, 107, 115; (victims of flood), 111; (victims of war), 96, 109-110;

his respect for clergy and religious, 124-125;

his service to the Holy See, 47, 125-126;

his service to the King and the French Church, 47;

in service to the Gondi family, 14, 17;

ABOUT THE AUTHOR

REV. EDWARD R. UDOVIC, C.M., PH.D., is a Vincentian priest from the Western Province of the Congregation of the Mission. Ordained in 1984, he has a Doctorate in Church History from the Catholic University of America. He presently serves as the Secretary, Senior Executive for University Mission, and Vice President for Teaching and Learning Resources at DePaul University in Chicago, the largest Catholic University in the United States. He is also an associate professor in the Department of History. Rev. Udovic has written extensively on Vincentian history, has published numerous articles, and is the author of *Jean-Baptiste Étienne and the Vincentian Revival* (2001).